Penguin Books

Gardens of a Golden Afternoon

Jane Brown lives in Hampshire and came under the influence of the Jekyll–Lutyens partnership while studying landscape design. She spent ten years visiting and researching the gardens she describes in this book. She was a consultant to the Lutyens Exhibition staged at the Hayward Gallery and prepared a parallel exhibition on Gertrude Jekyll at the Architectural Association in Bedford Square.

D1386298

GARDENS OF A GOLDEN AFTERNOON

THE STORY OF A PARTNERSHIP:
EDWIN LUTYENS & GERTRUDE JEKYLL

Jane Brown

Penguin Books

For Peter, as promised

PENGUIN BOOKS

Published by the Penguin Group
27 Wrights Lane, London w8 5TZ, England
Viking Penguin Inc., 40 West 23rd Street, New York, New York 10010, USA
Penguin Books Australia Ltd, Ringwood, Victoria, Australia
Penguin Books Canada Ltd, 2801 John Street, Markham, Ontario, Canada L3R 1B4
Penguin Books (NZ) Ltd, 182–190 Wairau Road, Auckland 10, New Zealand

Penguin Books Ltd, Registered Offices: Harmondsworth, Middlesex, England

First published in the USA by Van Nostrand Reinhold Company 1982
First published in Great Britain by Allen Lane 1982
Published in Penguin Books 1985
Reprinted 1988

Printed and bound in Great Britain by
William Clowes Limited, Beccles and London
Typeset in Clowes Dante

 CONTENTS

List of Colour Plates 6

List of Illustrations 7

Key to Garden Plans 10

Acknowledgements 11

Illustration Acknowledgements 12

Introduction 13

1 The Lady and the Architect 19

2 The Making of Munstead Wood
and the Early Surrey Gardens 33

3 The Gardens of the Golden Afternoon 64

4 Working Partnership 96

5 The War and Afterwards 132

6 A Reckoning 153

Appendix A
A List of Miss Jekyll's Commissions 188

Appendix B
Additional Notes on Lutyens's Commissions 192

Notes 193

Bibliography 204

Index 205

 LIST OF COLOUR PLATES

The page numbers given are those opposite the colour plates,
or, in the case of a double page spread, those either side of the plate.

1. Bramley Park, Guildford, Surrey (from a watercolour by Henry Sage)   *page* 24
2. The Taj Mahal (from a watercolour by Hercules Brabazon Brabazon)   24
3. Berrydowne Court, Ashe, Overton, Hampshire   24–5
4. Woodside, Chenies, Buckinghamshire: the vista down the slope to the pond court   25
5. Woodside: the canopied gate into the former garage court   25
6. Grey Walls, Gullane, East Lothian, Scotland: the south-east corner and rose garden   72
7. Orchards, Munstead, Godalming, Surrey: the view from the loggia terrace   72
8. Hestercombe, Kington, Taunton, Somerset: the return of Jekyll planting   72–3
9. Hestercombe: the Great Plat   73
10. Hestercombe: the view from the rotunda pool   73
11. Little Thakeham, near Storrington, Sussex: the entrance court   120
12. Little Thakeham: the vista through the west garden court   120
13. Folly Farm, Sulhamstead, Berkshire: a vista through the walls of the entrance
    and barn courts   120–21
14. Folly Farm: the formal canal garden and the 'Dutch' addition
    to the original farmhouse   120–21
15. Folly Farm: one of the 'platforms' raised at the four corners
    of the sunken rose garden   120–21
16. Folly Farm: the sunken rose garden and 1912 addition to the house   120–21
17. The Hoo, Willingdon, Sussex   121
18. The Hoo: the domed water-lily pool beside the lower walk   121
19. Marsh Court, Stockbridge, Hampshire: the pergola   168
20. Marsh Court: looking out from the entrance porch   168
21. Marsh Court: the entrance to the garden   168
22. Ednaston Manor, Brailsford, Derbyshire: the south terrace   169
23. Amport House, near Andover, Hampshire: the water terraces   168–9
24. Amport House: the water terraces   169

LIST OF ILLUSTRATIONS

Dorothea Strachey and Dinah the black kitten — *endpapers*

1. Bramley Park, near Guildford, Surrey — *page* 20
2. Gertrude Jekyll, from a photograph taken about 1880 — 29
3. Edwin Lutyens as a young man — 29
4. Lutyens's design for a cottage at Littleworth Cross — 31
5. Lutyens's design for a 'fowl house' at Littleworth Cross — 31
6. Munstead Wood: the north court — 35
7. Munstead Wood in Miss Jekyll's time (1896–1932) — 36
8. Munstead Wood: the Spring garden — 37
9. Munstead Wood: the Hidden garden — 39
10. Munstead Wood: the June garden — 40
11. The colour circle — 43
12. The colour triangle — 43
13. The basis of good 'architectural' order — 43
14. Munstead Wood: the main flower border — 44
15. Munstead Wood: the main flower border — 47
16. Munstead Wood: part of the main flower border — 47
17. Munstead Wood: textures and shapes — 47
18. Blagdon: the new border — 48
19. Munstead Wood: the house from the woodland garden — 52
20. Woodside: sketch layout of the site — 54
21. Woodside: looking east from the pond court towards the river garden — 55
22. Cartoon – 'I make obeysance' — 56
23. Orchards: sketch layout of the garden — 57
24. Orchards: layout of the Dutch garden — 57
25. Orchards: Lutyens's sketch for the gate to the Dutch garden — 58
26. Orchards: the garden in its heyday — 59
27. Orchards: the Dutch garden — 59
28. Goddards: the little garden within the arms of the house — 60
29. Witley Park: the bathing pavilion from across the lake — 61
30. Witley Park: detail of the pavilion — 61
31. A page from Miss Jekyll's plant catalogue — 62
32. Another page from the catalogue — 62
33. Cartoon – 'Aunt Bumps' — 63
34. Knebworth House: five-ringed herb garden — 65
35. Deanery Garden: Lutyens's original survey and plan — 66

36. Deanery Garden: terrace borders — 67
37. Deanery Garden: the house as it is today — 69
38. Deanery Garden: the garden front and mock 'bridge', looking west — 69
39. Deanery Garden: the garden front from the bridge level, looking east — 69
40. Lambay: sketch plan of layout — 70
41. Lambay: the view out over the west forecourt — 71
42. Lambay: the north court before planting — 71
43. Grey Walls: the path to the *clair voyée* — 74
44. Grey Walls: sketch plan of layout — 74
45. Marsh Court: sketch plan of layout — 75
46. Marsh Court: the steps leading out from the wood — 76
47. Marsh Court: the paving patterns that entice and entertain — 76
48. Marsh Court: the 'piazza' — 76
49. Marsh Court: the sunken pool garden — 77
50. Marsh Court: the lily pools below the lower pergola — 78
51. Marsh Court: the lead water tank in the pool garden — 78
52. Ammerdown: sketch plan of layout — 79
53. Ammerdown: the Italian garden — 80
54. Ammerdown: the vista from the Italian garden to Wyatt's orangery — 80
55. Ammerdown: the pergola — 81
56. Hestercombe: layout plan — 82
57. Hestercombe: the vista beneath the pergola — 84
58. Hestercombe: the restored planting of the Great Plat borders — 85
59. Hestercombe: details of 'dry stone' pool construction — 85
60. Heywood: the house (now demolished) — 86
61. Heywood: looking back across the Italian garden through the lime alley — 87
62. Heywood: the oval Italian garden in its prime — 88
63. Heywood: sketch plan of layout — 89
64. Barton St Mary — 90
65. Barton St Mary: planting plan for the kitchen garden borders — 91
66. Barton St Mary: the south garden plan — 92
67. Folly Farm: layout plan — 94
68. Folly Farm: the tank cloister — 95
69. Lambay: Lutyens's sketch explaining the north court — 100
70. Lambay: a detail of the planting scheme for the east court — 101
71. Edwin Lutyens: a photograph taken at Lambay Castle — 101
72. Abbotswood: Lutyens's conception of a garden — 102
73. New Place: sketch and discussion process at work — 105
74. Elevations to illustrate the placing of houses and their gardens on three sites — 107
75. Heathcote: 'conceal and reveal' layout — 109
76. The Salutation: the garden — 110
77. The Salutation: the sundial — 110
78. Hestercombe: footgate — 112
79. Ednaston Manor: footgate — 112
80. Castle Drogo: footgate — 112
81. The Salutation: entrance — 113

82. Berrydowne Court: entrance — 113
83. Millmead: sketch layout — 114
84. Millmead: the pergola — 115
85. Millmead: the entrance court — 115
86. Millmead: the garden front — 116
87. Dry-wall construction — 117
88. Millmead: the planting for the rose garden border — 118
89. Millmead: the planting for the retaining walls between the second and third levels — 118
90. Millmead: the planting of the lowest level — 119
91. Hestercombe: steps — 122
92. The Hoo: steps — 122
93. Hestercombe: steps — 122
94. Ashby St Ledgers: steps — 122
95. Munstead Wood: the millstone outside the workshop door — 123
96. Amport House: millstone and paving — 123
97. Pasturewood: millstone and brick-on-edge paving — 123
98. Pasturewood: millstone and tile-on-edge paving — 123
99. Marsh Court: the white stone necklace to the east lawn — 123
100. Munstead Wood: the craftsman's pride — 124
101. Gravetye Manor: Lutyens's sketch for a six-bay wooden seat — 125
102. Lutyens's garden seat – the larger of his two designs — 125
103. Temple Dinsley: garden house — 126
104. Millmead: garden house — 126
105. Hestercombe: the east rill garden — 128
106. Lutyens's ideal water garden with 'Emmie' and the children — 129
107. Putteridge Park: the plan for the rose garden — 130
108. Edwin Lutyens: portrait by Augustus John (1917) — 134
109. Gertrude Jekyll: portrait by William Nicholson (1920) — 135
110. Warlincourt Halte British Cemetery at Saulty — 137
111. Warlincourt Halte British Cemetery: sketch plan — 137
112. Gledstone Hall: the canal garden — 139
113. Tyringham Park: sketch plan of the garden — 140
114. Amport House: one of the lily pools and rills on the lower terrace — 142
115. Amport House: plan for the raised-bed rock garden — 144
116. Amport House: part of Miss Jekyll's original planting plan for the rock garden — 145
117. Plumpton Place: the rose borders — 148
118. Plumpton Place: the border by the lake — 149
119. Plumpton Place: astilbes and gladiolus by the lake — 149
120. Blagdon: Miss Jekyll's planting plan for the north part of the quarry garden — 151
121. Great Maytham: the rebuilt terrace — 179
122. Daneshill: how not to treat a Lutyens house with a Jekyll garden! — 181
123. The Dormy House: the approach from the golf club — 182
124. The Dormy House today — 182
125. The original plan for 100 Cheyne Walk, London — 184
126. John Brookes's 'revival' of Jekyll planting for 100 Cheyne Walk adapted as a Chelsea Flower Show garden — 185

Key to Garden Plans

—————— Enclosing or significant walls

/////// Enclosing or significant hedges

——————— Miniature hedges e.g. box

Grass

Border planting

Water

 Acknowledgements

I owe my sincerest thanks to very many people: to Geoffrey Collens, former editor of *Landscape Design*, for publishing my first article on this subject, and to Michael Packard, for suggesting that the article could be turned into a book.

To Michael Laurie and Stephen Tobriner of the College of Environmental Design at Berkeley, California, the home of the Reef Point Gardens Collection, and to David Dean and Angela Mace of the British Architectural Library, Margaret Richardson, Deputy Curator of the R.I.B.A. Drawings Collection, Mrs J. G. Links (Mary Lutyens), and Sarah Hann, sometime Librarian at *Country Life*.

To Caradoc King, of A. P. Watt Ltd, for recognizing that the book had a future when that seemed in doubt, and to Michael Dover and Annie Lee of Penguin, and Yvonne Dedman, the designer, whose combined talents have turned it into a reality.

My thanks must also go to all the owners of Lutyens/Jekyll gardens and to many other people who have given me their time and encouragement, especially Mr R. G. Bailey, Mrs Marjorie Barker, John Brookes, Frederick Burn F.R.I.B.A., Mrs Julia Edwards, Lord Hamilton of Dalzell, Lord and Lady Hylton, Gillian Jason of Campbell & Franks Fine Arts, Mrs Jane Kirby, Lucinda Lambton, the Hon. David Lytton-Cobbold, Mr David Nelson, Mr Nigel Nicolson and Dr Michael Tooley.

The last stages of the book's production have coincided with the Arts Council's exhibition on *The Life and Work of Sir Edwin Lutyens* at the Hayward Gallery, London; my final thanks go to my fellow members of the Lutyens Exhibition Committee, especially to Colin Amery, Piers Gough, Roderick Gradidge, Mary Lutyens, Margaret Richardson and Gavin Stamp, all of whose scholarship and enthusiasm have benefited my book in some way.

ILLUSTRATION ACKNOWLEDGEMENTS

COLOUR: 1, Coll. the Rt Hon. Lord Hamilton of Dalzell; 2, Campbell & Franks Fine Arts Ltd; 3, 4, 5, 6, 7, 10, 11, 12, 13, 14, 15, 16, 17, 18, 19, 20, 21, 22, 23 and 24, Peter B. Brown; 8 and 9, the Iris Hardwick Library of Photographs.

BLACK AND WHITE: 1, Coll. the Rt Hon. Lord Hamilton of Dalzell; 2, from Francis Jekyll, *A Memoir*; 3 and 71, Mary Lutyens; 4, 5, 25, 72, 101, R.I.B.A. Drawings Collection; 7, 8, 9, 10, 12, 13, 14, 18, 20, 23, 24, 34, 36, 40, 44, 45, 46, 47, 48, 49, 50, 51, 52, 56, 59, 63, 64, 65, 66, 67, 73, 74, 82, 83, 87, 88, 89, 90, 92, 97, 100, 102, 107, 111, 113, 115, 122, 124, 125, the author; 6, 15, 16, 17, 19, 31, 32, 116, 120, and endpapers, Coll. the University of California (Reef Point Gardens Collection), College of Environmental Design, Berkeley (Copyright the Gertrude Jekyll Estate); 21, 26, 27, 28, 41, 42, 60, 61, 62, 68, 112, 117, 118, 119, *Country Life* (I.P.C. Magazines); 29, 30, 37, 38, 39, 43, 53, 54, 55, 57, 58, 76, 77, 78, 79, 80 (by permission of the National Trust), 81, 84, 85, 91, 93, 94, 95, 96, 98, 99, 103, 104, 105, 114, 121, Peter B. Brown; 35, 69 and 70, Coll. the University of California (Reef Point Gardens Collection, Copyright Mary Lutyens); 75, from *The Lutyens Memorial*, Vol. 1; 86 and 123, from *Gardens for Small Country Houses*, 1st edn; 108, National Portrait Gallery (Copyright Miss M. Steen); 109, Coll. Viscount Ridley (photograph by Prudence Cuming Associates); 110, Commonwealth War Graves Commission; 126, from John Brookes, *The Small Garden* (Mitchell Beazley). The cartoons 22, 33, and 106 and the various quotations from Lutyens's letters are from the Lutyens Family Papers, B.A.L., R.I.B.A. MSS Coll. (the Misses J., S., and J. C. Ridley).

 INTRODUCTION

THIS is the story of an unusual and abundantly creative partnership. Much of its success was due to the mixing of experience with a young, unfettered talent, and thus my story concerns two lives that spanned a century: Gertrude Jekyll was born in 1843 and Sir Edwin Lutyens died on New Year's Day, 1944.

Miss Jekyll first met the young Lutyens in the spring of 1889, when she was forty-five years old. She had lived the first half of her life in the dedicated pursuit of all things artistic and beautiful, in the company of educated, spirited and successful people, many of whom, like herself, had adequate private means to adopt their chosen lifestyle. This freedom and the variety of her achievements were unusual for a Victorian gentlewoman, but in Miss Jekyll's personality any hint of the unconventional, or even 'bohemian', was subdued by her abiding love and understanding of the landscape and country ways of life of south-west Surrey, where she had been brought up. Her observation of this landscape was always her inspiration, and when in her mid-thirties her fading eyesight made it necessary to reduce the range of her activities, it was the prospect of a home of her own in Surrey which compensated for all she had to give up, and which gave her lasting contentment as a practical countrywoman whose chief occupation was gardening and writing about her garden. This transformation was almost complete when she met Edwin Lutyens; he was only twenty, and had little more as an augury for his career than an inner conviction that he could design beautiful buildings, and a few commissions from friends for cottages and lodges. Miss Jekyll had found her own garden, but still lived with her mother and now needed a house of her own and an architect to design what she wanted. Thus the partnership was formed in the making of Munstead Wood in the 1890s. Lutyens learned from Miss Jekyll not only the best way to design a garden but a good deal about designing houses, especially the kind of houses favoured by his new clients, many of whom were to be friends and connections of the Jekylls. He shared her love of the Surrey countryside, and exploring it together was the basis of their friendship; it was also the key to the dramatic character of many of his country houses and gave him understanding of the use of natural materials which was to be his mark.

The triumph of the partnership was in garden-making, and together they created over a hundred gardens, the real subject of this book, which are set out in the Survey on page 159. These gardens belong in essence, if not always in reality, to a small portion of the hundred years that is spanned by their makers' lives – the period from 1890 to the outbreak of war in 1914. They were gardens created for a rich and artistic coterie which inhabited what we like to think of as a golden age, made 'more radiant because it is on the other side of the huge black pit of war'.[1] Whatever the social shortcomings of that age, or the distortion of our memories by the events of succeeding years, it was certainly the last period in which there were clients with the freedom and wealth to indulge in a peculiarly English art. Lutyens's dream houses and their even more magical gardens were the expression of that art, the art of living elegantly, but not opulently, in the country – merely with everything of the best, a plentiful supply of domestic staff, and the time and innocence to relish the experience. In exploring the creation and design of the gardens – surely the last evocation of art into landscape that we have achieved in these islands – I have been unashamedly looking for the spirit of that golden afternoon, for I believe that it is in these gardens that it best survives.

The gardens were only a very small part of the tremendous output of Lutyens's career. In the 1890s he and Miss Jekyll would visit a site together, discussing how to make best use of it, where the house should go, how the garden should be laid out, and then combining their ideas into the finished design over tea or supper afterwards. Gradually, as she ceased travelling and he rose to the heights of Establishment and, finally, Imperial architect, they saw each other less and less, but the gardens carry on as an important recurring theme in Lutyens's career. Much of the inspiration for his work for the War Graves Commission sprang from his ideal of a garden as a place of peace and rest; his most fantastic garden of all was created for Viceroy's House, New Delhi. To the very end of his life, the opportunity to design a garden was a welcome link with youthful happiness and his early days as an architect at Munstead Wood.

As for Miss Jekyll, she had started designing gardens before she met Lutyens, and continued to do so long after the creative intensity of the partnership had faded. Her nephew and first biographer, Francis Jekyll,[2] gives a list of 346 commissions between 1868 and her death in 1932. This figure does, however, need some qualification. In many cases she did not visit the garden concerned; indeed for the last twenty-five years of her life she did not move far from Munstead Wood at all, certainly no farther than her pony cart would take her – a maximum of about twenty miles for the round trip. Many recommendations were confined to letters and plans after she had been provided with the essential details of the site and soil conditions. Many of the commissions were just for part of a garden, for a particular feature which displayed her special artistry, such as a border, a rock garden or a water garden. Though she contributed to many gardens in the 'stately home' class (planting schemes for Sutton Place and Loseley House in Surrey, a tiltyard for Arundel Castle, a herb garden for Knebworth House, flower gardens for Barrington Court), most of her commissions were for more modest houses, which have passed through many changes of ownership since her time. This has meant that in general her fragile creations have not survived, though her teachings, as set down in her books, and her influence have lived on. Only when she worked with an architect, when the designs were immaculately drawn out on paper and then physically contained in stone and brick as his more durable contribution to the scheme, has it been possible for her planting to have survived or be restored. Miss Jekyll did commissions for many of the architects of her day, and I have mentioned a few of these for the sake of comparison.

The Lutyens/Jekyll relationship was therefore a partnership in the broadest terms. For him, through Miss Jekyll and the people she knew, it was the true beginning of his career; for her, it was a new interest and a new challenge just when her life seemed to have lost some of its direction and purpose. They stayed the best of friends until her death, though after the war it was a somewhat distant friendship because of his globe-trotting eminence, and the links were maintained through friends. To the Lutyens family her image was that of a portly fairy godmother – 'Aunt Bumps' – made ethereal by her seclusion in the magical haven of Munstead Wood.

My introduction to the Lutyens/Jekyll legend, now a part of the folklore of west Surrey, came when I moved into a house of strong Lutyens inspiration at Abinger, just over ten years ago. The Abinger area has several Lutyens-designed buildings, some Jekyll gardens, and many Lutyens/Jekyll derivations. I first encountered Munstead Wood, Tigborne Court and Orchards, in the heart of the legendary land, on an outing organized by the Surrey Archaeological Society, the present-day guardians of Old West Surrey. I was enchanted. As I was also studying landscape architecture I used the Dutch garden at Orchards (see page 57) for a measured drawing project, and was rewarded by the amazing patterns of the geometry and the incredible accuracy of the craftsmanship still readily apparent despite 'three score years and ten' being a considerable age for a garden. It became a passion to list all the gardens that could possibly have a Lutyens/Jekyll connection, and I sought them out whenever the opportunity arose. In my obsession I became quite reckless – knocking on the most imposing front doors at awkward hours of the day or evening, simply because our routes to and from holidays in the North were always designed to pass a maximum number of distant gardens. I failed just once (being deterred by automatic gates and baying mastiffs in the drive), and can only express my gratitude again to all the patient and helpful owners I encountered. I hope that some of them will be as pleased as I am now that my obsession has inspired this book.

My Sources

Almost every book concerned with garden design in the last thirty years has given the partners' work some mention. The country houses and their gardens are blithely referred to as the climax of the Arts and Crafts Movement, but such elevation is usually followed by only the briefest reference to the most famous gardens – Deanery Garden, Folly Farm, and, following its restoration, Hestercombe. The most substantial source of information on the gardens in book form is Lawrence Weaver's *Sir Edwin Lutyens' Houses and Gardens*.[3] This book was based on articles published in *Country Life* magazine, which not only did a great deal to further the reputations of both Lutyens and Miss Jekyll, but also perpetuated the values of the country houses and their gardens. Lawrence Weaver was writing in the years before the Great War, and, more concerned to establish the pre-eminence of Lutyens's reputation as an architect, paid little critical attention to the gardens. Nonetheless the marvellous photographs, both in that book and in the *Country*

Life collection, have proved a valuable source of information about original designs and planting.

The other substantial source of information is the Reef Point Gardens Collection of Miss Jekyll's drawings in the possession of the University of California at Berkeley. I was allowed complete freedom of access to these drawings, for which I am extremely grateful, for much of the book could not have been written without the information gathered there. However, even in this priceless hoard, very few of the important gardens are covered by an anywhere near complete set of drawings, and it was disappointing to find that some of the Lutyens gardens are not included at all. With some bitterness I noted that there were often more complete plans for jobs done with other architects, and I came away with a feeling that the collection had been sifted many times before; it is likely that the 'best' drawings have been removed. The collection seems to be that which formed the basis for Francis Jekyll's list of his aunt's commissions published in the back of his *Memoir* of her in 1934. Quite what happened to them after he used them is a mystery – I have heard that they were thrown out in a waste paper collection – possibly when Munstead Wood was sold immediately after the war, or perhaps when Francis Jekyll's belongings were auctioned in the 1950s. I bless the memory of American landscape architect Beatrix Farrand, who had the foresight to rescue the bulk of the material from some further unhappy fate, even though she took them home with her and bequeathed them to a university thousands of miles from their home. There, thank goodness, they have a safe refuge, and the Garden History Society have recently acquired a catalogue and microfilm of the collection for reference in this country.

I have found only a small amount of Miss Jekyll's correspondence, the bulk of which I believe has been destroyed. In his *Memoir*, Francis Jekyll writes: 'To those who came as suppliants to her oracle, her reply was "Read my books"; she might have added: "Look around you if you seek my monument".'[4] As far as the gardens of the partnership are concerned, I am afraid that the first is only sometimes true, the second rarely possible. Her fourteen books are in many senses her life – they record her thoughts and doings about everything that would interest the garden-minded and they create marvellous impressionistic pictures of the magical doings at Munstead Wood. However, if one is seeking an all-round garden experience, they only tantalize – for very rarely are the beautiful gardening ideas related to an overall design (the only sketch design of Munstead Wood is in *Gardens for Small Country Houses*), and even rarer are the allusions to other designs which incorporate the features she recommends. Of course, if Munstead Wood had been preserved and cared for as she left it there would be a point of reference for all she advocated; but it has not, and so I have had to try, in Chapter 2, to convey a little of what it must have been like, for it was the begetter of all the other gardens.

Over the years, Miss Jekyll's planting theories have inspired much elaboration and re-interpretation by many experts, but you will find nothing of this kind here. With her planting plans for the gardens from the Berkeley collection we are back to original sources; I show simply what she planned. My view of her planting comes only from the plans, and my interpretation, where necessary, is intuitive rather than academic. Many of her plans are incompletely labelled (and anyone who has ever drawn up a planting plan knows how difficult it is to fit those last two or three plants in) and sometimes her writing is difficult to read; nonetheless, they are a model of professionalism far in advance of their time. The only way to make up for what is omitted or illegible is to 'get inside her mind' and follow her rules for colour and form in planting, which I have tried to explain in Chapter 2. Even her published plans, for instance those of Millmead in *Gardens for Small Country Houses* (see pages 118–19), are ambiguous, bearing in mind how names and hybrids have changed since Miss Jekyll's time. I have, in general, tried to illustrate the plans in understandable modern terms – this does not mean that every plant has been given its full Latin name, as in many cases this would be more misleading than leaving her old English version. If she has specified 'pink hollyhock' or 'white columbine' there seems to be little more to say (once you know the rules), and the chief difficulty of the present-day gardener will be sorting out the pink and white flowered seeds from the ubiquitous packet of mixed colours! Where there is room for doubt I have given the Latin and English names, and the variety and hybrid if she intended one in particular. Too often it will be a case of matching colour and form to her intention from a list of hybrids that bear no resemblance to those she knew, but I have not mentioned varieties that she could not have known, and I have not changed her names without being absolutely sure that we now use a new one. Finally, I do think the difficulties of following her old-fashioned plans are made too much of. The plans she made for clients were much simpler than those she dreamed up for Munstead Wood, and once armed with the vital rules, there would seem to be no insurmountable difficulties in their re-creation.

The British Architectural Library (R.I.B.A. Drawings Collection) has an enormous collection of Lutyens's drawings, but disappointingly little material on the gardens. There are some delightful sketches, which have found their way into this book. The B.A.L. also possesses a substantial collection of Lutyens's letters to his wife, covering the entire forty years that he knew her, but as she found lengthy mention of his work boring, there are only a few references of value concerning the gardens. The four-volume *Memorial* by A. S. G. Butler, George Stewart and Christopher Hussey (author of the *Life of Lutyens* which is Volume 4), published by Country Life in 1950, must rank as the most substantial tribute ever paid to a British architect. The three massive volumes illustrated with plans and photographs of Lutyens's life's works are now also collectors' pieces; I am the proud owner of what I believe was the last dust-jacketed and unopened set which came from the sale of Country Life publishing house to the repository of Lutyens/Jekylliana which is Mr Charles Traylen's bookshop in Quarry Street, Guildford. The list of Lutyens's works by A. S. G. Butler in Volume 1, and the plans and photographs of the houses and gardens, have been invaluable, but if the massive *Memorial* can be said to have a flaw, it is that Butler and Stewart (like Lawrence Weaver before them) were intent on leaving posterity with the image of an almost divinely faultless genius. In the *Memorial* all the plans have been re-drawn to perfection by George Stewart and all the photographs are set pieces. In reality, almost everything Lutyens ever built was conceived on scraps of blotchy and ash-scattered paper, with ink or pencil 'worm's-eye view' sketches of how the building, memorial or garden would actually look, and feel, in space and time; it was this moment of bright invention that gave a spirit of delight to his earlier works, and especially to the gardens. And it is in the gardens, rather than in any sombre building or on any page of involved analysis, that the spirit of this most delightful, and humanly frail, genius is most likely to live still. So, in the end, it is the gardens themselves that have told me most of all – some of them are still glorious, some have been blatantly despoiled, some are shabby with neglect and age – and though all their glories can never be captured within the pages of a book, I hope that an understanding of their creation can, and will, evoke a sympathy for their incongruity in our time.

Ashtead, Surrey   *Easter 1981*

1

THE LADY AND THE ARCHITECT

We met at a tea-table, the silver kettle and the conversation
reflecting rhododendrons.

Sir Edwin Lutyens[1]

A Surrey Childhood

GERTRUDE JEKYLL was born in London on 29 November 1843. She was the second
daughter and fourth surviving child of Edward and Julia Jekyll (pronounced
with the emphasis on the 'e' to rhyme with 'treacle'), an upper-middle-class
family whose forebears came from Lincolnshire[2] – one, Sir Joseph (1662–1738), was
Master of the Rolls to George I; his great-nephew, another Joseph (1754–1838), was a
barrister, pre-Reform M.P., founder of the Athenaeum and an elected Fellow of the
Royal Society of Arts. This Joseph's younger son, Edward Joseph Hill Jekyll, was
Gertrude's father; born in 1804, he served in the Grenadier Guards and was a keen
amateur yachtsman, inventor and engineer with a love of classical art and architecture.
His wife, Julia, was the daughter of Charles Hammersley, a banker, who had married
Emily Poulett Thomson of Waverley Abbey House near Farnham, the family's only
Surrey connection.[3]

Maybe it was Gertrude's maternal grandmother's suggestion that the family would be
better suited in the country; they moved to Surrey when Gertrude was four and a half,
and now had a younger brother Herbert (always to be her favourite) to make the
number of children five. (There was to be one more, Walter, born in 1849.) Their new
home was Bramley Park [1 and colour pl. 1], a sprawling neo-classical mansion with a
good garden and large park, close to Bramley village, beside the Horsham road south
from Guildford.[4]

Bramley, with its clustering deeply-roofed and tile-hung cottages, was a little world
of its own in the middle years of the last century. Its countryside is the fertile valley of
the River Wey and its tributaries, with lush green meadows edged with cow parsley and
filled with buttercups, where contented cattle grazed. Some of the drier fields grew
wheat, potatoes, hops and market crops for near-by Guildford; the cottagers and farmers
were thrifty and hard-working, and the village had its complement of essential
craftsmen (carpenter, saddler, wheelwright) in a land sprinkled with industries –
brickmaking, tanning, brewing, charcoal-burning and the remnants of Wealden iron,
made more prosperous by the coming of the Wey and Arun Canal which passed
through the village.[5] The railway, which was to kill off the canal trade and stifle
Bramley's self-reliance by turning it into a commuter village, was in the undreamed-of
future.

1. Bramley Park, near Guildford, Surrey: Gertrude Jekyll's home from 1848–68.

The Jekyll children, especially Gertrude, adored their new country life. As she grew older she was allowed to wander farther, but her first delight was the garden. The big house was surrounded by a certain amount of obligatory formal bedding (which did not seem to attract the embryo gardener), but in *Children and Gardens* she recalls how she loved the 'best shrubs and garden trees' – magnolias, rhododendrons, azaleas, kalmias, pieris (which she knew by the more dramatic name, Andromeda) and cut-leaved beech and ailanthus. She was allowed her own plot between the shrubbery and the field, with a cool damp ditch where the ferns loved to grow; this was also the home of her special rose, Blush Boursault, a thornless climber with enormous pink flowers. She remembers with 'special adoration' one tuft of large blue cornflowers. Here, certainly, was all the wonder and admiration of a small and spirited child set down in an exotically planted old garden for the first time; for years she did not know the names of the plants, but gave them her own names and greeted them as friends on her daily wanderings. Here she learned her gardener's feeling for plants – respect comes easily for things so much larger than oneself.

Beyond the garden was the park, with its streams, woods and mill-ponds.[6] This was the scene for tomboyish exploits with her brothers which are hard to imagine from the later pictures of the prim lady – she delighted 'to go up trees, and to play cricket, and take wasps' nests after dark, and do dreadful things with gunpowder . . .'[7] One of the mill-ponds 'had a large island near the upper end, but no bridge. In our earlier years we had no boat, but belonging to the house was a set of brewing-tackle, and among its items a beer-cooler – a wooden thing about five feet long and three feet wide, with sides eight or ten inches high, like a large shallow box or tray . . . and we children surreptitiously used it as a boat to make perilous journeys over to the island.'[8]

When her brothers were away at school, and her much older sister Caroline could not be bothered with her, she was left alone and would wander with her pony and dog for company beyond the park and along the lanes leading to the woods and heaths. Away from the river valley, the landscape of this part of Surrey has quite dramatic outcrops of sandstone which form small hills, and among the hills are the hollow lanes that have been worn by centuries of erosion and usage until sometimes they have 'cliffs' twice a man's height, and sometimes just a low sandy bank. The banks were traditionally planted with beech, and holly and oak have moved in too, and these banks are laced with contorted tree roots, struggling to support lofty beeches on thin air as the banks become further eroded. Gertrude was fascinated by the hollow lanes and the root formations, and when she took up photography she used these subjects over and over again.[9] In this sandy countryside she enlarged her knowledge of plants to include the wild flowers of heath and woodland. It is worth noting that the three types of planting in which she was to excel – water, woodland and dry-wall gardening – were exactly the habitats she knew and understood in her Surrey childhood.

She also visited the cottages and workshops of Bramley village; she talked to the villagers, watched them work, and helped, when she was allowed. Her fascination with rural life and the work of the countryside was to remain with her for the rest of her life – her innate respect for its thrift and good sense was always evident in her own personality and in her housekeeping and management. Later on, when she realized that this way of life was disappearing before her eyes, she recorded it in her books, *Old West Surrey* and *Old English Household Life*, and collected its artifacts.[10]

Despite all her leisurely wanderings Gertrude had a good education at home. The Jekylls were sensible enough to insist on competent governesses for their unusual daughter – 'my oddity', Edward Jekyll affectionately called her. She turned out to be proficient in languages, music and art, and in an age of liberal indulgence it was decided that she should continue to study all three.

The Lady as Artist and Craftswoman

'Liberal indulgence' was a phrase that came to mind in contrast to our own narrow educational specialization, but in 1861, when Gertrude Jekyll was seventeen, it was not usually a phrase applicable to the female half of the population. When she recalls, as I think she does in every book, that it was her greatest desire to be an artist, that was not the simple wish it sounds. Her parents must take a lot of the credit, not only for her free and happy childhood, but for allowing her 'higher education', for enrolling her for a two-year course at the School of Art in South Kensington (where the Victoria & Albert Museum now stands) and for continuing to support her in the independent life she wished to live. It was, after all, not long since Laura Herford had had to trick the Royal Academy Schools into accepting a woman by submitting a picture signed simply 'L.

Herford'. Helen Paterson (later Allingham)[11] and Barbara Leigh-Smith[12] (both future friends of Gertrude Jekyll) were among the first women to be taught at art school, and it was typical of Gertrude that she followed quietly in their wake. This quiet but determined pioneering, which she never alluded to and is rarely given any credit for, set the pattern for the rest of her life.

Towards the end of her time at art school, her father's friend Charles Newton, the Keeper of Greek and Roman Antiquities at the British Museum, asked if Gertrude would join his expedition to Greece as a companion for his wife, Mary. This expedition, in the autumn of 1863, took Gertrude to Corfu, Crete, Rhodes, Athens and Constantinople. In marvellous company, with the leisure to sketch and paint, with wonderful new wild flowers to be found as well as the fabled sites to be visited, she adored every minute. Mary Newton's sketches of her travelling companion show a short, rather plump, but sturdy-looking young lady, with her dark hair strained back into a bun (a style that was never to alter), and a bespectacled, blue-stocking appearance. From the descriptions of her friends it was undoubtedly the enthusiasm, good humour and common sense that shone through which lightened this rather stoical impression. The enthusiasm which had made her study so hard at her art, and make the most of every moment of this expedition, inspired her to work even harder on her return – she assiduously copied great paintings (especially Turner's) and visited exhibitions and lectures and artists in London during the week, returning to her workroom at home at the weekends. Through the Newtons she met John Ruskin (Mary Newton was the sister of Ruskin's faithful friends Joanna and Arthur Severn). Ruskin's books *The Stones of Venice* and *Modern Painters* and his exhortations on the virtues of the medieval artist-craftsmen, were having an all-pervasive influence on the artists and architects of the time. In the autumn of 1865 – the same year that she exhibited a painting of her brother's dog 'Cheeky – a native of Cawnpore' at the Royal Academy[13] – Gertrude recorded the first of several visits to Ruskin, and she must have been very much aware of the beginnings of the breaking of the new wave, later dubbed the Arts and Crafts Movement. She too found that painting was not enough; she visited William Morris in Red Lion Square, where Morris, Marshall, Faulkner & Company were established at the time, she met Edward Burne-Jones and Dante Gabriel Rossetti, and probably Morris's architect Philip Webb (later to be one of Lutyens's earliest influences) as well, and she started designing and making embroideries and craft work in metal and wood. Besides all this, her diary for the next few years mentions meetings with all the most famous names in Victorian art – G. F. Watts, Frederick Leighton, Frederick Walker, Albert Moore, William de Morgan, Simeon Solomon, Edward Poynter and William Holman Hunt were all known to her. She travelled each year, to France, Italy or Spain, and later Algiers, to see galleries, buildings and the great gardens of Europe – among them La Bagatelle, the Villas Taranto, Garzoni and d'Este, the Generalife and the Alhambra. In this Mediterranean landscape she found her abiding love for evergreen and aromatic plants: 'all that is best and purest and most refined, and nearest to poetry, in the range of faculty of the sense of smell' was her description of bay, rosemary, thyme, myrtle and 'incense-laden brakes of cistus'.[14]

When Gertrude was about thirty, she was described as a paragon of witty conversation, energetic activity and artistic talent, and master of 'carving, modelling, house-painting, carpentry, smith's work, repoussé work, gilding, wood-inlaying, embroidery, gardening and all manner of herb and flower knowledge and culture' – all carried on 'with perfect method and completeness'.[15] Not surprisingly she gained an artistic reputation even beyond that of her large circle of friends. The Duke of Westminster asked her to supervise the interior re-furbishing of the now vanished Eaton Hall in Cheshire. An exhibition of her silverwork attracted commissions from both 'high' aristocratic and artistic society – including Queen Victoria's fourth daughter, the Princess Louise, who became a friend (and a Lutyens client), Edward Burne-Jones and Lord Leighton. She joined the Blumenthals' circle[16] at 43 Hyde Park Gate, which was her London home for a while (and where Lutyens was to meet Lady Emily Lytton), and she made summer excursions to the Blumenthals' chalet above Lake Geneva. In this company she became firm friends with Barbara Leigh-Smith, an artist and later co-founder of Girton College, Cambridge.[17] She did some of her earliest garden designs for Barbara's retreat cottage, Scalands near Robertsbridge in Sussex. It was probably in Sussex that she met the painter Hercules Brabazon Brabazon, once hailed as the successor to Turner and more recently as 'England's Lost Impressionist',[18] with whom she was to remain close friends until he died in 1906. Brabazon's lifelong obsession with capturing light in his watercolour paintings, and his determined amateurism – which was to be his downfall – had a great influence on Gertrude Jekyll.

There are two threads, both of which have an important bearing on Miss Jekyll's reputation, which are worth close attention. Firstly, she had not only to counter the accepted limitations on the place of women in mid-Victorian society, but there was the delicate nature of *amateurism* as well. For all her variety of talents and undoubted hard work, for all the evidence that remains that her work was outstandingly beautiful (how could 'embroidered cushions with dandelion, mistletoe, pomegranate, strawberry' and 'embroidered periwinkles'[19] be otherwise?), the name of Gertrude Jekyll will not be found linked with the beginnings of the Arts and Crafts Movement. Just as Morris's name is unavoidable, so hers is invisible, though she would seem to have been just as talented. I think it was partly because she was a 'lady', partly because she spread her net too wide, but probably mostly because of the nature of this 'amateurism'. Though she secretly yearned to be paid for her work as a mark of its merit, the fact that she was a lady, known to be of independent means which made earning a living unnecessary, made this unthinkable; her amateur status, which meant that she was free to indulge all her whims, also meant that she would never be accepted by those for whom art was the serious business of earning a living. The last great bastions of the amateur versus the professional, Lords and Wimbledon, have long since given up the fight, and it is difficult for us to imagine just how great was the divide; perhaps Miss Jekyll's situation is best illuminated by the case of Lord Leighton's tablecloth. Leighton wrote to Gertrude's friend and cousin, Georgina Duff Gordon, some time in 1870:

I have seen today in the galleries of the International some embroideries on linen and serge by Miss Jekyll of such remarkable merit in point of colour and arrangement that I cannot refrain from writing to ask you more about them. I should add that one of them, a design with scrolls of fishes, is so good as decorative invention that I hesitate to attribute it to an amateur and presume it must have been borrowed. I should of course be rejoiced to be mistaken. Meanwhile I want very much to know from you whether Miss J does these things solely for her delight (being as I understand a lady of independent means) or whether they are accessible to outside admirers – and if so whether they are very ruinous.

In a second letter, having been encouraged by Georgina's reply, he goes on to say that he would like a tablecloth made for his dining-room, but fears 'it is a delicate matter to ask such a question of a lady'.[20] Poor Miss Jekyll, poor little fairly-rich girl, indeed, if this is what she was up against. Fortunately Georgina sorted it all out; Gertrude records starting work on the tablecloth, both hesitant painter and talented embroideress were made happy, and she was, presumably, eventually paid.

The second drawn thread which spoils the pattern, and will eventually bring this rich artistic life to an end, is her myopia. As far as I can make out her short-sightedness was about the same in extent as my own – and I can only see things exactly and clearly if they are less than one foot from my eyes, after which everything recedes into a blur. Apart from my own sympathy, there is now also Patrick Trevor-Roper's *The World through Blunted Sight*,[21] a miraculous revelation of the effect of myopia on the artistic mind, which enables us to see just how deeply Gertrude Jekyll's life and work were dominated by her myopic personality. For her, everything within the close, certain world that she could see clearly was easy and comfortable; myopes are usually well-read, for it is easy to 'stick one's nose in a book' and let the mind range afar into an imagined clear world, when reality is only hazily discerned. Perhaps even her childhood adoration of large plants and flowers was tinged by the fact that she could see them most clearly – part of the joy of her recollection may have been because she *did* see them more clearly when she was small, as myopia often intensifies with physical growth; and getting close to study the details and so discovering the textures and smells of leaves and flowers was to stand her in good stead when it came to gardening, but it was also typical of the myopic child. Perhaps she even felt the security of her beloved Surrey landscape because of its small-scale, hollow lanes, close hills and limited views – when her family moved to Berkshire in 1868 she hated it, 'because it was not Surrey', but possibly also because it was the expansive, spreading landscape of the Thames valley at Wargrave. Finally, there are her photographs, repeated studies of shapes, textures – endless studies of the contorted tree roots and the lane banks, studies of single branches of flowers and leaves, and the faces of Bramley people – but nearly always in close-up and very rarely the distant view.[22]

Even for such a practical and spirited personality, some of the typical myopic withdrawal into the world that is close and clear was inescapable, and to some extent this must have restrained her emotional development. From what we know of most of her friendships, they were based on shared interests rather than shared feelings. Certainly, she would not have brooked marriage to a man less talented or less capable than herself, but, as her tremendous intellectual and artistic activity was a mask for emotional shortcomings, then equally it was her myopic uncertainty which did not allow her to

1. Bramley Park, Guildford, Surrey:
the beautiful garden in which
Gertrude Jekyll spent her childhood
(from a watercolour by Henry Sage).

2. The Taj Mahal, from a
watercolour by Hercules Brabazon
Brabazon, represents much of what
Gertrude Jekyll learnt from her
long friendship with the painter,
and then contributed to the
partnership with Edwin Lutyens.
The highlights of white, the pinky-
creaminess of the most sublime
architecture, all balanced and reined
to the earth by dark greenery,
illustrate the beginning of the long
road to the 'enamelled carpets' of
Viceroy's House, New Delhi.

3. *(previous page)* Berrydowne Court, Ashe, Overton, Hampshire: a Surrey-style house translated – and not without difficulties – to the North Hampshire downs; however, the relationship between the house and the kitchen garden is typical and charming. Miss Jekyll's kitchen gardens were usually given wide flower borders flanking the paths which quartered the walled square, often with roses on looped ropes around a 'dipping well' in the centre.

4. *(above)* Woodside, Chenies, Buckinghamshire: the vista down the slope to the pond court, as it appears today in this, the first garden of the partnership, made in 1893.

5. *(left)* Woodside: the canopied gate into the former garage court.

kick over the traces of family approval to find happiness beyond the conventions of her time, as did her friend Barbara Leigh-Smith with her eccentric but magnificent Algeriophile, Dr Bodichon.[23]

Of course, she was in good company. Patrick Trevor-Roper has shown that short sight predominates among great artists, and is almost obligatory among Impressionists, many of whom would not wear spectacles because the blurring of details left their minds free to concentrate on colour and light.[24] Even Turner came into this category when he developed a senile cataract which had the same effect as myopia, and this coincides with the change in his style from the picturesque to objects 'dissolved' in light.[25] Thus her artistic loyalties were formed – and I like to think they may have been reinforced by a meeting with Claude Monet (who was a friend of Barbara Leigh-Smith) and perhaps a discussion over the beginnings of his garden at Giverny. Monet is, after all, famous because he did what Gertrude Jekyll perhaps failed to do – translate the glories of his garden on to canvas – but that is to anticipate the end of this story![26]

What she was to do – though it is rarely appreciated to the full – was to translate her impressionistic/myopic view of plants into marvellous gardens. It was, because of her myopia, a translation on two levels which are vitally important to the understanding of her planting ideas – firstly, because she was most comfortable working in close-up, she appreciated and used the textures and shapes of leaves, the perfumes of flowers, to their greatest advantage; secondly, because much of the distance was a hazy blur, her perception of sweeps of colour, of the habits of light, was uncluttered by details, and therefore the more devastatingly accurate and impressive.

It was inevitable that as she grew older her eyes would become more easily tired, and to maintain her ceaseless activity and beautiful fine work at embroidery and silverwork in the face of increasing pain and discomfort must have taken unusual energy and much courage. It could not have helped that she must have become aware of the approaching crisis just when she was breaking down the barriers of acceptance. By her late thirties she must have begun to realize that she would have to sacrifice all the things that gave meaning to her life – her painting, embroidery and silverwork – but even as this unlooked-for change was becoming imminent, two portentous things happened: she met William Robinson, and her family moved house again.

The Lady – 'To Munstead for good'

The Jekyll family had left Bramley Park (which they had only rented) in 1868, to live in a house at Wargrave in Berkshire which Edward Jekyll had inherited. In 1876 he died, and the family that remained 'at home' – Gertrude, her mother and her younger brother, Herbert – decided immediately that they would return to Surrey. They bought a plot of unlikely land high on Munstead Heath, south of Godalming and the Wey valley, and only a short crow's flight from the old home at Bramley. The Scottish architect J. J. Stevenson built Munstead House for Mrs Jekyll in a kind of Scots vernacular style, rather appropriate as the Surrey heathland has certain similarities with the then royally-favoured and fashionable Highlands. Gertrude records the moving day, 26

September 1878, in her diary – 'To Munstead for good',[27] and there could be no doubt that she was glad to be home; over the next ten years she was slowly to relinquish her London life and travelling, and Surrey was to gain more and more of her time. She had always retained her childhood interest in plants and now gardening was getting more of her attention, too – not only was she making the garden for Munstead House, but there were signs that she was entering the world of gardening with all the thoroughness with which she had encountered the world of art; if Ruskin had been the Olympus of the art world, this time she was starting with Vesuvius!

The gentleman rather prone to eruption was, of course, William Robinson, and Miss Jekyll met him at his office in Covent Garden for the first time in 1875; it is probable that she had gone there clutching her first contribution to his magazine *The Garden*, or perhaps to discuss some articles she wished to write, but for whatever reason, it was a vitally important meeting. Her attention had probably been first drawn to Robinson with the publication of his book, *The Wild Garden*, in 1870,[28] which must have come as a breath of fresh air into the gardening world of the time, extolling the beauties of English wild flowers to a society obsessed with ranks of geraniums and pelargoniums, palms and bamboo groves and monkey puzzle trees. Robinson had started *The Garden* the following year and she had been an early subscriber; after that first meeting they became firm friends. She probably discussed in advance the tirade that would be cannoned into the gardening world with the publication of *The English Flower Garden*,[29] in which Robinson was to destroy the most precious false gods of the Victorian gardeners; his ringing prose, more suitable to the battlefield than a supposedly gentle art, was to weaken the desire for stylized and exotic gardening which had fascinated England for over half a century. The preoccupation with novelty – adopted as a reprisal to 'Capability' Brown and the landscape movement who set their houses floating in seas of grass – was about to be countered by another return to naturalism. Robinson hated 'carpet bedding', which degraded flowers 'to crude colour without reference to natural form and beauty of the plants', and he felt it 'would be easy to fill a comic journal with the ugly monstrosities of the topiarist'.[30] Another shot was fired at rustic work, so beloved of Victorian villa owners – it was 'complex and ugly', with its only merit being that it rotted away within a few years. Terracing and sunken gardens were derided as spoiling the natural ground, and 'for various good reasons artificial water is best as far away from the house as possible'. 'It is rare to see a garden seat that is not an eyesore' makes a good parting shot.[31] These and other Robinsonian gems fired criticism not only at the details of the gardens of the time, but at the whole owner/designer/plantsman relationship – much of his advice about hedges, terraces, pools, pergolas and seats was taken to heart by the Lutyens/Jekyll partnership, and his wider analysis was also to affect the way they worked.[32]

But it was perhaps in her feeling that plants had merits of their own, the understanding of which could bring much beauty into a garden, that Gertrude Jekyll found Robinson's sympathy most heartwarming. Here she was pioneering again, for, though he might rail and roar, it was she who would encourage, both by reasoned description and by example, a more *intelligent* use of plants. For it must be admitted that up until this time the majority of gardeners were slaves to fashion. Nathan Cole's *Royal Parks and Gardens of London*, published in 1877,[33] with suggestions for private gardeners to copy the elaborate geometrical bedding plans that were a feature of Kensington Gardens and the like, was only echoing the advice in John Claudius Loudon's *Suburban Gardener and Villa Companion* of 1839. For over forty years, as long as the result was fashionable, the plants had been merely a means to a garish end. It was Gertrude Jekyll who would give them a value of their own. It may be that some of her ideas went into *The English Flower Garden* and came out as Robinson's – he certainly advocated wild spring gardens that were not confined to the fashionable tulips, pansies and hyacinths but included our own wild spring flowers; he liked clematis growing up through holly and other dark evergreens; he emphasized the importance of fragrance and that a garden should have an all-the-year-round appeal rather than just be bright for one summer's day alone, and he especially wanted to see more effective use of the newly-imported chrysanthemums, dahlias, lilies, yuccas and grasses to bring colour to early autumn. Many of these ideas turned out to be Jekyll favourites in the Lutyens gardens.

Knowing her difficulties with the amateur/professional status in the arts world, Miss Jekyll's close alliance with William Robinson at the outset of her gardening career is interesting, for he was the one professional in her circle of amateur gardening friends. She was later to pay a tribute to 'that wonderful company of amateurs and others who did so much for better gardening in the last half of the nineteenth century',[34] and this company were mainly her friends from the Royal Horticultural Society, who were in many ways bridging the gardening divides. Formerly, design had been the prerogative of the landed gentry and alter-ego architects who employed professional gardeners and so did not bother with mere plants themselves; on the other side of the chasm were the plant collectors and breeders, who knew little of complementary colours, contrasting textures or garden vistas. There was no one between these two extremes to advise the growing number of owners of moderately-sized gardens, who wanted both good overall design and the 'best use' (as Miss Jekyll always put it) of beautiful plants. She and her friends were to be this new band of mediators:[35] her friends included George Ferguson Wilson,[36] just beginning his garden at Wisley Common which is now the Royal Horticultural Society's Wisley Garden; the imperious Ellen Willmott (they must have made a formidable pair), author of *The Genus Rosa* and owner of a magnificent garden at Great Warley in Essex;[37] Professor (later Sir) Michael Foster, an outstanding writer on iris and iris breeding;[38] that lovely Christian gentleman, Dean Samuel Reynolds Hole of Rochester,[39] who had a passion for and great knowledge of roses; and another clergyman, owner of an idyllic vicarage garden in Gloucestershire, Canon H. N. Ellacombe.[40]

Finally, it must be noted that gardening was generally acceptable as an activity for ladies, not only as an adjunct to home-making, but even as a form of light work, and though Miss Jekyll was gently pioneering yet again, it would not be long before there were colleges and courses for lady gardeners.

Early in the 1880s it became clear that the increasing trail of friends descending on Munstead House was too much for her mother, and that Gertrude must have a place of her own. She was able to buy fifteen acres of land on the opposite side of the road (Munstead Heath Road), a triangular shaped sandy plot which was to become the legendary Munstead Wood. She was well-equipped for the making of her undoubted masterpiece – she had been learning about plants all her life, she had made careful notes about all the flowers and gardens she had seen all over Europe and while visiting her friends in England, and through her painting and embroidery she had developed her taste and understanding of colour and design. She had her new gardening friends at the Royal Horticultural Society who would keep her in touch with all that was going on, and she had plenty of friends around her too, both other 'gentle' gardeners and the tougher kind who would work to her instructions. Her old friends among the Bramley villagers down the road would see to that.

As the 1880s ticked away her life settled into a pattern. She occasionally went away to see old friends, but mostly she was at home, in her workroom making something or writing, or over in her garden planning the magic to come and supervising the labours that would achieve it. Though the garden could never be complete without her house in it, and though she knew exactly what she wanted, she had not yet found an architect. Nearly always in the afternoons she went visiting, driving the Surrey lanes in her pony and trap, often missing the ruts and fallen stones more by instinct than because she could actually see them, and occasionally coming to grief. It was on one of these visiting afternoons that she drove to a house in the woods at Littleworth Cross, half-way between Godalming and Farnham, to see Harry Mangles, rhododendron enthusiast and breeder of azaleodendrons.[41]

Enter the Architect

Edwin Lutyens was born in London on 29 March 1869, the tenth child in a family of thirteen. The name Lutyens (with which the English tongue has such difficulty and which is best pronounced with the 'Lut' to rhyme with 'hut') was probably of Dutch origin, and the family trace their ancestry back to a Bartholomew Lutyens, citizen of Hamburg, who settled in England in the middle of the eighteenth century.[42] Succeeding generations of the family seem to have been army men, and this was also true of Charles Henry Augustus (born 1829) who was to be Edwin's father. Immediately on taking his commission Charles Lutyens was sent to Canada, where in 1852 he married Mary Gallwey, an Irish girl, who was staying with her brother, the Governor of Montreal. That same year they returned to London, and five years later Charles retired from the army to devote his time to painting. He studied with, and became a close friend of, Edwin Landseer, after whom the ninth son was named – though he was always called Ned.[43] When the family was complete, the Lutyens bought The Cottage at Thursley as a country home – Mary Lutyens longed for a country home, and at the time, in the 1870s, Charles was a successful enough painter for them to afford it.[44] Thus it was at Thursley that Ned spent most of his childhood. Despite its name, The Cottage was a large house in the centre of the T-shaped village. Thursley is in the remotest part of Surrey, far down in the south-west, and though the A3, the Portsmouth road, passes

2. (*left*) Gertrude Jekyll, from a photograph taken about 1880, but very much as Lutyens was to remember her from their first meeting – 'cloaked propriety' in her 'Go-To-Meeting Frock' with the felt hat and curving, prancing feathers.

3. (*right*) Edwin Lutyens as a young man, looking much as he must have appeared to Miss Jekyll at their first meeting.

about half a mile away, it is quite secluded and completely surrounded by furze- and bracken covered heath. Along the valley opening to the south it looks to the Devil's Punch Bowl and Hindhead, and to the heights of Gibbet Hill and Blackdown, which melt into Sussex.

Partly because he had had rheumatic fever badly, Ned never had regular schooling and had to gather most of his education from his sisters' tutors at home. In her memoir of her father, Mary Lutyens tells of his delight in penny sherbets from the village shop, playing trains and fishing.[45] Clearly Ned was quite happy being left behind in peace while his gang of brothers were away at school; and his tutoring must have been fairly good, for he never seemed to lack mathematical know-how. However, it left him with a consciousness of a lack of *being educated* in the wider sense, and he was always frustrated because he could not express himself in words. He carried this through life; it meant that he developed a distrust in theories and a firm belief in doing things, and also that he was never without something on which to draw, whether to relieve his mind of the design for his next building or to make some cartoon comment on a particular moment in time. His limited vocabulary was enlarged by modifying words to suit his purpose, and his consequent shyness was masked by puns and jokes, all of which have contributed to the legend of his wit and good humour.

Even though Ned had obviously inherited the artistic side of his father's character, it seems unlikely that there was much sympathy between them; for one thing, Charles Lutyens spent much time painting, and talking about, horses – and Ned couldn't stand them. He adored his romantic Irish mother, and even if he later rebelled against religion as he had rebelled against horses, she instilled in him a deeply-held belief that he must trust in God. This belief was to make him something of a target for the goddesses of fate.

When he was old enough, Ned too was let loose on the Surrey countryside, and he spent much of his time cycling around the lanes. He always said that it was the drawings of Randolph Caldecott in his nursery books which had inspired him to architecture, and when he went out it was to find a certain similarity between the snug and happy houses the artist drew and the real-life architecture of the Thursley area. It is to our gain that he spent so much time wandering around, for he absorbed this traditional architecture into his growing body and mind; he saw the satisfaction in the fall of a roof which echoed the slope of its neighbouring hill, he developed a respect for the way the craftsmen he watched tooled their wood and sandstone, and he came to realize the intricate and indivisible relationship between cottage, garden and landscape. In the 1880s however, Surrey wasn't all cottages, but fast becoming the repository for the mansions of the English Domestic Revival. Most of the great Victorian architects decorated this county, but Ned Lutyens was particularly attracted by the work of Richard Norman Shaw and Philip Webb – he would have had the opportunity to see Shaw's Merrist Wood near Guildford and Burrows Cross at Shere, as well as Webb's Coneyhurst and Willinghurst, both near Cranleigh, either in the building or very soon afterwards. Some years later, Lutyens's lifelong friend and sometimes rival, Herbert Baker, was to muse about their early apprenticeship together in Ernest George's office: 'I first met Lutyens there, who, though joking through his short pupilage, quickly absorbed all that was best worth learning; he puzzled us at first, but we soon found that he seemed to know by intuition some great truths of our art which were not to be learnt there . . .'[46] Of course, we cannot know where genius comes from, but it would seem that he had absorbed at least some of these truths from his Surrey childhood; his long apprenticeship studying the building traditions and craftsmen of that landscape had instilled in him the deep conviction that he could design buildings, even if he could do little else.[47]

The first goddess of fate to enter Ned's life was Barbara Webb, a family friend and wife of the 'squire' of Milford, Robert Webb. Mrs Webb frequently rescued Ned from the crowded rusticity at Thursley and took him off to the elegant Queen Anne manor house, full of calm and culture, which still stands (though somewhat bereft of these two qualities) beside the Godalming/Milford road. It was undoubtedly her faith in him, and her influence and encouragement, which bridged the gap between childhood at Thursley and architecture in London. He was enrolled at the South Kensington School of Art to study architecture, but did not stay the course, and we already know that he did not stay long in Ernest George and Peto's office either. In 1889, when he was just twenty years old, he set up in practice on his own with an office in Gray's Inn Square. His first

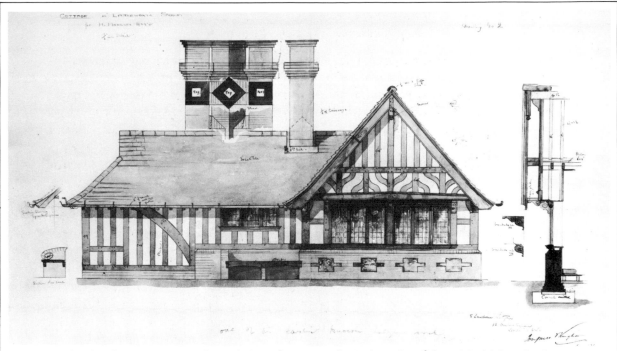

4. 'Design for a cottage at Littleworth Cross for H. Mangles Esq': a print of the original ink and colour-washed drawing which may have convinced Miss Jekyll that she had found her architect. This represents one of the earliest surviving Lutyens drawings.

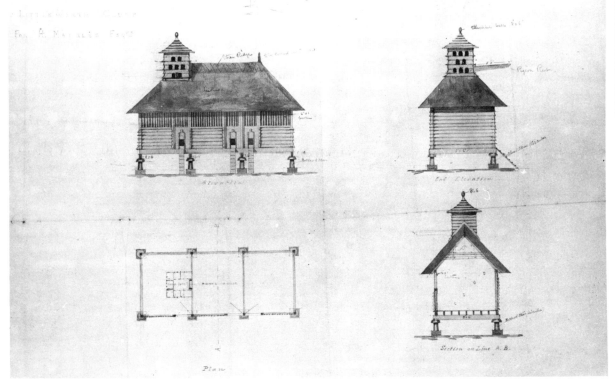

5. Lutyens's design for a 'Fowl House' at Littleworth Cross, which may also have appeared at the tea-table in May 1889, and which Miss Jekyll would have appreciated for the architect's eye for detail, and also his sense of humour.

commissions all came from Surrey friends – some alterations to a cottage in Thursley, some small lodges at Park Hatch in the near-by village of Hascombe, and, possibly because Charles Lutyens had painted a portrait of a family friend, Agnes Chapman, sister of Harry Mangles of Littleworth Cross, Mr Mangles commissioned a cottage as well [4, 5].[48]

Lutyens's description of his meeting with Gertrude Jekyll in the garden at Littleworth Cross, with which I opened this chapter, was written years later as part of his tribute to her. He continued: 'She was dressed in what I learnt later to be her Go-To-Meeting Frock – a bunch of cloaked propriety topped by a black felt hat, turned down in front and up behind, from which sprang alert black cock's tail feathers, curving and ever prancing forwards.'[49] Remembering that he was an enthusiastic if somewhat skittish twenty-year-old, and she clearly very prim – even stern when her face was in repose – there is a certain warm assurance in the knowledge that kindred spirits *will* recognize each other, however unlikely the outward guise. Apparently she did not speak to him all through the tea-party, nor still when she was preparing to leave for her drive home – and then, 'with one foot on the step of her pony cart and the reins in her hand, she invited him to Munstead Wood the very next Saturday'.[50]

2

THE MAKING OF MUNSTEAD WOOD AND THE EARLY SURREY GARDENS

It is roughly triangular in shape, widest to the south, and slopes down to the north-west. There had been a close wood of Scotch Pine lately felled in the upper nine acres, then a wide strip of Chestnut coppice, and at the narrow end a small field of poor sandy soil.

Gertrude Jekyll writing of Munstead Wood as it was when she bought it[1]

FROM this beginning, as can be followed from my reconstruction of the plan of Munstead Wood [7],[2] the small field was trenched and manured to become the kitchen garden, and the chestnut coppice was to be the site for the house and flower garden. The upper part, where the pines had been felled, was to become the woodland garden, a place of patient labour and observation of which she would never tire; the pines had been felled some fifteen years before and 'young trees of natural growth, seedling pines, birch, holly, oak, mountain ash and Spanish chestnut' were growing up. Her 'first care' was to keep these several kinds a little apart 'in order to get natural pictures' of one kind of tree at a time, which she felt was most soothing.

This basic work of garden making was well advanced by the time Ned Lutyens arrived for his first visit. His picture of her on that occasion is of a lady very much at home: 'genial and communicative, dressed in a short blue skirt that in no way hid her ankles', with a blue linen apron, blue-striped blouse, 'box-pleated like a Norfolk jacket', and a straw hat trimmed with a blue ribbon and bow.[3]

On that first visit, and probably on almost all subsequent ones, he was given a tour of the embryo garden to mark the various stages of progress; in the conversations that followed she found confirmation of her first instinct, formed at the tea-table in Harry Mangles's garden, that she had found her architect. Their shared interest in old Surrey buildings blossomed into friendship and there were frequent expeditions, Ned braving her rather psychic driving of the pony cart, to examine the construction of cottages and farmhouses, and to make inquiries – of a philosophical and practical nature – into the habits of their occupants. They would go southwards through the sandy lanes to Hascombe – Ned proudly pointing out his new lodges by the side of the road at Park Hatch – and on into the thickly-wooded edge of the Weald beyond Dunsfold and Chiddingfold; to the south-west they went across the heath to Hambledon, Witley,

Brook and eventually Thursley, and on really distant excursions south to Haslemere and the valley fastnesses of the broom squires.[4] Ned adored rivers and Miss Jekyll was also fond of the Wey valley, so they went west of Godalming – to Eashing, Peper Harow, Elstead and Tilford, where the monks of Waverley Abbey built the stone bridges over the river which are still in use today. This is the heart of legendary Surrey – the lanes and villages where they found the deep-roofed cottages, with sandstone-flagged paths between flower borders leading to the front porch, and inside, in the heat of a summer afternoon, all cool and quiet, smelling of beeswax and home-made cider. I imagine that the advent of the pony cart, and the imminent descent of the stout lady with her rather dashing but shy young companion, was the cue for much wiping of hands on aprons and straightening of caps at cottage doors!

And so, out of the Surrey countryside traditions, and perhaps from her memories of other retreats – Barbara Bodichon's Scalands and the Blumenthals' chalet – Miss Jekyll's dream house was born. For Miss Jekyll and Lutyens the designing of it became 'a witty and exciting sport with full discussions and great disputations'.[5] Building actually started in 1895. It was an intensely happy and productive time; she would emerge from The Hut, the small wooden cottage that Lutyens designed for her as a temporary home on site, at the same early hour as the workmen started, and then busy herself in the garden where she could both keep an eye on them and enjoy watching them work. The solid walls of Bargate stone (which came from a near-by quarry)[6] steadily rose higher and higher, to be topped with enormous sailing chimneys and draped with a deep roof of hand-made tiles; doors and window-frames were of English oak, and inside all was formed into beautifully proportioned spaces for living. As the house rose 'it took on the soul of a more ancient dwelling place'[7] and looked as if it would endure for ever. Everything was designed for harmony and peace. Down to the last window-catch and door-latch there was to be no clashing of styles, no substitute for honest hand-work, and though this might take more time and trouble (and expense) the outcome would be right – 'and to see and know it is just right is a daily reward and never-ending source of satisfaction'.[8] Inside the house there was (and still is) an immense feeling of refuge. It is a kind of sophisticated burrow, which says a great deal about the inner needs of an outwardly spirited lady. Munstead Wood house is the ultimate expression of a house designed to fit a personality and a setting. Though she always gave all the credit to her architect, and he was to go on to evolve the Munstead style into a high art, so much of its character comes from its being created for Miss Jekyll – her tastes, her lifestyle, her values, her fading eyesight – in an age when such things mattered more than the cost.

The house is welded to its garden by the formal north court, which provides a secluded and shady sitting place beneath the gallery overhang [6]. This small court was paved with a circle of precious water-marked sandstone, and surrounded by box-edged borders of shade-loving greenery, brightened with the addition of pots of lilies and pink hydrangeas in their season. Steps from the court led down past a tank surrounded by ferns, to a path through the nut walk – a path, thirteen feet wide, between a double avenue of *Corylus maxima* (Munstead was not only pretty, but productive) underplanted

6. Munstead Wood: the north court, marked as (3) on the layout plan on page 36. The seat is one of Lutyens's designs, and this or one of a smaller design was to become a feature in most of the larger gardens. The planting scheme of enormous glaucous-leaved hostas, ferns and white lilies was set out in pots, with great care as befitted this very special part of the Munstead garden.

with hellebores, primroses, anemones and pale daffodils. This was the only part of the garden to be formally designed with the house, the rest having been taken in hand at various times and treated on its merits – much as William Robinson had advised when he wrote of the ideal owner getting to know his ground and suiting its possibilities.[9] The layout of Munstead Wood never approached the ingenuity amply demonstrated in the later gardens; in some ways its abundant naturalness was in complete contrast to the sophistication to come, but it was the source and inspiration of all the planting plans and many of the design ideas. Here, in the early years of their friendship, the young Ned Lutyens had the time to appreciate the succession of garden pictures that Miss Jekyll created, and – though he never had the time to learn anything much about plants – he absorbed her experience of a garden's purposes and refined them into his future designs. At Munstead Wood they learned to see each other's point of view, and so formed the basis of a working partnership.

Flower Gardening at Munstead[10]

One of the Munstead themes was that every part of the garden was capable of giving a virtuoso performance at distinct times of the year. When the first warm days of spring

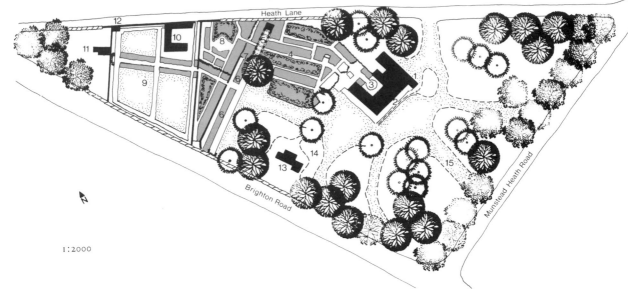

1:2000

7. Munstead Wood as it was in Miss Jekyll's time (1896–1932). The entrance was from Heath Lane to a porch in the south-east corner (1). In the centre of the south side of the house was the garden door (2), leading on to a sandstone terrace edged with briar roses, with a wide flight of steps to the lawn. The north court (3) led to a path through the nut walk (4) to the pergola (5) – this was the only part of the garden to have been formally designed with the house. The borders on either side of the nut walk were used for various shrub and flower schemes. The main flower border (6) was at right angles to the nut walk, with a high wall behind it – the large stone seat which looked down the border at (7) was probably that christened 'The Cenotaph of Sigismunda'. Through the door in the wall were more borders, including the Spring garden at (8) and the kitchen garden with a vista of flowers (especially Michaelmas daisies) through it (9). The potting sheds and workshops were at (10), the head gardener's cottage at (11), and the Thunder House (12) was a roofed but open-sided gazebo on top of the wall, where Miss Jekyll loved to watch the storms passing along the Wey valley. To the south of the house was The Hut (13), with the June garden around it and the Hidden garden (14) in the bushes beside it. The south-eastern half of the Munstead plot was the woodland garden, divided by walks through the trees; the chief of these walks, the Green Wood Walk (15), was described by Miss Jekyll as her 'most precious possession'.

encouraged the use of a seat in the sun, but shelter was still needed, there was the enclosed Spring garden to visit – at the end of the nut walk, through a gate from the pergola. The path led to a footgate on to Heath Lane or back to the main path to the kitchen garden, so it was easy to look in, and for those with time to stay there were seats at the edge of the small lawn. My reconstruction of the plan[11] of the Spring garden [8] shows a rectangle (though it may not have been exact) with the spring flower beds backed by borders of tree peonies underplanted with *Stachys lanata* for later interest.

The effect of the Spring garden in bloom must have been magical, as some of the old photographs show, but there was nothing mysterious about its making. Miss Jekyll's success here, as in other parts of the garden, was that she allowed her plants to show themselves to the best of their ability, either *en masse* or in subtle contrasts of texture, shape or colour, within an area suited to their scale, rather than diffused in dribs and drabs. She felt that spring flowers too easily had a 'temporary' look – for their nature is ephemeral – and needed good strong base planting to establish a foil. Hence the clumps of *Myrrhis odorata*, *Veratrum nigrum* and *Euphorbia wulfenii* which were the basis of the planting are marked on the plan. In the side borders these were underplanted with drifts of colour, beginning with pale yellow primroses (polyanthus), *Tiarella cordifolia*, pale

8. Munstead Wood: the Spring garden. The larger trees were oaks, the smaller ones hollies and hazels (*Corylus maxima*). The choice of paths through the garden revealed its twin characters, the first spring flowers being beside the right-hand path, with beds of tree peonies undercarpeted with silver foliage for later effect beside the other paths. The bold *Yucca gloriosa* (1) and *Acanthus spinosus* (2) were for later effect, but *Euphorbia wulfenii* (3), *Myrrhis odorata* (4) and *Veratrum nigrum* (5) were the heart of groups of base planting, with *Bergenia cordifolia* and *Helleborus niger*. At (6) were the most vivid colours – red and scarlet tulips, orange Crown Imperials and brown wallflowers; at (7) the colours toned down to rose pink tulips, *Dicentra eximia* with drifts of white arabis, white primroses and white daffodils leading to and mixing with (8), the yellows – tulips, wallflowers, daffodils, doronicum and Crown Imperials. The palest colours were in drifts in group (9) – all pale lemons and whites: tulips, aubretias, wallflowers, pale yellow iris, pale daffodils, *Tiarella cordifolia*, a dreamy and luminous green, and pale primroses with a dash of palest lilac aubretia. The final group, behind the veratrum and mingling with it, were the purple wallflowers and dull red tulips (10). Opposite the path from the pergola a large rock was embedded for height, and was almost covered with carpets of iberis and lithospermum with white tulips; at (11) the colours changed to blues – forget-me-not, blue iris and *Phlox divaricata*. At (12), beneath garlands of *Clematis montana* strung on ropes beneath the nut trees, grey antennaria and *Stachys lanata* merged with pink aubretias and *Phlox amoena*, into (13), honesty and purple wallflowers. At (14) were yellow tree peonies with *Stachys lanata* and white tulips, *Hebe brachysiphon*, *Ruta graveolens* and *Leycesteria formosa*; at (15) pink tree peonies with *Stachys lanata* and white tulips, with R. 'Mme Alfred Carrière' on arches. At (16) were red polyanthus with *Heuchera richardsoni*.

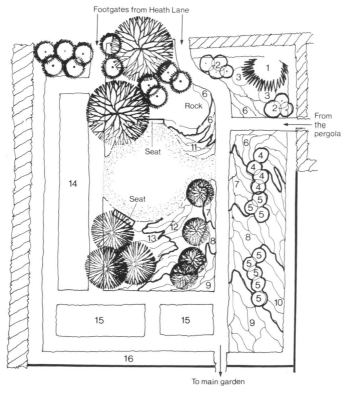

yellow daffodils and iris, double *Arabis albeda*, *Iberis sempervirens*, white anemones and pale lilac aubretias. These are backed by strong colours – dull red wallflowers, double purple tulips, and these in turn with clumps of veratrum. Another swathe of pale profusion followed, steadily getting stronger in colour with the addition of yellow doronicums and yellow Crown Imperials. The climax of colour – orange Crown Imperials, orange tulips and brown wallflowers – is saved for the corners of the path from the pergola.

Around the little lawn the sun filtered through tall oaks and more hazel bushes. Two judiciously placed rocks added height to the borders, allowing tumbling iberis, aubretias, and alpine phlox to contrast with short-stemmed white tulips and small blue iris. The contrast between spike and carpet was a feature of the Spring garden planting, and so many spring flowers fall into one or other of these forms. Beneath the seats a scheme of grey *Antennaria minima* with pink aubretias, a phlox of darker pink, and purple honesty was encouraged to spread beneath the hazels.

The Spring garden was of interest until early May; then, as a retreat from the activity of a large number of gardeners and garden boys (she is said to have employed seventeen at one time), Miss Jekyll had a Hidden garden, surrounded by evergreens, with no direct path leading to it and the entrance easily missed. Inside the evergreen walls (yew, holly, *Quercus ilex*) all was very informal – rough sandy paths, sandstone steps and retaining walls, and the main beds built up as rocky earth mounds. The flowers were planned for the end of May and early June, and, in keeping with the atmosphere, their colours were subdued and quiet, though there were many contrasts in texture and shapes. Roses – Paul's Carmine Pillar and *Rosa brunonii*, the heavily-perfumed Himalayan musk rose with white flowers – were encouraged to climb into the hollies and yews.

Though very limited in its scope, the plan of the Hidden garden [9][12] shows some lovely colour and plant relationships: pale lilac pansy, flanked by *Nepeta mussinii* (the beloved Munstead cats also needed a retreat!) and London pride with St Bruno's lilies (these were white, and with a cloud of London pride represented the best plant relationship she found), drifting into pale lilac iris and hartstongue ferns with *Iberis sempervirens* tumbling from the rocks above – such delights seem a world away from serried ranks of petunias. So does a patch of *Anemone sylvestris* floating among stonecrop, catmint, plume hyacinth, fern and asphodel. Here woodland and flower gardening met, with masses of Solomon's seal drooping elegantly in the shade with iris and hostas at its feet.

As the years passed and the evergreens and overhanging trees cast more shade, this garden plan was abandoned. The Hidden garden became a fern garden; now only ghosts of ferns and evergreens remain.

In direct contrast to this quiet hideaway, the June garden around The Hut was Miss Jekyll's version of a cottage garden, a riot of colour and perfumes. The planting plan [10][13] shows a rather basic layout which belies its charm, for at Munstead everything grew in such profusion that it spread beyond the bounds of its allotted space, so that

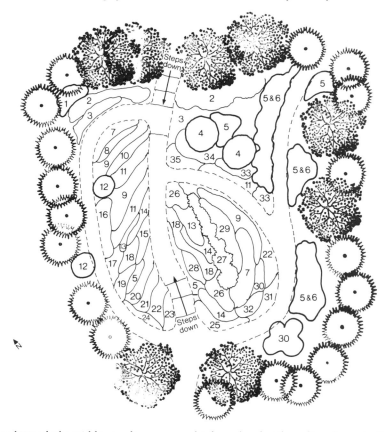

9. Munstead Wood: the Hidden garden was completely enclosed with unclipped yew, holly and *Quercus ilex*. The whole atmosphere was 'natural', with rough sandy paths and stone steps, and the 'beds' banked up with large stones in order better to display the tumbling drifts of flowers, many of which were favourites from the wild.

Key to the planting:

1. *Myrrhis odorata* (sweet cicely)
2. *Polygonatum multiflorum* (Solomon's seal)
3. Purple May-flowering iris
4. Salmon pink and rose pink tree peonies – 2 groups of 3
5. Lady fern (*Athyrium felix-femina*) and male fern (*Dryopteris felix-mas*)
6. *Lilium rubellum* (pink), *L. testaceum* (buff), and *L. szovitzianum* (yellow with black spots)
7. Pale lilac iris
8. *Camassia esculenta*
9. *Phlox divaricata*
10. Yellow iris
11. *Corydalis ochroleuca* (cream-flowered fumitory)
12. *Olearia phlogopappa* (*gunniana*) (Tasmanian daisy-bush)
13. Blue iris
14. *Anthericum liliastrum major* (*Paradisea liliastrum*) (St Bruno's lily)
15. *Achillea umbellata*
16. Pink *Rosa spinosissima*
17. Aquilegias (columbine), pale yellow, cream with touch of purple
18. *Arenaria montana*
19. *Asphodelus luteus*
20. *Cerastium columnae*
21. *Muscari comosum monstrosum* (large tassel hyacinth)
22. *Nepeta mussinii* (*faassenii*) (catmint)
23. *Sedum telephium*
24. *Anemone sylvestris*
25. *Saxifraga umbrosa* (London pride)
26. *Phyllitis scolopendrium* (hartstongue fern)
27. Mauve alpine rhododendron and *Pieris japonica*
28. *Iris cristata*
29. *Iberis sempervirens* (candytuft)
30. *Geranium ibericum*
31. Pale lilac pansy
32. *Onoclea sensibilis*
33. *Uvularia grandifolia*
34. *Hosta sieboldiana elegans*
35. *Asarum europeum*

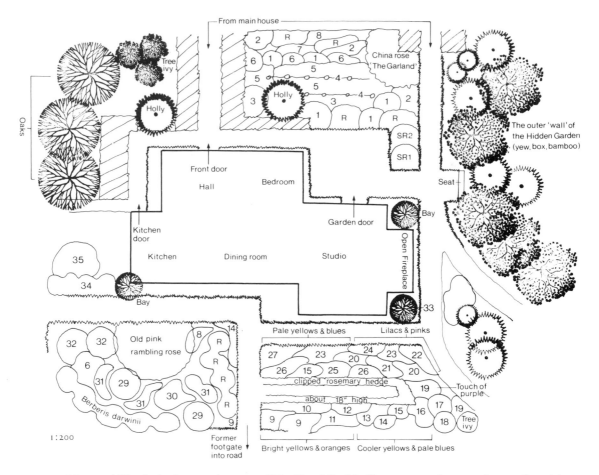

10. Munstead Wood: the June garden around The Hut, Miss Jekyll's cottage garden – a mixture of special plant relationships and old friends. The Hut was in constant use after the main house was built – as a workroom, a pot-pourri 'factory', or let to friends.

Key to the planting:

R. Old shrub roses, mainly *R. damascena* 'Celsiana' and *R. centifolia*

SR. Standard roses [1] 'Celeste'; [2] 'Madame Plantier'

1. *Paeonia officinalis* (pink and white)
2. Snapdragons (pink and cream)
3. Underplanting of orange lilies, ferns and white foxgloves
4. Roses on hoops – *R. moschata* and *R. chinensis*
5. Underplanting of male fern, *Myrrhis odorata* and white aquilegias
6. White foxgloves
7. *Penstemon barbatus* (these and the snapdragons [2] to carry on flowering)
8. *Bergenia cordifolia*
9. *Papaver orientalis* (apricot and oranges)
10. Deep orange lilies
11. Warm yellow iris
12. Yellow tree lupin
13. Cream foxgloves
14. Clear yellow iris and white lupins
15. *Aruncus sylvester* (meadowsweet)
16. Pale blue anchusa
17. *Olearia phlogopappa* (*gunniana*) (*Tasmanian daisy-bush*)
18. *Kerria japonica*
19. Pale yellow iris (Dutch hybrid)
20. Lupins (creamy, bluish lilac and a few purple)
21. *Paeonia lactiflora* (flesh pink)
22. *Iris pallida dalmatica*
23. *Saxifraga umbrosa* (London pride)
24. *Iris pallida* (pinky lilac variety)
25. *Nepeta mussinii* (*faassenii*) (catmint)
26. *Campanula lactiflora*
27. Creamy lupins
28. *Geranium ibericum* (purple-blue cranesbill) with pale yellow and white Spanish iris
29. *Crataegus monogyna* (whitethorn)
30. *Verbascum bombyciferum*
31. *Heracleum giganteum* (*mantegezzianum*) – highly prized but well-controlled!
32. *Thuya occidentalis*
33. *Viburnus tinus*
34. *Berberis darwinii*
35. *Prunus lusitanica*

luxuriance was another dimension of design. Harold Falkner, the Farnham architect who was a frequent visitor to Miss Jekyll in her later years, recalls some of this quality: 'the main colour schemes . . . were purple geraniums, white oriental poppies, sages and lavenders, with a secondary scheme of lupins and iris. Lupins have since been developed . . . but I do not think they were ever better grown than in this border, particularly Munstead blue – with very large flowers of forget-me-not blue and medium spikes, and Munstead white, which was really a cream with white wings and thick petalled bells'.[14]

The Hut garden was approached across the lawn from the house; through an arch in the hedge was a world arranged on a much smaller scale than the main garden – with single-file sand paths between box edging to borders overflowing with foxgloves, roses, columbines, lupins and herbs. Wherever Miss Jekyll gardened, the China rose, The Garland, followed; it was always planted for effect, as here, guarding the entrance to the June garden, assaulting the newcomer with its perfumed fountain-sprays of small blushing flowers. As well as The Garland, this front border (The Hut faced the house) was crammed with dusky flowered roses on looped ropes, with masses of male fern, white columbines, pink and white double peonies, white foxgloves and creamy snapdragons at their feet. The colours were predominantly warm and gentle, the whites always creamy, the pinks always pale and salmony, with a splash of orange lilies to enhance the effect, and, as always, a solid surround of yew and holly.

The small border on the far side of The Hut, backed by the hedgerow trees of the boundary with Heath Road (the main road to Godalming) and set for viewing from the window of The Hut's sitting room (called the Studio), was a late spring version in miniature of the main herbaceous border. To examine it in detail is a good preparation for the complications to come! The border was too wide for convenience, so it was divided by a low clipped rosemary hedge; if we take this gardener's way in rather than viewing from afar, the first groups are of apricot and orange poppies with deep orange lilies. Beyond them and some warm yellow iris, a paler yellow tree lupin marks the change to cooler colours – clear yellow (by which she meant sulphur) iris, white lupins and foxgloves, then a punctuating clump of ferny, cream *Aruncus sylvester* (meadowsweet) before the introduction of blue with the anchusa. The blues are strengthened to purples with the clump of lupins at the head of the rosemary alley, and then the pinks and pinky lilacs are brought in. The border returns through lilac-blue iris, flesh pink peonies, blue and silver catmint, a balancing meadowsweet, to pale yellow, white and blue iris again.

In the far corner of the June garden the cottage atmosphere was maintained, and large favourites could find a home where they would not be in the way of the show and could be sought out when their company was needed; here resided some old roses, much loved whitethorns, *Verbascum bombyciferum* and a great prize, *Heracleum giganteum* – a descendant of this last giant still survives.[15]

The Rules of Colour

It is evident that various laws of colour association ruled the Munstead estate. The colour theories which formed the basis of Miss Jekyll's rules were the product of years of research by a Frenchman, Michel Chevreul. Already an eminent chemist, he was appointed director of the Gobelin tapestry factory in 1824 and given the task of investigating the causes for complaints about the qualities of the dyes.[16] The result was a long and detailed report, which was translated into English and published in London in 1854 with the title *The Principles of Harmony and Contrast of Colours and their Application to the Arts*; it was received with acclaim, and has remained the basis of teaching about colour in arts and crafts ever since.[17] Chevreul's principles must have been the guiding theories in Gertrude Jekyll's education in the early 1860s; they also had a great effect on the painters she admired most, and their influence is particularly strong in the paintings of Delacroix, Pissarro, Monet and Cézanne.[18]

The Chevreul theories are based on a colour circle made of the primary colours (red, yellow and blue), the secondaries (orange, violet and green), and any number of tones between these, attainable in a given medium. Given the order of the circle [11], there are certain rules that can be applied to planting design in the following ways:

The colours on the *warm* side of the circle are more dynamic and evoke the greatest appreciation from the eye (this is enhanced in myopic eyes).
A small area of bright reds and oranges attracts, exhilarates and yet disturbs repose.
Harmony is achieved from various relationships within the colour circle.
Adjacent and analogous colours give emotional harmony because they are based on the warm or cool side of the spectrum when arranged in proper sequence.
There is also *harmony* in the opposite colours of the circle, and a more refined harmony between a colour and the ones either side of its opposite.
There is a further harmony in triads (which brings in the dark green of yew as a satisfactory foil for pinks and yellows).

A complication is added by the misty blue daylight of England which can add a blue tint or shadow where least required; it is essential, therefore, to examine and place reds, in particular, carefully, so that the strongest reds give way to flames and oranges in one direction, and purples and violets *in the other*. In our most admired contemporary gardens bright reds and vivid blues vie with each other – something that was *never* allowed to happen at Munstead Wood!

Chevreul also pointed out, very conveniently for gardeners, that the colours of nature scale through harmonious adjacents in the circle – those of autumn – red, oranges, yellows, golds, browns and purples. Less prosaically, *beauty*, the colour rules stated, *is the natural product of good order*. Any given colour plus black and white produces set shades, tints and tones – for these there is a given form, and the straight lines of this triangular form [12] govern what is natural and concordant. Valid sequences also must regard *stability*, which means using a heavy base colour [13] and gives the cue for so much use of dark green, especially the heavy green of yew, for permanent background and base planting.

The final rules dictate the importance of white, as it was beloved by the Impressionists and by Miss Jekyll's friend and mentor, Hercules Brabazon Brabazon [see colour pl. 2]. *White is the colour of light and makes most things beautiful*. It is almost impossible to find

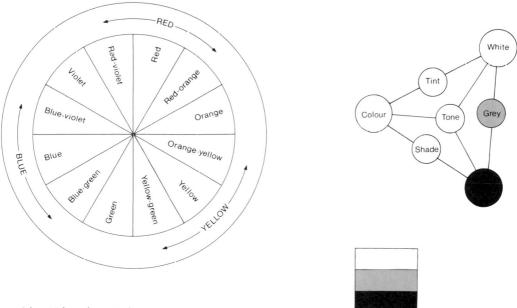

11. *(above)* The colour circle.

12. *(above right)* The satisfactory sequences: the straight line sequences of the triangle are naturally beautiful to the eye, as long as they are in order. Thus most border plans and planting sequences started with white, moving to pale colours, i.e. tints, before the colour itself was added. Reversing the order is also beautiful, Chevreul decreed, but disrupting it never so.

13. *(below right)* The eye seeks stability, therefore black or a heavy colour is the basis of good 'architectural' order – hence the great drifts of *Acanthus spinosus* or *Bergenia cordifolia* leaves at the front of so many borders.

discord in a combination of a pure colour, plus its tint, plus white; the most refined and eloquent sequence is from tint to tone to shade – chiaroscuro – the use of which especially affected Miss Jekyll's woodland planting. Though all colours gain in their association with white, there is also an accepted order of the greatest beauty – light blue and white are best, followed by rose pink and white, then deep yellow and white; bright green, violet and orange respectively with white were less beautiful. The harmony of pure colour, tint and white is a frequently used planting combination – pure blue, pale blue and white (bright blue ageratum, pale nepeta and white gypsophila) were included in grey gardens, which were a great favourite.[19] Rose pink was added to make perhaps the most delicately pretty borders, as the plan for Deanery Garden [36] shows. A green border contained perhaps the most sophisticated planting scheme of all, with tints, tones and shades of green enriched with textures, and the triad harmony introduced with touches of pale yellow and dark red flowers. This was the colour scheme used by John Brookes for his Gold Medal Award-winning recreation of planting *à la* Jekyll for the 1978 Chelsea Flower Show [126].[20]

However, Miss Jekyll's real canvas for her experiments with the colour theories, the source for so many of the schemes that are described in this book, was her large

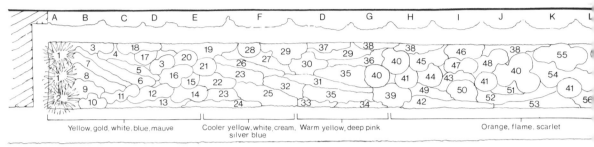

Yellow, gold, white, blue, mauve | Cooler yellow, white, cream, silver blue | Warm yellow, deep pink | Orange, flame, scarlet

14. Munstead Wood: the main flower border was the Munstead masterpiece, the pride of a lady who felt that the best place to be in July and August was at home.

Key to the planting:

A. Crimson rambling rose
B. *Robinia hispida*
C. *Viburnum tinus*
D. *Nandina domestica*
E. *Abutilon vitifolium*
F. *Eriobotrya japonica*
G. *Laurus nobilis*
H. *Punica granatum*
I. *Ligustrum japonicum*
J. Pyrus (hybrid *P. salicifolia*)
K. *Chimonanthus praecox*
L. *Fuchsia magellanica gracilis*
M. *Vitis coignetiae*
N. *Magnolia conspicua*
O. *Choisya ternata*

P. *Cistus ciprius*
Q. *Piptanthus laburnifolius*
R. *Carpentaria californica*
1. *Yucca recurvifolia*
2. *Yucca filamentosa*
3. White everlasting pea
4. Blue delphinium
5. Pale pink astilbe
6. *Elymus arenarius*
7. White snapdragon
8. *Campanula lactiflora*
9. *Lilium longiflorum*
10. *Crambe maritima*
11. *Clematis davidiana* (*heracleifolia*)
12. *Iris pallida dalmatica*

13. *Iberis sempervirens*
14. *Ruta graveolens*
15. White lily
16. *Salvia officinalis*
17. *Ligustrum ovalifolium* 'Aureum'
18. *Verbascum olympicum*
19. *Thalictrum angustifolium* and *Rudbeckia speciosa* 'Golden Glow'
20. *Miscanthus sinensis* 'Zebrinus'
21. *Aruncus sylvester*
22. *Iris orientalis*
23. Yellow snapdragon
24. *Bergenia cordifolia*
25. *Tagetes erecta* (primrose yellow African marigold)

herbaceous border at Munstead; this is where she pursued her painstaking task of ordering the multitudinous colours of nature (let alone the variations dreamed up by plant breeders) into the sequence of colourful beauty. Obviously she was constantly experimenting, and her garden always changing, but the main border that she described in Chapters 6, 7 and 8 of *Colour in the Flower Garden* (1908) is very similar to the border described in Chapter 16 of her first book, *Wood and Garden* (1899), where she refers to her search for beauty and harmony everywhere, especially the harmony of colour.

Herbaceous Border Planting

The high point of the Munstead garden year was when this herbaceous border, 200 feet long and 14 feet wide, backed by the 11 foot high sandstone wall which almost enclosed the main garden at its western end, began to bloom at the beginning of July [14].[21] Against the wall, with a path in front of them for maintenance, were planted the shrubs which were the carefully chosen backdrop to each section of the border – *Viburnum tinus*, *Choisya ternata*, *Eriobotrya japonica*, cistus, bay, privet and magnolia. The border itself

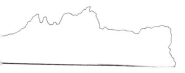

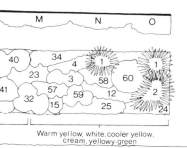

M N O

Warm yellow, white, cooler yellow,
cream, yellowy-green

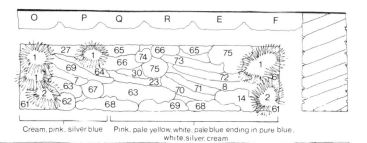

O P Q R E F

Cream, pink, silver blue   Pink, pale yellow, white, pale blue ending in pure blue,
white, silver, cream

26. *Filipendula ulmaria flora plena*
27. Foxgloves (*Digitalis ambigua*) (yellow or white) and *Verbascum olympicum*
28. Tall yellow dahlia
29. *Helianthus multiflorus*
30. *Achillea eupatorium*
31. *Monarda didyma* (scarlet) and ligularia (yellow flowered variety)
32. *Eryngium oliverianum*
33. *Helenium pumilum magnificum*
34. *Rudbeckia speciosa newmanii*
35. *Coreopsis lanceolata*
36. *Helenium striatum*
37. Helianthus (tall single hybrid)
38. Dark red hollyhock
39. *Kniphofia galpinii* (dwarf variety)
40. *Kniphofia uvaria*

41. *Gypsophila paniculata*
42. *Salvia superba*
43. *Lilium tigrinum*
44. *Canna indica* (scarlet)
45. Dahlia 'Cochineal'
46. Dahlia 'Lady Ardilaun'
47. Dahlia 'Fire King'
48. Dahlia 'Orange Fire King'
49. *Lychnis chalcedonica*
50. Orange hemerocallis
51. *Phlox paniculata* 'Coquilot'
52. *Gladiolus brenchleyensis*
53. *Celosia thomsonii* (red)
54. *Tagetes erecta* (orange African marigold)
55. *Canna indica* (tall red)
56. *Tropaeolum majus* (dwarf yellow variety)
57. *Eryngium giganteum*

58. *Clematis recta*
59. Peony unspecified but certainly yellow
60. *Euphorbia wulfenii*
61. *Stachys lanata*
62. *Crambe maritima*
63. Blue hydrangeas
64. *Saponaria officinalis*
65. Sulphur yellow hollyhock
66. *Echinops ritro*
67. *Dictamnus* (*fraxinella*)
68. *Cineraria maritima*
69. *Santolina chamaecyparissus*
70. *Geranium ibericum*
71. *Aster acris* (*sedifolius*) (blue)
72. *Aster shortii* (pale mauve)
73. *Aster umbellatus* (tall cream)
74. *Clematis jackmanii*
75. White dahlia

had a vital base planting of interesting plants – yuccas (stemmed and sprouting varieties) at the corners, generous edgings of *Bergenia cordifolia*, santolina, *Salvia superba* and the eternal iberis, and carefully spaced *Gypsophila paniculata*, *Euphorbia wulfenii*, blue hydrangeas, *Miscanthus sinensis* 'Zebrinus' and more meadowsweets to calm everything down. For the rest, it was an embroidered cavalcade of the flowers which make up our dreams of an English garden in high summer – lilies, peonies, snapdragons, delphiniums, sweet peas, foxgloves, red hot pokers in various hues, daisy faces, gladioli and dahlias.

Keeping this border in flower from the beginning of July until October was an achievement not only of careful planning but of constant attention to trimming, seed collecting, and removal of those plants which were past their prime and infilling with potted ones. This involved a number of tricks learnt over the years, such as training the gypsophila clouds down over the chopped off stems of the Oriental poppies which had given early colour to the border. White everlasting pea similarly disguised the chopped-off delphiniums, and vertical plants (Michaelmas daisies, dahlias and rudbeckias) were carefully trained horizontally to cover the bare patches. Obvious spaces among the perennials were filled with ordinary bedding from the greenhouses – calceolarias, pelargoniums, salvias, begonias, gazanias. The half-hardy annuals were added as required – white petunias, tall ageratum, striped maize, and the bright orange and sulphur yellow African marigolds (tagetes) so beloved then, as now, of park-keepers. In August the pot-grown hydrangeas and *Lilium longiflorum* were brought out to replace the lost colour amongst the grey and silver foliage. Without the colour rules this would all be rather indigestible, but the border was carefully graduated (the graduations are marked on the plan) from a groundwork of grey at each end – grey being flattering to all primary and secondary colours – to grey-blues, pale blue, pale yellow and the introduction of palest pinks, all in distinct massings, and passing to stronger warmer yellows and the splash of fiery oranges and reds in the centre. The colours then recede in inverse order along the second half of the plan, and instead of blues, purples are used with greys and silvers at the far end. Her own photographs [15, 16, 17] give an idea of the texture and abundance of the borders, but only imagination can conjure up the brilliance, the perfumes, the contented drone of the Munstead afternoon, when, with a kitten cavorting at your feet, you view the borders to the lively commentary of the artist describing her effects. When you have admired the sentinel yuccas, experienced the sheer visual delight of a cloud of gypsophila settling onto spikes of hemerocallis or a carpet of yellow African marigolds, and then noted the afternoon sun flaming the gorgeous company of red and orange dahlias, red hollyhocks and tiger lilies at the heart of the border, she will walk you to the quiet ending, with more glaucous foliage and pink flowers (sometimes pink gladioli and japanese anemones, sometimes, as in this plan, pink astilbes and white snapdragons). 'It is important,' she is saying, 'in such a border of rather large size that can be seen from a good space of lawn, to keep the flowers in rather large masses of colour. No one who has ever done it, or seen it done, will go back to the old haphazard sprinkle of colouring without any thought of arrangement, such as is usually seen in a mixed border.'[22]

Nor did she, of course. The plans she was to make for other people may not have been so complicated or labour-intensive as her prized borders at Munstead, but the rules were always the same. Her gardening life was completely dominated by the struggle to order the colours of nature, and it is interesting to look forward, across nearly thirty years, for her last virtuoso performance makes an intriguing comparison with these early struggles at Munstead. In 1929, when she was almost blind and more than ever seeing in her mind's eye, she designed an extraordinary and magnificent border on the grand scale for Lutyens's daughter Ursula, Viscountess Ridley of Blagdon in Northumberland.[23] The designs were discussed during a long and painstaking correspondence, which shows a tenacious old lady clinging to her ideals to the last; this border (though that seems a singularly inadequate word) was contained in an elaborate framework of interlocking hexagonal yew hedges (designed by Lutyens), planted to range through the same sequences as the Munstead herbaceous border. Again, it can only be explored in the imagination (for it has long gone in reality) and I have tried to present the plan [18][24] in a way which makes this a pleasant journey, rather than like working through a knitting pattern. The progress down the painted path was through pale yellow, pale blue and white, stronger yellows and warm pinks to purples and blood reds; the emphasis was on

15. Munstead Wood: the main flower border.

16. (*left*) Munstead Wood: the main flower border. Eryngium, yuccas, euphorbias and lilies by the path to the door in the wall.

17. (*right*) Munstead Wood textures and shapes: *Olearia gunniana* (*phlogopappa*) with hostas, ferns and bergenias in a shrubbery border.

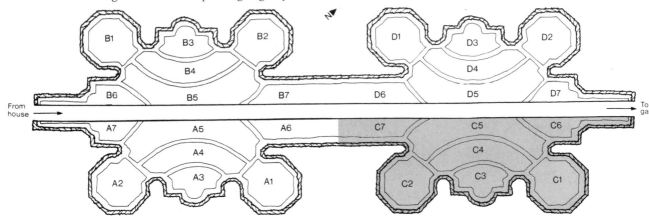

18. Blagdon new border: planting of groups A, B and D. Section C is named in detail on p. 49.

From house →

To garden →

Diagram labels: B1, B3, B2, B4, B6, B5, B7, D1, D3, D2, D4, D6, D5, D7, A7, A5, A6, C7, C5, C6, A4, C4, A2, A3, A1, C2, C3, C1

A1. *Prunus cerasifera* 'Pissardii' (purple-leaved plum) in the centre, with red hollyhocks and dahlias, eupatorium (hemp agrimony), purple rhus (*Cotinus coggygria*) and Japanese maples (*Acer palmatum* 'Atropurpureum').

A2. *Sorbaria tomentosa* in the centre supporting *Clematis flammula,* surrounded by white hollyhocks, white and a few purple Michaelmas daisies, with white asters and *Chrysanthemum maximum* and *Gypsophila paniculata.*

A3. Eupatorium and rhus, white dahlias, pinky-purple hollyhocks, *Campanula lactiflora* 'Loddon Anna' and a large sweep of *Acanthus spinosus.*

A4. In the centre another large sweep of acanthus as a backdrop for white achillea, pink phlox and snapdragons; to the left the colours turning to salmon pink (hollyhock) and orange (double sunflowers, dahlias, and orange African marigolds) with a sweep of lighter yellow cephalaria. On the right, steely-blue echinops with *Clematis flammula,* white Japanese anemones, eryngiums and blue and white Michaelmas daisies.

A5. Another central mass of acanthus with pale yellow and white snapdragons, primrose African marigolds, a yellow day-lily and *Geum chiloense* 'Lady Stratheden' with ageratum and blue statice next to the path. On the left, red dahlias, orange African marigolds and kniphofias, yellow iris, gladiolus 'Brenchleyensis' (yellowy-orange) and thyme and trollius in the front. On the right, acanthus at the back, with blue campanula, peach astilbe, white *Aster amellus* and phlox 'Elizabeth Campbell'.

A6. Geum 'Mrs Bradshaw', geranium 'Paul Crampel', salvia 'Fireball', orange snapdragons, red dahlias, gladiolus 'Brenchleyensis', scarlet penstemons, and rhus with a generous backing of senecio (*Ligularia clivorum*).

A7. Pale pink phlox, pale pink and tall white snapdragons, erigeron, *Campanula carpatica,* catmint, *Stachys lanata* and bergenias.

B1. *Sorbaria tomentosa* in the centre, with *Clematis flammula,* white dahlias, white and purple Michaelmas daisies, eryngium, *Campanula cordifolia* (*alliariifolia*), gypsophila, *Aconitum napellum* and *Chrysanthemum maximum.*

B2. A variation on A1 with the addition of oriental poppies (scarlet) and *Berberis thunbergii.*

B3. Purple hollyhocks, rhus, *Chrysanthemum uliginosum,* lythrum 'roseum' (possibly 'Rose Queen'), purply-red and white Michaelmas daisies, lavatera, and *Aconitum napellum,* acanthus and eryngium in the front.

B4. A central sweep of acanthus, with pink lavatera, lythrum 'Rose Queen', peach astilbe and aster 'Lady Lloyd'. On the left, gypsophila, white Japanese anemones, echinops with *Clematis flammula,* and *Campanula lactiflora*; on the right, *Daphne cneorum* as a backing for kniphofias, orange day-lilies, heleniums (orange striped-crimson var.) with tall white snapdragons in the front.

B5. Acanthus sweeping all round the curve as a backing for pink and white phlox and snapdragons at centre front with statice and pale pink annual phlox, *P. drummondii* at the path edge; on the left, pink and white snapdragons, white campanulas, pink Michaelmas daisies, *Aconitum napellum* and erigeron; on the right, red snapdragons, kniphofias, orange African marigolds, pinky/orange bedding geraniums.

B6. *Aconitum napellum,* tall white snapdragon, 'small blue' asters, *Geranium ibericum,* shorter white snapdragon, statice, nepeta, bergenias, white pinks and *Stachys.*

B7. The same as A6 plus kniphofias and red day-lilies.

D1. A dark-foliage berberis marked 'fruity' for centre, with blood red hollyhocks, tall red dahlias, Japanese maples, eupatorium, red poppies, 'Fire King' dahlias, *Ricinus communis gibsonii* and *Berberis thunbergii.*

D2. *Sorbaria tomentosa* in the centre with *Clematis flammula,* white dahlias and hollyhocks, *Artemisia lactiflora,* white delphiniums and Shasta daisies, and a variegated holly in the front (creamy-white leaf margins).

D3. Golden elder, golden rod, primrose-yellow helianthus, rudbeckia 'Golden Glow', *Artemisia lactiflora,* golden privet, mulleins, acanthus and *Euonymus japonicus.*

D4. Again the acanthus in the centre, with primrose-yellow African marigolds, *Salvia nemorosa,* yellow snapdragons, gaillardia with white astilbe. On the left, mulleins, *Berberis thunbergii,* dahlia 'Queenie', orangey-brown snapdragons and heleniums; on the right, mulleins, *Aconitum napellum* (monk's hood), gypsophila, *Anthemis tinctoria* and acanthus.

48

D5. Acanthus in the centre, with *Anthemis tinctoria, Helenium pumilum,* azure scabious, purple sage and nemesia 'Blue Gem'. On the left, *Berberis thunbergii* and *Ligularia clivorum,* tall African marigolds (orange), kniphofias, heleniums, coreopsis and Shasta daisies; on the right, white astilbe, yellow African marigolds, monk's hood, white snapdragons, aster 'Little Boy Blue'.

D6. Dahlia 'Fire King', kniphofias, orange snapdragons, double scarlet zinnias, gladiolus 'Brenchleyensis', fiery orange nemesia and rich orange dwarf French marigolds.

D7. White astilbes, hostas, yellow snapdragons and heleniums, with *Stachys lanata,* catmint and statice.

NB. *Mahonia aquifolium* at the foot of yew hedges by entrance and exit.

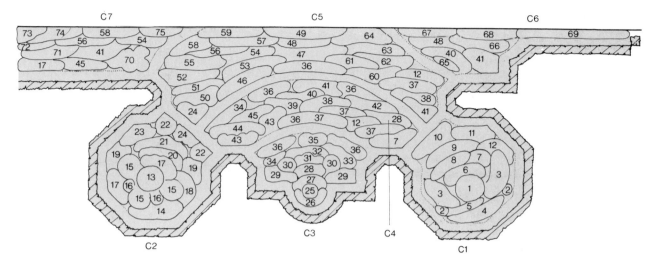

Key to the planting of Section C of Blagdon new border plan:

NB. Where the colours are in brackets they are my suggestions, otherwise Miss Jekyll stipulated the colour on her plan.

1. *Sorbaria tomentosa*
2. *Clematis flammula* (to trail over delphiniums)
3. Delphiniums (pale blue)
4. White hollyhocks
5. Solidago (lemon yellow golden rod)
6. *Chrysanthemum uliginosum* (white)
7. White delphiniums
8. Tall yellow snapdragons
9. Delphinium (pale blue or white)
10. *Zea japonica* (maize)
11. *Chrysanthemum maximum*
12. Double meadowsweet (*Aruncus sylvester*)
13. Berberis with dark foliage (unspecified)
14. Blood red hollyhocks
15. Japanese maple (*Acer palmatum* 'Atropurpureum')
16. Clematis (unspecified but presumably rose red)
17. Red dahlias
18. Orange dahlias
19. Eupatorium

20. Red poppies
21. *Ricinus communis gibsonii* (red-leaved castor-oil plant)
22. *Cotinus coggygria*
23. Malope (orange)
24. *Berberis thunbergii*
25. Golden elder
26. Solidago (golden rod)
27. Primrose yellow helianthus
28. *Artemisia lactiflora*
29. Golden yellow dahlias
30. Golden privet
31. Pale yellow dahlias
32. Tall white snapdragons
33. Cornflower blue snapdragon
34. Double helenium (golden yellow)
35. *Euonymus Japonicus* (golden-leaved)
36. *Acanthus spinosus*
37. Delphinium 'Belladonna'
38. Tall yellow snapdragons
39. *Helenium striatum*
40. Chrysanthemum 'Morning Star'
41. *Spirea callosa alba*
42. Polemonium (pale blue)
43. Dahlia 'Queenie'
44. Tall French marigold (orange)
45. *Ligularia clivorum*
46. Orange African marigold

47. Primrose African marigold
48. Shorter yellow snapdragon
49. Nemesia 'Blue Gem'
50. Tall dark (brown) snapdragons
51. Scarlet poppies
52. Tall red snapdragons
53. Day-lilies (striped orange/yellow)
54. Snapdragon 'Orange King'
55. Red penstemon
56. Gladiolus (orange)
57. Helenium (short, yellow)
58. Orange nemesia
59. Variegated golden mint
60. Coreopsis (yellow)
61. Day lilies (yellow)
62. *Oenothera fruticosa* (yellow)
63. Lemon yellow helenium
64. *Glyceria aquatica* 'Variegata'
65. Anchusa
66. *Hosta ovata*
67. Cobalt blue lobelia
68. *Agathea coelestis* (*Felicia amelloides*)
69. *Mahonia aquifolium*
70. Kniphofias
71. Dark scarlet zinnias
72. Scarlet penstemons
73. Geranium 'Paul Crampel'
74. Soft red geranium
75. Dwarf French marigold (orange)

the warmer colours, to cheer the Northumberland climate which Lady Ridley found so trying. The progressive harmony of adjacent colours revealed by walking through the garden is enhanced by the harmony of opposites and the satisfaction of after-images, by placing the golds opposite the purples. The gorgeous companions from the heart of the Munstead border – blood-red hollyhocks, scarlet dahlias, purple *Rhus cotinus* – are the culmination of the border experience, glimpsed from the farthest point in either direction. Conversely, the pure white flowers in their dark green surround are the final crisp and pure image remaining in the mind.

Miss Jekyll's struggles to satisfy her own ideals, and her final efforts to please Ursula Ridley, were in themselves partly the reason why neither of these gardens survive for us today. Because she put all her changing experiences into her books, her planting ideals have been handed down as a sort of national, or international, heritage. We have adopted the generalities and lost the originals because gardening is such an individual art; her successors have carefully read her theories – and then adapted them to their own time and purpose. In the end, we have become so appalled at the thought of seventeen gardeners, and such labour forces, and so mesmerized by trying to equate her names and varieties with the plants available to us now, that we have in truth abandoned the essence of Jekyll gardening. The vast majority of flower borders are back to sprinkling again. Munstead Wood garden as she knew it is unrecognizable, the Blagdon border has gone, and so have the demonstrations of adherence to the colour rules in nearly all the gardens she planned in between; it seems that no faithful disciples of equal artistic and horticultural knowledge have been content to perpetuate her works of art, least of all in the places where her gardening belongs. This is all the more hurtful when we realize that both Claude Monet's paintings (and she was to be cruelly criticized for failing to put her garden pictures on canvas as he did) and his garden at Giverny are carefully treasured; also, the gardens which Miss Jekyll must have in some way inspired, such as Hidcote Manor and Sissinghurst Castle, are elaborately maintained in the way their makers would have wished. That is why, with one or two notable exceptions which will make a welcome appearance later, any appreciation of the flower gardening at Munstead, and in the Lutyens-designed gardens, has to be in the imagination. I sincerely hope it will not always be so.

Woodland Gardening at Munstead

The largest proportion of the Munstead acreage – just over half – was devoted to wild or woodland gardening; this was the upper and south-eastern half of the plot where the Scots pine had been felled for timber about fifteen years before, leaving two or three strangely shaped or double-stemmed trees which Miss Jekyll used as focal elements. The soil was basically acid sand, with a thick peaty covering from which seedling trees had sprouted. Her first task was to thin these into considered groups. Her way of doing this will please those who believe that plants have ears – it was 'to appeal to the little trees themselves and see what they had to say about it',[25] which meant that wherever she found an especially good young tree or a happy plant relationship she let that dictate the species for a particular area. In general terms this was determined as silver birch with holly, as beautifully contrasting neighbours in the nearer part, changing in the space of a hundred yards into oak wood; then came the beeches, and on the farthest and highest ground the Scots pine were allowed to return. The western part of the wood had some Spanish chestnut. Miss Jekyll was particularly careful that the changes in species should have no harsh frontiers, so the divisions were very flexible, and the final arbiter was the relationship of any single tree with those around it. Having decided that the woodland would be of these four distinct types – 'the preponderance of one kind of tree at a time [gives] a feeling of repose and dignity' being her main reason – she next decided how the woodland experience would be revealed. During countless visits, at all seasons, she had undoubtedly made random paths to a special spot or favourite tree; these random paths were organized into five walks radiating from the lawn near the house. The wide green walk, opposite the garden door in the south front, was her 'most precious possession' – this was treated most boldly. The beginning of this walk was flanked by rhododendrons, grouped carefully as to colouring, with pink, rose and white flowering varieties kept carefully away from the purple *Rhododendron ponticum* and the magenta colourings. The ground in front was planted with ferns and pieris (*floribunda* or *japonica*) on the shady side of the path, and *Lithospermum diffusum* and *Calluna vulgaris* in the sun. The rhododendrons were planted around the young birch trees, so that in maturity the heavy green would provide a superb foil to the silver trunks. This main path was wide enough for two people to walk comfortably side by side, and thus it was also light enough for the grass to grow; it was kept mown to emphasize the importance of this walk. In fine weather it was possible to see to the end of the path, where a double-stemmed Scots pine, backed by a more distant wood, closed the vista, giving a sense of security and repose; in misty weather, green melted into green in the bluish distance, creating a sense of the mystery and magic that we believe all woods should have.

The other paths radiating from the lawn were more enclosed and sandy, with more meandering paths crossing them in the wood; however, the planting was carefully controlled to give each path character. The fern walk, through birches and oaks, was naturally carpeted with bracken, but groups of *Blechnum spicant* and *Osmunda regalis*, the royal fern, were added for distinction. Another path through birches and oaks passed drifts of daffodils, ranged regularly in sequence according to their kind, with the hybrids standing between their parents, and all especially planted to catch the rays of slanting sun. The rock wood path was decorated with lumps of sandstone, large and very carefully placed (no doubt with the aid of Jack the donkey and his garden cart) about which were planted pieris, skimmia and alpenrose so that glimpses of the rocks seemed totally unremarkable. Gaultheria (probably *G. shallon*), a showy relative of the heathland whortleberry, was a favourite because of its liking for heavy shade on acid soil, and found a place in the wood. (Where it remains, the successors of Miss Jekyll have reason to curse her quietly for this affection, for she introduced it to Leith Hill and Hydon Ball and in both places and adjacent gardens it now rampages happily over everything else.[26])

Throughout the woodland garden the effect of light coming through the trees was exploited to illuminate what Miss Jekyll called 'flowery incidents' [19] – a patch of white

19. Munstead Wood: the house from the woodland garden, with some of the 'flowery incidents' in view.

foxgloves, a sweep of lily-of-the-valley or poet's daffodil or the white blossoms of *Rubus parviflorus* and *Amelanchier laevis*. Her impressionistic obsession with white as the colour of magical light was allowed full play in the woodland garden. Colour, too, played its part – the azaleas were planted beneath the chestnuts in one grove, so that the russets of the fallen leaves made a perfect scheme with the creams, golds, oranges and reds of the flowers; there was an abundance of *Azalea pontica*, both for its perfume and for its ability to merge naturally into the surrounding wood. Another feature of Munstead in spring was the polyanthus patch in the oak wood; Miss Jekyll had first found yellow and white bunch primroses, as she called them, growing in a cottage garden in the 1870s. From these first flowers she developed the large-flowering Munstead strains, and though different colours were used in other parts of the garden, the planting beneath the oaks was purely yellow and white – the oak stems 'being bare to a considerable height giving, at the time when the primroses were at their full glory, a faint greenish light from the young oak foliage'[27] – creating a picture of translucent primroses which would long be remembered by those who saw it.

Woodland gardening at Munstead was carefully organized – no less so than the flower borders or vegetable garden – but with Miss Jekyll's restraining hand and deep respect for plants nothing appeared contrived; it was merely that nature was given the opportunity for displaying glories that so often go unmarked and unseen. The woodland garden was a constantly changing experience of delight to all her visitors and friends, its springtime pleasures followed by others throughout summer and autumn. A holly laced with flowering honeysuckle, *Lilium auratum* blooming at the feet of a rhododendron, the clearing that was full of pink and white cistus in flower, or clumps of magnificent lupins at the wood edge – all these were 'flowery incidents' to be chanced upon unawares. They were not, I hasten to add, for picking – Mary Lutyens remembers that her father would never allow cut flowers in the house, and she imagines that he never recovered from Miss Jekyll's tirade when he casually plucked a Munstead flower during one of those early youthful visits!

Of all kinds of gardening perhaps woodland gardening is the most personal, and thus a peculiar prey to time and a stranger's hand. The battered ghosts of Miss Jekyll's woodland survive, but little of its spirit. She did design woodland schemes for other like-minded clients (to start them off), and one of these, of which much of the atmosphere remains, was for her friend the Hon. Emily Lawless, for whom Lutyens designed a house, Hazelhatch near Shere, in 1896.[28] Others will be met along the way. There are also other gardening ideas which had their source at Munstead Wood – Miss Jekyll's delight in dry-wall gardening, and her decided views on the all-important kitchen garden – but these are explored in connection with designs to come. The dream of Munstead Wood was the setting for their partnership, but the partnership was already working for clients by the time Miss Jekyll's house was finished in 1896.

The Surrey Houses and Gardens

Miss Jekyll recorded her first garden client as the boy from a Rochdale mill for whom she planned a window box and sent the plants by post.[29] But she had also given advice on the gardens of a dozen friends, mostly in Surrey, before she met Lutyens. While Munstead Wood house was still in the 'disputations' stage, she apparently offered tentative advice on the garden for Lutyens's first major house, Crooksbury, on the slopes of Crooksbury Hill, near Farnham. He was to build this for old family friends, Arthur and Agnes Chapman (Charles Lutyens had painted Agnes Chapman, Harry Mangles's sister), who wanted a small home in south-west Surrey to be near their family and friends. Crooksbury is rather an enigma – certainly as far as the garden is concerned. It was to be a continuing commission, with several additions to the house and subsequent alterations to the garden, but because it was in the early days before presages of fame made every sketch and drawing precious, none of these have survived. Because it was built at different periods it was also ripe for division, and splitting a house is death to a garden because of conflicting tastes and the need for artificial boundaries. So all that remains at Crooksbury are portions of brick terracing and a brick pergola, apart from the fig court, a pergola'd covering between the arms of the house (where, presumably,

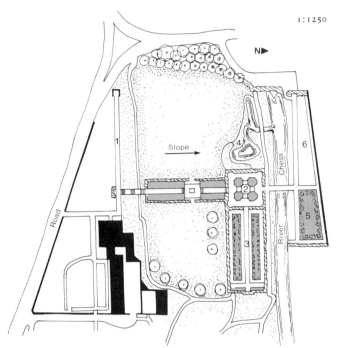

1:1250

20. *(left)* Woodside: sketch layout of the site, which slopes to the river with the steepest slope below the terrace (1). The purpose of the axial design was to unite house, garden, river and the extra land on the farther bank. This was done by leading from the new west door of the house to the terrace at the top of the slope, from where a stepped path, with bordering yew-enclosed flower beds, led down to the pond court (2). The pond court, with set-in seats and flower beds round an arbour (which originally sheltered a round pond), introduces a choice between the river garden, with wide herbaceous borders and a seat at the farther end (3), or crossing the bridge to the formal rose garden (5) and the mill lawn (6). The water garden at (4) was planted with irises, marsh marigolds, arums, rushes and arrowheads.

21. *(opposite)* Woodside: an original *Country Life* photograph looking east from the pond court towards the river garden. The intricate paving and brickwork, using the 2-inch narrow bricks, can be clearly seen.

figs were grown), of which many photographs survive. The house is surrounded by rhododendrons and birches – but here, as in many of the less consciously designed Surrey gardens, it is impossible to say that they were Miss Jekyll's planting, for they are plentiful in the surrounding sandy woodland countryside.

The first 'official' garden of the partnership is in a much happier state. In 1893 they were asked to design a garden for an existing house, Woodside, on the outskirts of the village of Chenies in Buckinghamshire, for Adeline, Duchess of Bedford (widow of the 10th Duke who had died earlier that year and presumably a contact through Miss Jekyll's London friends). I have reproduced a sketch plan of Woodside [20], which illustrates how Lutyens re-organized the house. The main door originally faced the road, but Lutyens removed the focus to the west front, where a path leading on to the terrace, down the slope to a bridge over the River Chess and thus linking the garden on the other bank, formed the main feature of the design. Woodside is a sculptured garden, very much in the Italian style, and one can imagine Miss Jekyll's particular pleasure in its making. No planting plans seem to have survived, but it is possible to create suitable schemes from old photographs and from her favourite ideas – the yew-enclosed borders along the sloping paths would have been filled with silvers and greys, with pale pinks and pale blues in the way of delicate spring and summer flowers. Woodside is an important and precious garden, for it gives glimpses of themes, especially in the formality and craftsmanship of the pond court, which will be refined, reiterated and embellished over and over again; what is perhaps more important, it demonstrates how a garden with a definite architectural framework and with continued respect and care can survive for almost ninety years. [See 21 and colour pls. 4 and 5.]

The early work of the partnership was of the 'Surrey School' of garden design, not always within the county, but mostly so. Crooksbury and Munstead Wood launched Lutyens on his career as a country-house architect, building the houses which have not only become synonymous with Surrey, but *grew out of* Surrey. They were designed in the vernacular traditions he had known throughout his childhood, and built in the main of the warm golden Bargate sandstone which is found in small patches in south-west Surrey.[30] Just as the greensand yielded stone for houses, it was used in gardens for paths and walls. The acid dryness of the soil indicated the kind of planting that would succeed (in this they were mostly Munstead's children), and the low fertility ensured that 'natural' planting could be kept under control. The commissions themselves were dictated initially by a particular circle of friends and acquaintances. The building of Orchards is an apt example; the future owner, Julia Chance, an artist and sculptress and member of the Strachey family, has written her description of what happened:

We intended to build on a piece of land about a mile down the lane [from Munstead Wood] but by an unhappy choice we had hit upon an architect whose plans we disliked so much that for the moment we had actually given up the idea of building at all, rather than make the irreparable mistake of letting the wrong kind of house materialize. Then a miracle happened. One day on our way to visit our still virgin acres, we walked up the hill from Godalming. Passing through a sandy lane we saw a house nearing completion, and on the top of a ladder a portly figure giving directions to some workmen. The house was a revelation of unimagined beauty and charm, the like of which we had never seen before, and we stood entranced and gazing until the figure descended from the ladder, and we found ourselves, after due explanation, being welcomed as future neighbours and shown over the wonderful house – as a result of this meeting we became the owners of a Lutyens house with a Jekyll garden.[31]

The Chances, William and Julia, and their belief in the integrity of art and life, illustrate well why many of the people who were to give their names to history as Lutyens's clients (and often a large part of their fortunes as well) were labelled *fastidious*. Though Orchards is quite large, and to modern eyes a grand house, the philosophy of its makers, the design and the materials used, give it the earthborn quality which is the special aura of these Surrey houses. Orchards, as the creation of a house and garden in a landscape according to the dictates of that landscape, is one of the greatest triumphs of the partnership. And I believe that here, for the first time for a client, Miss Jekyll did far more than merely plant the garden.

22. 'I make obeysance'.

The whole designed layout of Orchards [23] makes obeisance to the site; the house was laid out in a quadrangle, and both the interior progress and the paths and terraces around the house led inexorably to the glorious eastward view over the Thorncombe valley [colour pl. 7]. The view was to be enjoyed from the loggia, purposely sought and savoured from comfortable cane chairs; that it could be glimpsed from the windows of the east side was merely incidental, for the windows were small (as were the windows of the Munstead burrow) and leaded as was essential to the detailed character of the design. The view from the loggia looked across the top of the sunken Dutch garden; this was the one man-made feature of luxurious sophistication in all this adoration of the landscape [24]. The contrast of the Dutch garden, with its intricate geometrical paving in brick and stone, delicate and perfumed planting of white roses and lavender, sight and smell mingling with the sound of water trickling from a mask designed by Julia Chance into a raised pool by Lutyens, added the dimension of the divine orders [25, 27]. Below the Dutch garden a simple yew-hedged path creates an axis across the view and a means of getting to the flower and vegetable gardens. Orchards (the name was chosen because of extensive fruit orchards on the estate) was country living of a kind that demanded a degree of wealth, but where thrift and rural economy still ruled, and self-sufficiency in flowers, fruit and vegetables was expected. In truth Orchards garden [26] – the formal part of the design at least – is largely productive: vegetable plots bordered and decorated with flowers and herbs in a manner that derived partly from monastic traditions, partly from the French *jardins potagers*, and partly from Miss Jekyll's belief

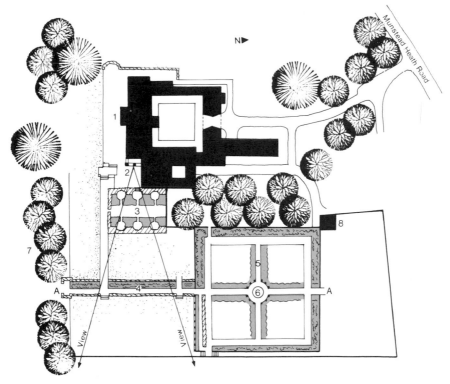

23. Orchards: sketch layout of the garden. From Munstead Heath road the drive led directly into a plain and unadorned quadrangle. From the right of the entrance arch a path led, past Julia Chance's studio with its north light, around the house to the south terrace (1). The path, stone-flagged and raised, continues to the loggia terrace (2) which gives entrance to the sunken Dutch garden (3). It is from the loggia terrace that one can see half of Surrey laid at one's feet [see colour pl. 7], but the lower level of the Dutch garden is now completely enclosed by the yew hedges, which have grown to a height of over 7 feet. The directional path (A–A) leads via a yew-enclosed and bordered walk (4) to the kitchen garden (5), of which the centre-piece is a dipping-well (6) surrounded by roses trained on hoops and chains between oak posts. The edges of the kitchen garden beds were planted with a luxuriant cottage-garden mixture of silver lavenders, santolina, catmint and *Stachys lanata*, with clumps of *Iris germanica* and an abundance of other pink and blue flowers – thus the impression through the vista was of a long flower-filled walk. The south lawn (7) was planted with azaleas and rhododendrons, with paths cut between the beds. The gardener's cottage is at (8).

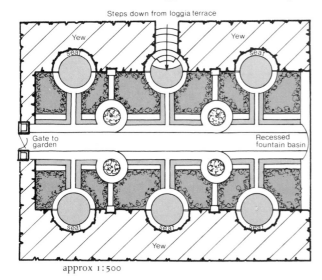

24. *(left)* Orchards: the Dutch garden plan showing the pattern of the herring-bone brick (shaded) and stone paving, and how paving, semi-circular seats and steps are all part of the related radii of the circles in the design. The planting was originally simply white bush roses surrounded with lavender.

25. Orchards: Lutyens's ink and watercolour sketch for the gate to the Dutch garden. The annotation is typical of the young Lutyens at work: 'Tile posts with tile multigonals on top on a cement core and apologies for yews! An iron gate'.

that flowers and vegetables were a benign influence on each other. Miss Jekyll must have spent a great deal of time at Orchards, both in the designing and building stages, for she and Julia Chance had much in common and became great artist-companions. Lutyens's marvellous use of his sites (for *he* must get the credit) is much in evidence at Orchards. The total harmony of building and grounds reflects William Robinson's ideal partnership at work – an owner who loved, and certainly wanted to understand, her soil; a garden designer who understood the soil completely and knew what the owner and her friends would like; and an architect prepared to let his own beloved landscape dictate his art.

Munstead Wood and Orchards were the first of a gilded quartet of Surrey houses. In one of Miss Jekyll's photo albums, there is a picture showing Theodore Waterhouse having breakfast on the Chalet balcony which I think makes the connection with the other two. Theodore was a relative of the architect Alfred Waterhouse, but his particular branch of the family were founders of the city accountants Price Waterhouse & Co., and they lived in an Alfred Waterhouse-inspired house, Feldemore at Holmbury St Mary, about eight miles south-east of Guildford.[32] Just over the road from Feldemore is Pasturewood,[33] then the home of merchant banker Sir Frederick Mirrielees – and it would seem likely that it was via the Waterhouses and Miss Jekyll that Lutyens was called to Pasturewood to discuss the design of Goddards, a holiday home for lady social workers 'of small means', which Miss Mirrielees wanted her father to finance at near-by Abinger Common. Goddards was built on Abinger's green, a beautiful rough-cast house with finely-detailed brickwork. Miss Jekyll's planting for the ornate little courtyard garden [28] is exactly identifiable, and the character of the garden seems to fit the house's purpose exactly. While staying at Pasturewood (and writing home that the horses were better treated than the guests but the connection would be good for him professionally!)[34]

26. Orchards: an original *Country Life* photograph of the garden in its heyday.

27. Orchards: the Dutch garden, with its complex paving pattern of stone and brick. The yew hedges have now grown to the height of the climber-covered wall on the right, making a 'garden room', as can be seen in colour pl. 7.

28. Goddards: rich planting and contrasting textures of stone and brick in the little garden held within the arms of the house. The dipping-well in the centre was one of Miss Jekyll's favourite features, and evidence of her gardener's common-sense understanding of the dry, sandy Surrey gardens.

Lutyens designed a 'folly' extension to the Flockhart half-timbered, half-tiled house, and an elaborate pergola. Miss Jekyll planted an enormous rock garden on the slopes of the tree-covered hillside, of which birches, rhododendrons, pieris and gaultheria are the most persistent survivors.

The last of the quartet, Tigbourne Court, now rather too close to the A283 just south of Witley, was built for Edgar Horne, M.P. for Guildford and chairman of the Prudential insurance company. The house has a famous tripartite gabled front with soaring chimneys, but the garden is quiet – an arched loggia leads on to a level flagged terrace and through a curving pergola of brick piers and oak crossbars. No original planting plans survive (as is the case with so many of these early houses) but rhododendrons, azaleas and other acid-loving shrubs and climbing roses proliferate.

It seems that, as a rising young architect, the name of Edwin Lutyens fast became the equivalent of a good tip in the city – Sir Frederick Mirrielees and Edgar Horne led to a trail of bankers and financiers, who were to be an important group of Lutyens's clients. He built the two Overstrand houses, Overstrand Hall and The Pleasaunce, near Cromer in Norfolk, through banking connections (Miss Jekyll had nothing to do with these, probably feeling that Norfolk soils and exposure were alien to her gardening), and Berrydowne at Overton in Hampshire [see colour pl. 3] for another financier, Archibald Grove. Archie Grove was to become a firm friend – in spite of what happened at

Berrydowne, one feels, which suggests that the partners did not have the measure of the Hampshire downland landscape quite as well as that of Surrey. Berrydowne is walled and rough-cast in a creamy-grey which is exactly the right colour, but it has no view nor is it secluded – it seems to be at cross-purposes with its site. The planning of the garden seems to have gone awry; in August 1899 William Robinson was called in, and the end result (though by whose order is not recorded) was that tons of peat were imported to provide the obligatory rhododendrons and azaleas at all costs. The following year 'the 19th solution' to Berrydowne was tried, and later the same year Archie Grove sold it. The partnership did suffer the occasional failure.[35]

It was during the 1890s, when so much happened so quickly, that Miss Jekyll and Lutyens settled into a working partnership. At the beginning of the period, while Munstead Wood was being planned and built and most of the jobs Lutyens had were in Surrey, her influence on him was obviously at its strongest. It was a matter of cause and effect – because so much work was in Surrey he spent quite a lot of time at Munstead, where he had a workroom, and in turn many of his commissions came from Miss Jekyll's friends or friends of his family at Thursley or the Webbs at Milford. Towards the end of the decade, with commissions from a number of bankers and financiers taking him farther afield, Lutyens's life assumed a pattern of almost frantic hard work: a continual succession of travelling, site visiting, discussing by day, working at his drawing-board – scattering it with ash from his eternal pipe as he did so – far into the night. A number of commissions were completed outside of the informal partnership – Miss Jekyll did about twenty-eight gardens between 1890 and 1900 which were not

29. (*left*) Witley Park: one of Lutyens's earliest garden buildings, the bathing and boating pavilion from across the Witley Park lake. This was built in 1897 for Whitaker Wright, who spent a fortune on a house and park at Witley in the 1890s, only to commit suicide in 1904 after being sent to prison for fraud.

30. (*right*) Witley Park: detail of the bathing and boating pavilion. The doorway makes an interesting comparison with the gate at Woodside of four years earlier [see colour pl. 5].

31, 32. Pages from Miss Jekyll's plant catalogue, entitled *Some of the Best Hardy Plants for Border, Shrub and Rock Garden*, printed by Craddocks of Godalming, but undated. Munstead Wood potpourri was offered at 20s. a gallon ('one gallon will fill a large bowl'), or 5s. a pound, postage extra.

Lutyens's concern.[36] In 1898 she designed a garden for the headmaster of Charterhouse School near Godalming (some of which survives) and this led to an interesting commission for both of them – the Red House in Frith Hill Road, just by the school, for a retired master, the Rev. H. J. Evans.[37] Because of the cliff-like site, the Red House is an early, miniature brick version of Castle Drogo, hanging above its garden, which was so steep that the only resource was to erect tier upon tier of retaining walls of sandstone, planted with lavenders, sun roses, pinks, hyssop, rosemary, ferns, santolinas, senecios and miniature campanulas in the crevices and all over the walls themselves. A more informal woodland garden clothed the bottom of the slope. In this case there seems to have been little consultation; it was clearly a Lutyens-only house and a Jekyll-only garden, but this was rarely so. Later correspondence shows that it became a habit to discuss the relationship between house and garden: where the views from the windows should be directed, where the paths from the doors should lead – all as a result of a first examination of the site, which in Surrey, until after the turn of the century, was in most cases done together. From this discussion Lutyens would draw up the plan of the whole site, and while he retired to work on the house details, Miss Jekyll would adapt the shapes of the areas to be planted to a scale which was comfortable to her weak eyes, and proceed to fill in the planting details. In many cases she would also supervise the supply of some plants from Munstead Wood, for by this time her small army of gardeners was paying its way, and her business was developing [31, 32]. In *Pot Pourri from a Surrey Garden* (1897) Mrs C. W. Earle wrote:

Dec. 10 – there has been in this year's Guardian a succession of monthly papers on a Surrey garden written by Miss Jekyll of Munstead Wood, Godalming. I give her address as she now sells her surplus plants – all more or less suited to light soils, to the management of which she has for many years past given her special attention. The papers have much illuminating matter in them and are called 'Notes from Garden and Woodland'. All the plants and flowers about which Miss Jekyll writes she actually grows on top of her Surrey hill. Her garden is a most instructive one and encouraging too. She has gone through the stage so common to all ambitious and enthusiastic amateurs, of trying to grow everything, and often wasting much precious room in growing inferior plants, or plants which even though they may be worth growing in themselves are not yet worth the care and feeding which a light soil necessitates if they are to be successful.[38]

This rather barbed appraisal of Miss Jekyll's efforts may have just been the gentle rivalry of two ladies who wrote about gardening, or it may reflect the crisis over Ned's romance which was the talk of the Jekyll circle at the time. Mrs Earle was a friend of the Jekylls, but she was also the sister of the Countess of Lytton (widow of the 1st Earl who had died in 1891), and it was the Countess's youngest daughter, Emily, with whom Ned was in love. They had met at a musical evening at the Blumenthals' house, 43 Hyde Park Gate, in the early summer of 1896 – Ned had found Emily looking cross and unhappy and had vowed to make her happy.[39] Knowing the rather patronizing attitude Mrs Earle adopted towards Miss Jekyll, it takes little guessing to assess the Lytton attitude to her racy young architect friend – to whom, wrote the Countess, she had *not* been introduced. Emily was a spirited and romantic girl, and though at first their cause seemed hopeless, she and Ned were determined – friends and relatives came to their aid, the Countess was eventually appeased and finally delighted, and they were married at Knebworth on 4 August 1897.[40] Emily was always to remain his greatest inspiration. Though Miss Jekyll was at first concerned lest Emily should prove a frivolous influence on Ned, she soon accepted his adoration of Emily and became their firm ally. After her first visit to Munstead Emily wrote: 'She is the most enchanting person and lives in the most fascinating cottage you ever saw. Mr Lutyens calls her Bumps, and it is a very good name. She is very fat and stumpy, dresses rather like a man, little tiny eyes, very nearly blind, and big spectacles. She is simply fascinating.'[41]

For a time Emily must have coloured every conversation and the partnership must almost have been a triumvirate, but it was not to be so for long.

33. 'Aunt Bumps'.

3

THE GARDENS OF
THE GOLDEN AFTERNOON

I am the garden, and every morn I am revealed in new beauty.
Observe my dress attentively, and you will reap the benefit of a
commentary on decoration.

From a wall in the Alhambra, Spain[1]

NED LUTYENS's marriage to Emily Lytton added the element of a spiritual quest to
his professional ambitions; he was deeply in love, and determined to scale the
heights of his art for Emily's sake and for the sake of their baby, Barbara, who
was born a year after their marriage. Emily believed in, even adored, his idealism,
though she may not have quite understood the quirk in his personality which made him
believe, with equal fervour, that his was a pilgrimage of zest, and that 'creating a furore'
was essential to playing the game.[2] With the acquisition of a family, and a new home
and office combined at 29 Bloomsbury Square (which had been Norman Shaw's office),
it was a game that had to be played hard. The Lytton connection was clearly useful, and
the first delightful outcome was Fisher's Hill, on Hook Heath, near Woking, a house
built for Emily's eldest sister Betty, who was married to Gerald Balfour, M.P.[3] Though
Fisher's Hill is now divided and neglected, it is still beautiful, and must have been
exceptionally so. Its garden falls away to what was a wooded dell. The only indication of
large flower borders in the Munstead style around the house is the survival of Miss
Jekyll's list of plants, divided into what she could supply (Dundee Rambler and The
Garland roses, rosemary, lavender, bergenias, *Achillea* 'The Pearl', santolinas, southernwood, *Eryngium giganteum* and pink hollyhocks among them), and others that she could
not, along with instructions to grow French and African marigolds and zinnias from
seeds. Mrs Earle was now an ally – and she was to be the source of *Stachys lanata* and
pinks from her garden at Cobham.[4] The Lytton connection led Lutyens to Knebworth,
and a portfolio of work which included some possible alterations to the formal gardens
at Knebworth House – though his sketch designs have been rubbed out by some
nameless present-day garden consultant. He also built Homewood for his mother-in-law
the Countess, now appearing to be a likeable if rather eccentric lady, who made a daily
pilgrimage down her garden path to pay homage with a curtsey to the sun at the field
gate, and likewise acknowledged the *Iris stylosa* on her return.[5] Ultimately it was this
Lytton connection which led via international exhibitions to the pinnacle of his career,
the Delhi commission.

However, perhaps more important to garden-making was another association which came into bloom with the new century. Some time at the end of the 1890s Miss Jekyll had introduced Lutyens to Edward Hudson, the founder and owner of *Country Life* magazine, to which she had been contributing gardening articles. The two men struck up a friendship, based on shared feelings and failings (Hudson, too, was inarticulate, but good craftsmanship and an insistence on high quality in life were shared objectives), which was to last for the rest of Hudson's life.[6] Lutyens built Deanery Garden, in the centre of the Thames-side village of Sonning in Berkshire, for Hudson in 1901. With this house he demonstrated his ability to accept the challenge of the 'new' architecture – as a later critic, Nicholas Taylor, described it: 'A miraculous and short-lived flowering between immaturity and the fatal reversion to Classicism.'[7] As the name implies, Deanery Garden is more than just a house. Its site was a walled orchard, almost surrounded by village streets, completely enclosed and with no outlooks. When Lutyens first surveyed it [35] he carefully noted the positions of the trees and left a large part of

Key to the planting:
A. Alecost or costmary (*Tanacetum balsamita*)
R. Rosemary
L. Lavender
M. Marjoram
S. Southernwood
SS. Summer savory
WS. Winter savory

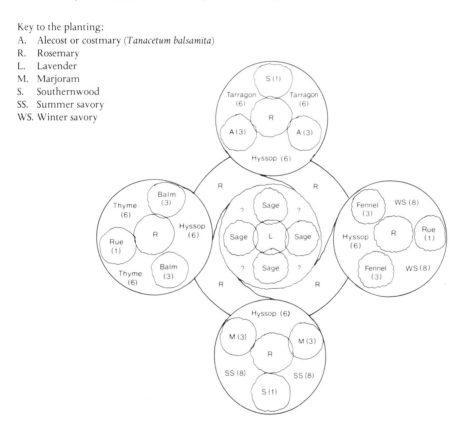

34. Knebworth House: the plan for a five-ringed herb garden in the *quincunx* pattern made by Miss Jekyll in 1907. There is no evidence that she did any other work at Knebworth and this plan may have been inspired by Emily as a present for her brother, the Earl of Lytton. The figures in brackets on the diagram refer to the number of plants used; most of the herbs are in the list of those Miss Jekyll sold, and in her plant catalogue [pl. 31].

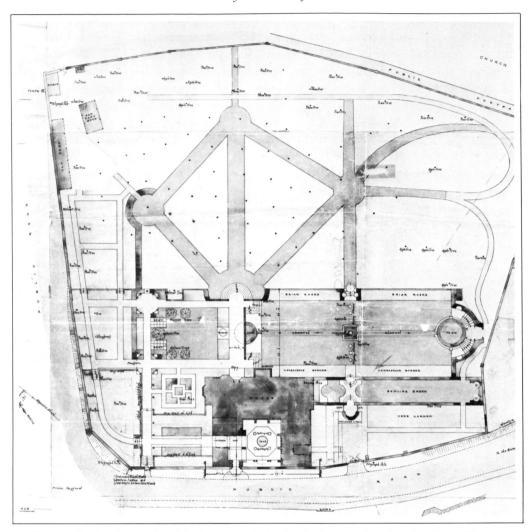

35. Deanery Garden: Lutyens's original survey and plan for the house and garden, dated 27–28 June 1899.

the orchard undisturbed; he fitted the house logically on to the side of the main street, and both house and garden were fitted into the orchard. Deanery Garden is an entity, united and indivisible, inside its walls – the flowers intrude into the house via a court, the flower beds in the open are only a step away from the carpet, all are united in their seclusion from the outside world. And a vital key to the harmony of Deanery Garden is that the motor car has been kept out – there was no room, and therefore the stables, now garages, are out of the way across the road. In return for a slight inconvenience on wet nights (though I presume Mr Hudson was always dropped at his street door), there is a complete and undisturbed harmony of people, trees and flowers at peace within their own world. A retreat indeed.

Deanery Garden usually earns uncritical architectural acclaim because of its asymmetry. The beautiful oriel window, with more than a touch of the days of Gloriana about it, is balanced by the concentric recessing of the garden door and the massive chimney beside it. The formal garden, too, is asymmetrical: features treated in detail – parterres, the pergola – are on the south-east corner, answered by the cool sweeps of lawns in the other direction. But the strongest impression from the plan is of the uniting influence of that central axis, from the door, across the mock bridge, down the circular steps and through the orchard (losing some of the trees in the process), which brings reason and peace to the whole design. The asymmetry lifts any hint of claustrophobia from the confined space, but out among the grass and trees the old order rules again.

36. Deanery Garden: planting plan for terrace borders. The planting scheme for the borders of the terrace at Deanery Garden typifies the delicate, refined, old-fashioned planting that was so right for this whole garden – with touches of sophistication provided by the yuccas, iris and gladiolus. The colours are kept to the delicate pinks, pale blues and silver, with occasional touches of purple; the plants on the south wall – santolina (1), pink snapdragon (6), pink centranthus (8), rock pink (9), rosemary (16), catmint (17) and *Veronica prostrata* (18) – would hang over the retaining terrace wall. (21–28) are flowering water plants in the iris canal – cream, rose and purple flowers with a touch of yellow from the *Iris pseudo-acorus*.

Key to the planting:

1. *Santolina chamaecyparissus*
2. Pale blue delphinium
3. Blue pansy
4. Blue iris
5. *Reseda odorata* (mignonette)
6. Pink snapdragon
7. *Echinops ritro*
8. Centranthus (pink valerian)
9. Pink hybrid rock pink
10. Lavender
11. Pink hollyhock
12. Lilac pansy
13. White snapdragon

14. Pink China rose
15. Dwarf lavender
16. Rosemary
17. *Nepeta mussinii* (catmint)
18. *Veronica prostrata*
19. *Filipendula ulmaria flore pleno*
20. Centranthus (white valerian)
21. *Sagittaria sagittifolia*
22. *Myosotis palustris*
23. *Sparghanium ramosum*
24. *Iris laevigata*
25. *Butomus umbellatus*
26. *Iris pseudo-acorus*

27. *Menyanthes trifoliata*
28. *Alisma plantago*
29. Hydrangea
30. White rock pink (dianthus)
31. *Stachys lanata*
32. *Yucca filamentosa*
33. *Yucca gloriosa*
34. Purple gladiolus
35. *Clematis jackmanii*
36. *Chrysanthemum maximum*
37. *Clematis flammula*
38. *Hamamelis mollis*

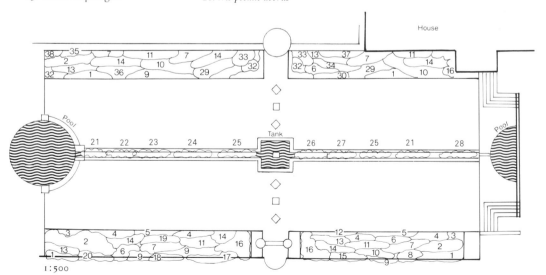

1:500

And Edward Hudson was rich enough, and Deanery Garden was small enough, for games to be played – the delightful mock bridge that served the garden door, which is really only a means of overcoming a difficult change of level, was given an arch beneath to make it look more like a bridge, and thus was born the first idea for the domed pools which were to become a garden symbol. Hudson enjoyed games – he obviously liked bowls, so there is a bowling green ordered in yew; he apparently did not like croquet, so the only usable lawn was crossed with an iris channel, an idea Miss Jekyll brought back from Moorish Spain, which made the pool beneath the 'bridge' logical and led across to a balancing circular pool at the other end. The iris channel was planted with water forget-me-nots, flowering rush, arrowhead, and *Iris pseudo-acorus* – just to lower the level of stratagem, for though games might be played with bricks and mortar they were never played with living plants. The other planting, of which the plans of the terrace borders [36] are an example, was delicate, refined and rather old-fashioned: The Garland grew triumphantly over the terrace walls, and there was a profusion of lower walls of brick, with spaces left for plants, all dripping with pinks, saxifrages, stonecrops, santolinas and lavenders. The orchard was ideal for 'meadow gardening', and daffodils, fritillaries and meadow saffron were among the species naturalized here. Planting apart, Miss Jekyll seemed to think Deanery Garden rather modern (it has aged little in eighty years), and it has rarely been surpassed for the provision of a heart's desire within four walls – refuge and warmth, sun and shade, flowers and fruit, the contemplation of water still or rippling, enticement and repose to fit every mood and season. [See 37, 38, 39.]

Almost as soon as Deanery Garden was completed, Edward Hudson found Lindisfarne Castle in need of care and attention, and asked Lutyens to convert it into a holiday retreat. Here Lutyens met, for the first time, a defensive architecture of a much tougher kind than the Surrey sandstone cottages. As can be seen from the interiors of Lindisfarne[8] – the stone-vaulted ship room and dining room, the arched and beamed long gallery – he was undeterred by the change in scale. Lindisfarne proved 'much more of an expensive amusement' than Hudson had anticipated, and despite a site visit by Miss Jekyll the extensive lake and water garden he envisaged never materialized. Instead, Miss Jekyll provided planting plans for a walled garden below the castle, the venue for a short excursion on fine afternoons. Ever practical, for it seemed that these excursions would be rare and that the need for fresh salads and vegetables in a place cut off by the tide for much of the time would be more important, these plans show another *jardin potager* with beds of spinach, lettuce, carrots, peas, broad beans and early potatoes with a cheerful disguise of gladiolas, roses, hollyhocks, sweet peas, fuchsias and mallows.

Hudson was always on the look-out for new possibilities (often it was Lutyens who did the looking), and over the years they considered Lympne Castle in Kent, Huntercombe Manor, at Burnham in Buckinghamshire, and the seventeenth-century Crossways Farm at Abinger in Surrey (George Meredith's setting for *Diana of the Crossways*). All to no avail (in the latter case perhaps this is a blessing), but in 1920 elaborate garden plans were prepared by the partners for Heath House at Headley, on the downs behind Box Hill; again nothing came of it. Finally, in 1927, Hudson bought

37. (*top*) Deanery Garden: the house from the orchard as it is today.

38. (*above left*) Deanery Garden: the garden front and the mock 'bridge', looking west.

39. (*above right*) Deanery Garden: the garden front from the bridge level, looking east. The lawn with the iris rill and borders [see pl. 36] is below the parapet.

Plumpton Place in Sussex, a home for the dreamed-of lake and water garden at last. Lutyens was too busy and too famous to do much to the garden design, but Miss Jekyll and Hudson conducted a charming and elaborate correspondence which resulted in beautiful gardens, described in more detail in Chapter 5.[9]

Though the problems of gardening in a strong prevailing wind were not really faced at Lindisfarne, there were two other commissions where exposure provided the key to the design, Lambay Island [40, 41, 42, 69, 70] and Grey Walls. In both cases Lutyens

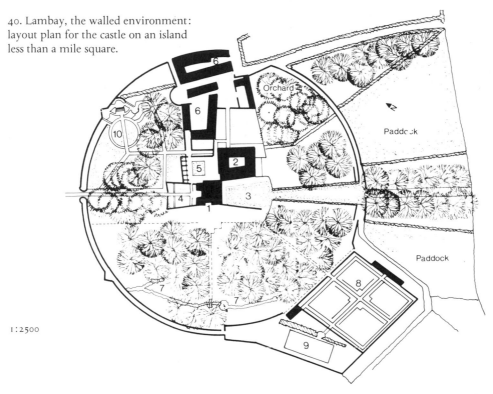

40. Lambay, the walled environment: layout plan for the castle on an island less than a mile square.

1:2500

1. The castle.
2. The new wing with staff and service quarters around the kitchen court.
3. The east court, a simple grass court with paving surround and a wide herbaceous border containing santolinas, rosemary, peonies, lilies, snapdragons, penstemon, hydrangeas, the bush *Clematis davidii*, and sentinel yuccas under the wall of the kitchen wing.
4. The west forecourt – level grass, but decorated with

an iris rill across it filling a small tank on the north side.
5. The north court, with a pergola adapted from the large pillars of an old barn and planted with clematis, roses and jasmine.
6. The stables, yards and farm buildings.
7. The water supply from wells.
8. The walled kitchen garden.
9. A hard tennis court.
10. The Memorial added after the War.

Among the buildings, the many high walls and small scale of the courts give a feeling of warm enclosure, the garden courts really being roofless rooms with green lawn carpets and flowers and stonework for decoration – 'on a fine day in summer the differences between being in or out-of-doors can be hardly noticeable', Professor A. S. G. Butler notes in *The Memorial*. Miss Jekyll never visited Lambay; the office ground floor plan was sent to her, and Lutyens visited Munstead to explain the castle. The plan is covered with his perspective sketches, and she then added her planting suggestions. [See pls. 69, 70.]

41. Lambay: the view out over the west forecourt.

42. Lambay: the north court before planting.

created his own micro-climate, and he did it on a massive scale. Grey Walls is not a castle, but a house by the sea. It was built for another M.P., Alfred Lyttelton,[10] a keen sportsman and golfer, and it stands on the famous Muirfield Links, facing the Firth of Forth and the north-east winds. The entrance to Grey Walls is via an enormous courtyard on the leeward side of the house. It is a well-devised plan, more easily understood and appreciated on paper [44] than in reality; the geometry of the court and the way the approach is directed to the sheltering angle of the house, the pleasing proportions and the lodges which seem convenient despite the awkward intrusion of the existing road and the clubhouse which had to be circumnavigated, are ingenious. Beyond the entrance court, the gardens have walls of their own. The most sheltered is the formal rose garden next to the house [colour pl. 6], with a tea-room, a delightful name for what Christopher Hussey called 'delicious garden architecture' in the north-east corner.[11] From the rose garden a central vista cuts straight through the south gardens to an oval stone *clair voyée*, set high to frame the distant Lothian hills [43].

Marsh Court

Architecture and the depiction of houses had been a feature of *Country Life* from its inception, and after Hudson met Lutyens his houses were of course included. It was as a direct result of seeing Crooksbury in *Country Life* that Lutyens was approached by Herbert Johnson, who wanted to build a house for himself on land near Stockbridge in Hampshire. Johnson was the son of a clergyman, and his natural flair for the stock market had earned him half a million pounds by the time he was forty-four. He was the quintessential Lutyens client – the adventurer. It was for such clients that Lutyens was to do his best work.[12] 'Johnnie and Ned', so the story goes, 'perceiving one another's greatnesses' became lifelong friends.[13] Perhaps because of his dream of sharing a little white house with Emily, perhaps because of his feelings for Herbert Johnson and his wish to design a house symbolic of 'adventurous traditionalism', or perhaps because of his avowed affection for the gentle, open landscape of the Test valley,[14] Marsh Court is where Lutyens most delightfully displays his genius for designing striking and beautiful houses and gardens.

Just as the early sandstone houses nestled among their Surrey hills, so Marsh Court reflects its landscape, only this time it is the luminous glow of the white Hampshire chalk, and even among Lutyens's highly individual houses it is unique. It can be seen, clinging to the chalk knoll on which it stands above the Test valley, from the hills to the west of Stockbridge's wide High Street, but by the time we are down in the village the house has disappeared and it is not easy to find again. A narrow lane leads off by an ancient and overgrown churchyard, giving the impression that it has no more purpose than reaching a few cottages and an old quarry, until – with only a plain wooden nameboard to indicate arrival – we reach a steep-sided drive, cut off to the left between high trees. This narrow drive winds even more tortuously before arriving at a pair of barn-like lodges – and for a moment we might be back in Surrey again – but there is still no sign of the house. Imagine an Edwardian summer afternoon – a garden party is our

6. Grey Walls, Gullane, Lothian, Scotland: the south-east corner of the house and the sheltered rose garden.

7. Orchards, Munstead, Godalming, Surrey: the view from the loggia terrace illustrates the *raison d'être* of the planning of both house and garden. The enclosed Dutch garden is below eye level, as are the yew walls which organize the rest of the garden, and the distant prospect over the Thorncombe Valley has been retained, its beauty only enhanced by the ordered yew.

8. *(previous page)* Hestercombe, Kington, Taunton, Somerset: the return of Jekyll planting – white lilies and bergenias making striking contrast in the borders, following Somerset County Council's completed five-year plan for restoration.

9. *(above)* Hestercombe: the pattern of the Great Plat laid out below the terraces.

10. Hestercombe: the view from the rotunda pool.

goal, but by now the inauspicious approach and the utter confusion caused by meeting with a returning trap or, even worse, a motor car in the narrow driveway will have turned our joyful expectation perhaps to frustration and anger, for the appointed hour for arrival has slipped past. When at last the house comes into view, beneath an arch of yew and across a stone, balustraded bridge, its enormous roof broods disapproval across a deserted courtyard and the great front door is firmly shut. At such stressful extremes of circumstance, Marsh Court's garden is a supreme example of a garden designed to be kind [45]. On our right a break in the yews shows a grass clearing, and across the clearing we find ourselves at the top of a magnificent semi-circular flight of steps, ornamented with an extension of the front courtyard balustrade [46]. Down the steps, and a long paved path leads by the side of the court, then along beneath the windows of the house – but they are too high to see in or be seen from. The pattern of the path, squares and rectangles of herring-bone brickwork set in stone, entrances us and leads us down to another flight of steps, and with our progress the sounds of the party come nearer. On the left, at the end of the house wall, is a door, but to burst through might well be to find ourselves centre stage, so we will continue, this time up a flight of steps – again of stone embroidered with flint insets – and now the path is completely walled in high yew hedges. At the corner a left turn brings us to the garden front of the house. From the sheltering yew the backs of groups of people can be seen gathered on the piazza [48]; the hedge becomes wall again and an opening reveals what was on the other side of the door in the house wall – the enclosed and sunken pool garden, its pool surrounded by steps and flower borders [49, 50, 51]. On the right the view opens out to reveal the River Test far below, and straight ahead is a pergola through which the paved path continues. We can stop to admire the circles and segments of water cut as pools beneath this pergola, still quite hidden from the party above, and finally, after climbing the steps at the other end, we emerge amongst the flower borders of the piazza, as if we had been there all the time.

Marsh Court's garden is not only kind, it is solicitous and entertaining. It is wrapped around the house, and all the paths, steps and doors entice and direct. The garden leads, occasionally giving choices, and all the visitor has to do is follow. The great white house, bejewelled with flint, tile, brick and stone, with soaring twisted chimneys, towers above; the repetition of its materials, the pale stone and patterned bricks of the piazza, the flint-studded steps and walls beneath the balustrades, and to some extent the complementary geometry, make the garden the magical shadow of the house itself. The guests who had arrived on time would have been ushered through the front door, into the long, low vestibule, might perhaps have registered a twinge of disappointment at the cityish grandeur of the pillared hall and dining room, but would soon have recovered their delight beneath the brick-domed loggia. The view over the misty valley is saved for the piazza itself, and it is preserved, in the old Orchards manner, by sinking both the pergola which was our escape and the formal pool garden below eye level. [See colour pls. 19, 20, 21.]

Planting might seem *embarras de richesse* at Marsh Court, but Miss Jekyll would have been undeterred. We do not know just how she counterbalanced all this pattern and

43. Grey Walls: the path to the *clair voyée*, set on high for framing the Lothian hills.

44. Grey Walls: sketch plan of layout, showing the geometrical and rhythmic layout of the walled entrance court and how the flower and kitchen garden was sheltered from the North Sea winds. The rectangular 'wing' on the east side of the building is the drawing room – an 'island' room which has views north over the golf course to the sea and south into the flower garden. The extension into the garden is a large-windowed tea room. The only garden on the north side of the house was a formal sunken lawn which led to the golf course.

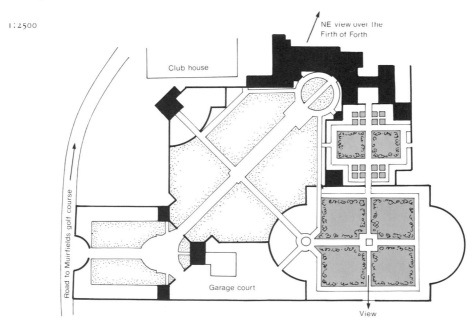

74

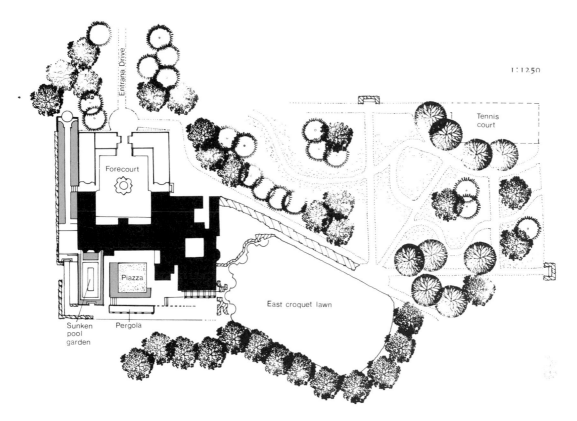

45. Marsh Court: sketch plan of layout. No planting plans for the formal garden have survived. In April 1915 Lutyens asked Miss Jekyll to suggest planting for 'the ground to the east of the big house' which falls from the north-east to the south-west 'between the drive and the new dry tennis court' – a large area of bank with quite a steep fall which she planted informally with ilex, bay, arbutus, roses, bamboo and box. The banks of the drive were to be covered with soapwort, rock pinks, eleagnus, valerian and *Clematis vitalba*, in long drifts for which spaces were to be cleared.

texture, for no planting plans have been found. Would the piazza borders have been filled with grey and silver herbs, with tumbling pink roses over the balustrades, and delicate pink and blue and perfumed cottage garden flowers – or with a more sophisticated scheme of creamy and yellow hybrid tea roses edged with the short-stemmed and dark-flowered Munstead lavenders, for there is a touch of the Elizabethan here, as at Deanery Garden? Or would the glowing russet of the herring-bone brickwork have been reflected in flaming gladiolas, dahlias, fuchsias and kniphofias? On balance, and the fine social balance that was so important, it would have been the former, for the Johnsons would most likely have been far away from Hampshire in late summer. The formal pool garden at Marsh Court bears a strong resemblance to Miss Jekyll's 'ideal' of this type, described in her article 'Some Problems of Garden Planning':[15] she envisages a square, or, as in this case, rectangular tank, with steps on all four sides – easy steps with a suitable wide path as a landing on which to walk, with the lower steps leading down into the water. This last idea she seems to have brought back from Italy or Spain, and easily convinced Lutyens of its merit, and of it being a safeguard against children falling into the pools. This ideal walled garden was the best setting for water-lilies, the

46. (*opposite left*) Marsh Court: the beginning of the garden sequence, the steps leading out from the wood.

47. (*opposite right*) Marsh Court: the paving patterns that entice and entertain.

48. (*opposite below*) Marsh Court: the 'piazza' on the garden front, an embroidery of paving, lawn and flower borders with a central sundial, its plinth ornamented with inlaid flowers.

49. (*above*) Marsh Court: the sunken pool garden from a house window above – the ideal formalized setting for water-lilies, with complementary borders of lilies, crinums, hostas and ferns round the sides.

50. (*left*) Marsh Court: the lily pools beneath the lower pergola, which Miss Jekyll planted with *Nymphaea marliacea carnea* at each end, *N.m. chromatella* in the circular pools, and water plantains in the centre.

51. (*right*) Marsh Court: the lead water tank in the pool garden, with a favourite Lutyens trellis motif, Herbert Johnson's initials and the date, 1904.

nymphaeas, which were then being developed in lovely colours – she wanted *N. marliacea chromatella*, with large yellow flowers and mottled foliage, and *N.m. carnea*, with flowers varying from blush-white to pink, for the pools beneath the lower pergola, and perhaps the latter for the bigger pool as well. She felt that water-lilies 'would exactly accord with masonry of the highest refinement, and with the feeling of repose that is suggested by a surface of still water'.[16] The colours of the water-lilies were to be reflected in surrounding border planting – pink and coppery lilies, pink crinums, with hostas (*sieboldiana grandiflora*) and hartstongue and lady's ferns. Photographs of Marsh Court's pool garden show figs, wisteria and clematis on the walls, with santolinas and *Stachys lanata* edging the borders, so these could have been the survivors of the original scheme.

The Game's the Thing

A feature of the gardens thus far is their unity with their houses. In the early years of this century, however, the partners were concerned with three gardens which were garden designs in their own right; in these three gardens in particular – Ammerdown (1902), Hestercombe (1903) and Heywood (1906) – Lutyens let his *penchant* for geometrical games take over. Both at this time and in the years to come, the existence of a house offered a challenge to be upstaged with the garden design, and it is a feature of the designs where the game was the thing that they are perhaps more impressive on paper than they are in the garden experience. A sort of natural justice.

The major exception to this rule, where both experience and geometry are equally exhilarating, is Ammerdown Park, just south-east of Radstock in Somerset. Ammerdown was built for the 1st Lord Hylton by James Wyatt in 1788, and so was worthy of Lutyens's respect. When he first visited it the house was surrounded by its park in the true landscape style and the deer came up to feed from the windows. There was a small orangery, also by Wyatt, and a walled kitchen garden at some distance from the house. The only way from the house was by a door at the south-east corner which led from the drawing-room, but when Lutyens drew the axis from this door it met the corresponding axis from the orangery at an awkward obtuse angle. Both this problem and the solution to it are seen clearly on the plan [52] – the dominant feature of the garden design is a circular garden which allowed two exits to the north, one to the orangery door and one into an enclosed rose garden. The balancing exits on the south side lead via steps down into the park. The wonder of it all is that this great pattern is enclosed with yew hedging, kept to optimum height by skilful trimming which is the special care of the present Lord Hylton. The large enclosure which holds the axial pivot of the layout is patterned with box-edged gardens of intricate design, with statues set against the dark yew in the Italian tradition [53, 54, 55]. These box-edgings – which have to be kept to a certain

52. Ammerdown: sketch plan of layout. The garden geometry in a framework of yew which unites Wyatt's house and his little orangery.

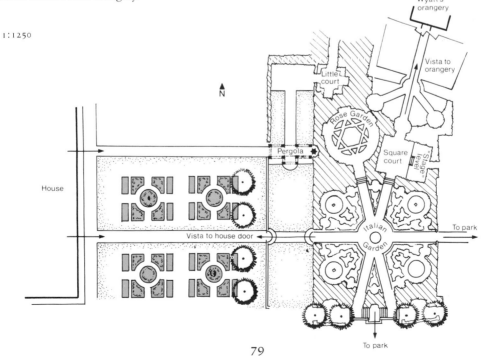

53. Ammerdown Park: the Italian garden from the house roof.

54. Ammerdown Park: the vista from the Italian garden to Wyatt's orangery.

55. Ammerdown Park: the pergola.

height not to look ridiculous in comparison with the yew surround (and are also 'drawn up' by the yews) – make the planting of the beds rather a problem; in the mid-1920s they sported a scheme of red and pink pelargoniums with variegated grasses, and today they are set with dahlias of flame colours. There is no proof that Miss Jekyll had a hand in this design, though the commission for Ammerdown probably came via Lutyens's great friends the Horners at near-by Mells, to whom Miss Jekyll was also related by marriage.[17]

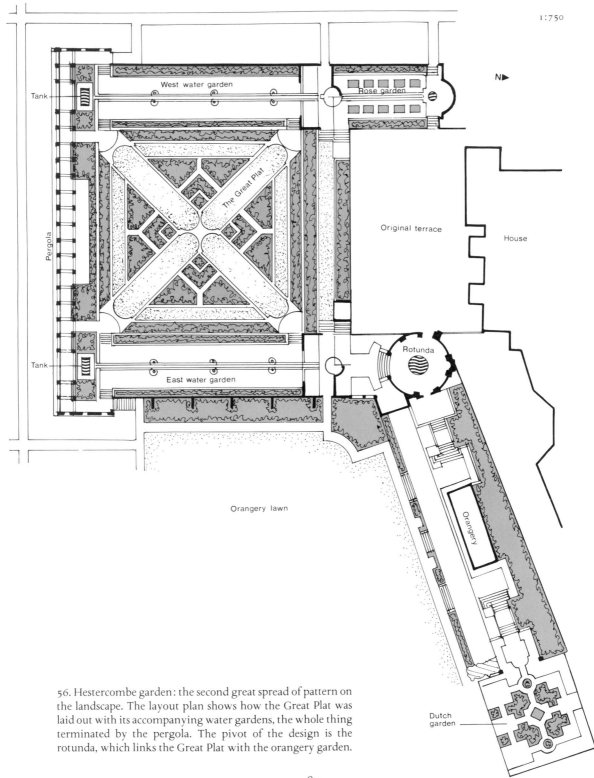

1:750

Tank

West water garden

Rose garden

N▶

The Great Plat

Pergola

Original terrace

House

Tank

East water garden

Rotunda

Orangery lawn

Orangery

Dutch garden

56. Hestercombe garden: the second great spread of pattern on the landscape. The layout plan shows how the Great Plat was laid out with its accompanying water gardens, the whole thing terminated by the pergola. The pivot of the design is the rotunda, which links the Great Plat with the orangery garden.

Ammerdown and Mells together undoubtedly conspired to produce Hestercombe, farther west, to the north of Taunton, where Lord Portman had rebuilt his house in the 1870s. The house is gaunt and ugly, and if at Ammerdown Lutyens had to be careful, here he had no need for restraint. As can be followed on the plan [56], the Hestercombe design is in two carefully integrated parts. The house had a single terrace, and this was elaborated to descend to the meadow where the Great Plat, 125 feet square with flanking water gardens and enclosing pergola, was laid out. With Wyatt's little Ammerdown orangery in his head, Lutyens gave Lord Portman a much larger and more impressive orangery in a garden of its own, set at an angle from the Great Plat garden to enjoy the view across the lawn and meadows. Here the pivot was smaller and stronger – the rotunda – heavy with stone textures and details, massive walls and a patterned floor with a central round pool.

Hestercombe has the whole gamut of Lutyens devices. Near the house, coming down the terraces, the intricate changing of levels displays an infinite variety of details, views and open and closed vistas. The texture of the stonework has been carefully graded to the importance of the elements – finely finished Ham Hill ashlar is used for pool edges and door frames and curving surfaces, selected but rough stones for most of the paving and some pillars, and rough stone from a near-by quarry for the gigantic walls which relate the garden to its surrounding landscape. Each side of the Great Plat are two iris channels, grown in emphasis since Deanery Garden, which carry water 140 feet from matching domed tanks at the terrace ends to pools beside the pergola. The pattern of the Plat is emphasized by stone paving outlining the flower beds; these shapes are further enhanced and solidity is given to the layout by the thick surround of *Bergenia cordifolia* enclosing pink roses and lupins. The pinks of the flowers tone beautifully with the pink-grey stone and the pink-brown earth to shed a rosy happiness over all.

Hestercombe's massive pergola, which is an experience in its own right, is 230 feet long, with alternating round and square pillars of slivered stone and oak cross-beams, all softened with roses, clematis and Russian vine [57]. And, not to be outdone, the orangery is approached by wide and stately steps, down to the orangery from the rotunda, down again to the lawn, and on and up to a parterre (called the Dutch garden again but very different from Orchards), set on top of a bastion wall. Finally, as my photographs show [58, 59; colour pls. 8, 9, 10], Hestercombe has been miraculously restored to its full glory by Somerset County Council, its owners, and justifiably awarded many honours. The County Council, who use the house as a headquarters for their fire brigade, took this unique initiative in 1973. The first priority was the crumbling stonework, but now the major part of the planting has been restored, and here you can see the confirmation of all I have described: the lilies and the bergenias, the yuccas, lavenders and santolinas, and many more of Miss Jekyll's favourite plants, just where she intended them to be. The only aspect to which Somerset County Council's energy and resources have not yet extended is the water rills and pools. Lutyens's water systems are a source of despair and expense to many present-day owners, who face a constant battle to stop leakages after so many years. At Hestercombe the water was collected in reservoirs on the hill behind the house and brought down in pipes to fill the pools at terrace level;

57. (*opposite*) Hestercombe: the vista beneath the pergola.

58. (*above*) Hestercombe: the restored planting of the Great Plat borders beside the pergola.

from there gravity took it through the rills to the lower pools, whence it drained off to the meadow. The reservoirs have now become overgrown and have silted up, and during their prolonged neglect the rills and pools have contracted and their stones and bricks have become loose as their mortar – presumably puddled clay – has disintegrated, so that they no longer hold water. It cannot be that such a difficulty will defeat the Somerset Fire Brigade for long.

59. Hestercombe: detail of 'dry stone' pool construction. The water was retained with a mixture of skilful stonework, puddled clay and constant flow! What could be seen underwater was just as important as any of the open-air stonework, and vital to the basic integrity of the garden.

60. Heywood: an original *Country Life* photograph showing the house (now demolished) on its confined site. The buttress wall in the front holds up the lawn [see pl. 63], and both the pergola Lutyens set into the west side and the pillars leading to the pleached lime alley on the east side can be identified.

The last of the trio is an important garden and draws many visitors each summer. It was built for Heywood House, Ballinakill, near Port Laoise in Ireland. When Lutyens designed the garden, Heywood was a large gaunt house on an elevated site in a beautiful park. However, the house has since been destroyed by fire, the shell demolished and buried beneath a bank of earth, and only the garden remains in the care of the Salesian Fathers' Missionary College. As the old photograph shows [60], the house was set high, with room for a terrace and lawn on the south front, but then the land dropped away steeply to the west and south-west and more gradually to the east. The steep slope was supported by an enormous cliff-like buttress, which incorporated a half-level pergola'd walk on the west side, with antique Ionic pillars and oak cross-beams. The lawn was emphasized by crisp paving, with wide flower borders at each end. On the eastern side the garden could spread, and does so via a pleached lime alley, with adjacent small enclosed gardens fitted to an existing wall which leads to the Italian garden [61, 62, 63].

61. (*opposite*) Heywood: looking back across the Italian garden through the lime alley.

62. Heywood: the oval Italian garden in its prime, a splendid *Country Life* photograph, *c.* 1910.

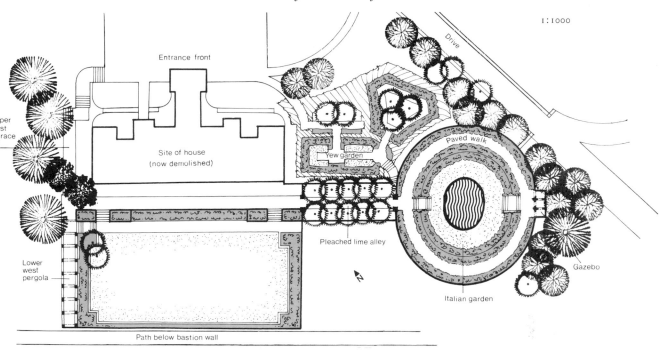

63. Heywood: sketch plan of layout: geometry enhancing a dramatic site and uniting the pergola'd walk cut into the terrace on the west with the spread of pattern to the east culminating in the oval Italian garden.

This Italian garden is a walled oval, with tiers of retaining walls and borders, and a perfect oval pool guarded by stone turtles in the centre. What may not be appreciated on the ground, but can be seen from the plan, is the subtle change of shapes from the outer walls of the garden to achieve the perfect oval for the central pool.

Barton St Mary

Despite their refined geometry, these gardens of a golden afternoon never lost their quality of innocence, the hallmark of their period. This was partly because of the partnership's allegiance to the decrees of landscape form and history (and here it was impossible to tell where Miss Jekyll's faithfulness ceased and that of Lutyens began), and partly because their planting schemes were very simple. Miss Jekyll was not to be fooled into ostentation just because she was becoming fashionable (it is probable that she fell out with Sir George Sitwell and later with Julius Drewe of Castle Drogo over just this point), and she was fully aware both of the capabilities of her clients' gardeners and of the fact that if her clients had been experts themselves they would not be asking her for planting plans.[18] She went to great efforts to make her schemes answer particular needs – not only those of soil, shelter and aspect, but social requirements as well.

This simplicity of planting for particular needs is demonstrated in the plans for a little-known garden, Barton St Mary, on the borders of Wadhurst clay and Tunbridge

1:1250

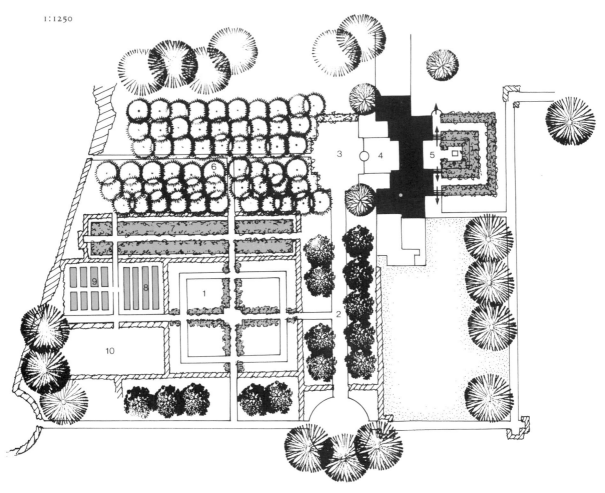

64. Barton St Mary: the site was planned around the existing kitchen garden (1) [see pl. 65]. The entrance drive (2) was planted with strong groupings of shrubs (laurel, weigela, brooms, forsythia, golden privet, Scotch briar rose, *R. lucida* and rhododendrons); the gravel court (3) was surrounded with dry retaining walls and 'Millmead' type planting; the sunken paved court (4) was flanked by the groupings of scrub oak and shrub roses; and the intricate raised south garden (5) is shown in detail as pl. 66. The fruit trees were ranged at (6), the herbaceous borders (for which no plans have survived) at (7), roses in borders at (8), with 'cutting and reserve' at (9) and the frame yard, compost, etc. at (10). A gardener's garden indeed!

Wells sand on the southern outskirts of East Grinstead in Sussex. Here, the requirement was not so much geometry as fruitfulness, and Lutyens, undeterred, seems to have fitted the whole plan round an existing walled kitchen garden [64, 65]. Having come round this walled garden there was a rectangular gravelled court outside the front door with a rose border enclosing it at the far end. To each side of the door there was an unusual grouping of evergreen scrub oak (*Quercus dumosa*), twenty-five plants on each side, with some old shrub roses, which may have already been there. On the opposite side of the court, steps led up to an avenue of fruit trees – quinces (and walnuts), the edible crabs

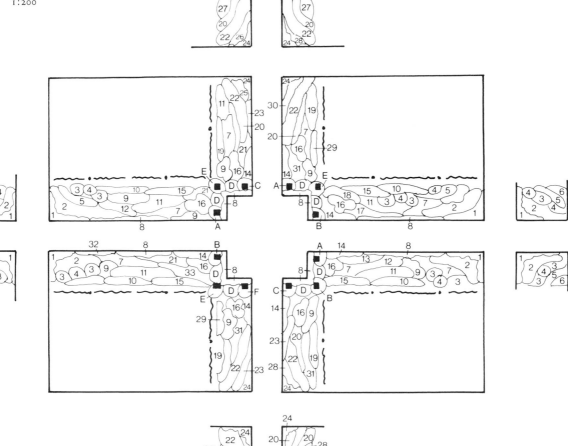

65. Barton St Mary: the finest surviving planting plan for the flower borders which were given to many kitchen gardens.

Key to the planting:

Roses: the climbers and ramblers were trained on to metal and rope loops around the path crossing.

A. 'The Garland'
B. 'Aimée Vibert'
C. 'Dundee Rambler'
D. Standard roses (unspecified)
E. 'Reine Olga de Wurtemburg'
F. 'Psyche' (the description has been cut out of Harkness's 1912 catalogue and I have found no other reference)

1. *Santolina chamaecyparissus*
2. Sulphur yellow African marigolds
3. Anchusa (pale blue variety)
4. White everlasting pea (*Lathyrus* 'White Pearl')
5. Pale blue delphinium
6. *Elymus arenarius* (blue lyme grass)
7. White snapdragon
8. White pink
9. *Galega officinalis* (goat's rue)
10. Sulphur yellow hollyhock
11. Coreopsis (paler yellow variety)
12. Yellow day lily (*Hemerocallis flava*)
13. *Chrysanthemum maximum*
14. *Dicentra formosa* (bleeding heart)
15. Rudbeckia 'Golden Glow'
16. Double yellow peony
17. Yellow snapdragon
18. Purple snapdragon
19. Red hollyhock
20. *Lychnis chalcedonica* (scarlet campion)
21. Pink snapdragon
22. Orange African marigold
23. *Rudbeckia speciosa* (orange)
24. *Bergenia cordifolia*
25. *Helenium pumilum* (orange/yellow variety)
26. Lychnis 'Haag' (fiery red?)
27. Tritoma (red hot poker)
28. Monarda (bergamot) (scarlet)
29. Pink hollyhock
30. Senecio (*laxifolius*)
31. Rose pink snapdragon
32. *Stachys lanata*
33. *Spirea venusta* (pink astilbe)

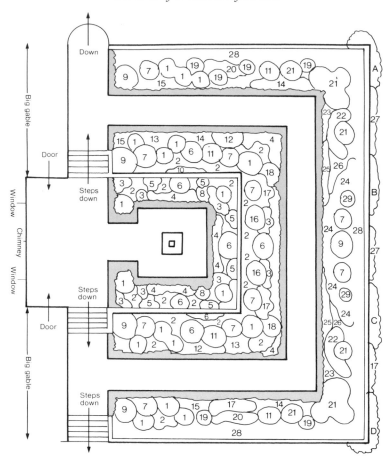

66. Barton St Mary: the south garden plan.

Key to the planting:

All borders of *Stachys lanata*, shaded.

1. Lavender
2. China rose
3. *Santolina chamaecyparissus*
4. *Nepeta mussinii (faassenii)* (catmint)
5. *Echinops ritro*
6. *Phlomis fruticosa* (Jerusalem sage)
7. Rose 'Madame Plantier'
8. Iris (unspecified, probably Dutch hybrid white or pale yellow)
9. *Fuchsia magellanica riccartonii*
10. *Clematis flammula*
11. White tree lupin
12. *Dicentra eximia*
13. Yellow snapdragon
14. Rose pink snapdragon
15. Pale pink snapdragon
16. *Euphorbia wulfenii*
17. Centranthus (pink valerian)
18. Clematis 'Dawn' (shrubby clematis?)

19. *Galega officinalis* (goat's rue) (possibly a pinky-mauve variety 'Lady Wilson')
20. Mauve-blue delphiniums
21. Tritoma (red hot poker)
22. Coreopsis (no variety specified, but bright yellow and one of the taller ones)
23. *Helenium pumilum* (orangey-yellow variety)
24. Orange African marigold
25. Rudbeckia 'Golden Glow' (double yellow gold)
26. Gladiolus (probably *brenchleyensis*, a scarlet)
27. *Iris stylosa (unguicularis)*
28. A complete edging of *Fuchsia magellanica gracilis* – a profusion of small scarlet and violet flowers

Roses on wall:

A. 'Reine Olga de Wurtemburg' (vivid red flowers, strong climber)
B. 'The Garland'
C. 'Dundee Rambler' (white flower with pink edges)
D. 'Gloire de Berkeley' (but I cannot trace this variety)

Dartmouth and John Downie, and a mouth-watering selection of apples including Newton Wonder, James Grieve, Blenheim Orange, Irish Peach, Duchess of Oldenburg, Devonshire Quarrenden and the cooking apples, Bramley Seedling and Alfriston.

The dry stone walls edging the gravelled court in front of the house were decorated very simply, with pinks and blues and lots of silvers and herbs – pink and white snapdragons, London pride, iberis, aubretias, ferns, phlox and campanula, valerian and plumbago, santolina, lavender and sedums, with clumps of *Iris stylosa* (Miss Jekyll's name is so much nicer than the new one – *I. unguicularis*) around the base of the walls.

The final Jekyll scheme for Barton St Mary was the 'wilderness' she planted beyond the house as a shield from the railway line; mown paths rambled through clumps of holly, *Amelanchier laevis* (with fragrant white flowers and pinky foliage in spring), *Azalea pontica*, white broom, with a 'special' feature plant for different areas – *Arbutus unedo* in one, *Rosa polyantha* in another, and water elder on the damp clay patches.

Folly Farm

The last garden in this chapter is that of Folly Farm, one of the most famous and most loved gardens of the partnership. This garden evolved over the vintage years of creation before the War, and somehow it absorbed the spirit of happiness that belonged to those years, a spirit which has survived and may still be met there on summer afternoons. Miss Jekyll's contribution was, yet again, much more than just the planting, for Folly Farm has not one but six gardens, and it has them as the gift of her memories of Moorish Spain, for here the sun-drenched and dark-shaded courts of the Alhambra have been transmuted to surround an old farmhouse in misty blue England. That this transformation has worked is due largely to Miss Jekyll's belief that imitation must never be slavish, but that a little spark of similarity between two places may be encouraged and enhanced without overstepping the bounds of good taste. To her beliefs and memories must be added – especially in the case of Folly Farm – Lutyens's undoubted ability to treat old buildings with respect, whilst somehow elevating their essence to high art – an ability for which he usually earns unstinting praise.

The original Folly Farm was a long Georgian house sideways on to the road, on a bend in the middle of Sulhamstead, a village in the lush Kennet valley south-west of Reading. In front of the house was a deep-roofed, black-boarded barn. In 1906 Lutyens added a symmetrical double-fronted 'Dutch' extension to the southern end of the old house [colour pl. 14], the centre of this being occupied by a double-storeyed hall, with a sitting-room and library on each side, and two rather small bedrooms above – this touch of impracticality, the impressive hall and little else, was often tolerated by clients for the sake of their architect! The building of the Dutch house enclosed the courts around the old house [colour pl. 13], the barn, and an entrance court between the new house and the road. These courts were separately walled and given a series of brick-arched doorways and brick herring-bone paths flanked by small lawns and flower borders. The planting was, of course, old-fashioned – borders of aquilegias, poppies, gypsophila, *Iris foetida* and white campanulas (the other colours confined to pale pinks, pale blues and pale yellows) against a background of cistus, jasmine, clematis, lauristinus, hardy fuchsias and roses (Aimée Vibert, a perfumed white rambler, Dorothy Perkins and The Garland) which formed the permanent base planting against the walls. It almost goes without saying that the borders were edged with box. From the entrance court there was an exit through an arch to a formal walk, parallel with the road wall, which led to a small sheltered sitting area. The road wall was bordered with rhododendrons, but there were beds of Michaelmas daisies (mauves and purples) and yellow tree lupins for summer interest. The rest of the garden at this time was occupied by a croquet and tennis lawn.

When Folly Farm changed hands around the end of 1911 the new owner, Zachary Merton (whom Lutyens may have met through James Barrie, for he too was a benefactor of Great Ormond Street Hospital), required a dining-room and a decent-sized bedroom. Lutyens, equally understandably unwilling to spoil his Dutch symmetry, built on in the only direction he could with the sort of devastating comment in asymmetry that leaves modern architects gasping [colour pl. 16]. The 1912 addition to Folly Farm, a large dining-room with a large bedroom above (including a sleeping balcony for those balmy nights which seem redolent of the period), was linked by a corridor which is all roof and supporting pillars. *Now*, the garden design could really take off [67]. The Dutch front

67. Folly Farm: sketch plan of the garden as completed by 1916. The original farmhouse (1) was given a 'Dutch' addition (2) in 1906, creating the entrance and barn courts (3 and 4). The rhododendron walk (5), axial on the entrance court, was also made at this time, but otherwise only croquet and tennis lawns occupied the south front of the house. In 1912 Lutyens added the linking corridor and west wing (6), and the garden design was subsequently completed with the canal garden (7) on the 'Dutch' front, the tank court (8) beside the corridor cloister, the parterre garden (9) on the 1912 front, with the axis completed by the walled kitchen garden (10). The finale is the enclosed rose garden (11).

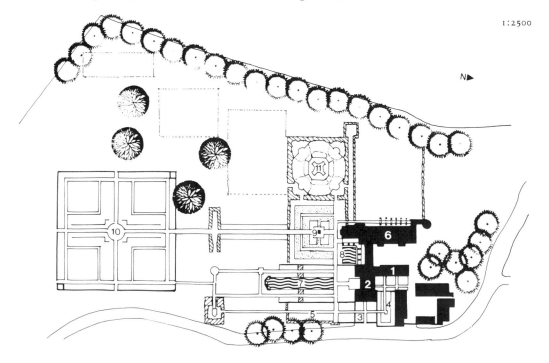

1:2500

94

68. Folly Farm: the tank cloister, a most sophisticated piece of garden architecture.

was given a formal canal garden suited to its character. Into the recess of the corridor Lutyens fitted the tank court – still, dark water which created the perfect foil for the curtain roof and the swelling pillars which support it, and doubled the visual drama by reflection. This tank 'cloister' [68] is probably Lutyens's *pièce de résistance* in garden architecture, totally dictated by its surroundings, of particular surprise in the garden of a 'farm', and something uniquely his own. After the experience of it, rather as a frothy dessert succeeds the chef's superlative entrée, the path leads to the rose garden [colour pls. 15, 16], surrounded by yew – patterned, perfumed profusion that delights the senses. It is an embellishment of the Dutch garden at Orchards, which now seems so long ago.

There are many gardens which could not find a place in this chapter, because of the limitations of space and because I have not wanted any hint of incompleteness or decay to mar these special gardens, the outstanding milestones of the heady years when over seventy gardens were made. As I said at the very beginning, this was the period to which all the gardens really belong, the time when the lavish expense, labour and care that went into their making was at one with the values of the Edwardian society for which they were made. The year 1910 was to see the gathering storm clouds which presaged the end of the golden afternoon, and the gardens to come must be recognized as an impossible attempt to perpetuate a vanishing dream in a changing world.

4

WORKING PARTNERSHIP

Often when I have had to do with other people's gardens they
have said 'I have bought a quantity of shrubs and plants, show
me where to place them' – to which I can only answer, that is
not the way in which I can help you – show me your spaces and
I will tell you what plants to get for them.

Gertrude Jekyll, 1900[1]

A garden scheme should have a backbone – a central idea
beautifully phrased. Thus the house wall should spring out of a
briar bush – with always the best effect, and every wall, path,
stone and flower bed has its similar problem and a relative value
to the central idea.

Edwin Lutyens, 1908[2]

T HESE two quite simple statements contain the seeds of the small revolution in
garden design prompted by the partnership.[3] After almost a century of plant
mania, in which the latest acquisitions were shown off according to various fads,
Miss Jekyll advocated a charter of dignity and integrity for plants, insisting that the
setting must inspire their use *naturally*. Lutyens added (perhaps he should have said it
first, but he didn't) that every feature of a garden was worthy of inclusion in the basic
design theme of the house – and thus the implication was that even if there was no
house, a garden was worthy of a central theme *in itself*. As it happens, the circumstances
of his utterance rather governed what he was saying, for it was part of a reply to an
address by the landscape architect Thomas Mawson at an Architectural Association
meeting in April 1908. The subject of the meeting could be loosely described as 'new
minds on an old theme' – that of the natural versus the formal in design – but the notes
for this meeting represent Lutyens's only substantial written comments on the subject
of garden design.[4] If the phrasing – 'always the best effect' and the mention of the briar
bush – has a Munstead ring about it, that was because he had spent the previous
weekend at Munstead Wood so that Miss Jekyll could help him with his notes for his
speech at the debate.

But how did the partners' ideas find formal expression? The gardens described so far
are a good basis on which to discuss the actual *how* and *why* of their creation. Orchards,
Deanery Garden, Marsh Court, Hestercombe, Ammerdown and Folly Farm are the
universally admired high points of the partnership's work, the product of two minds
working in close harmony. There is very little contemporary paper evidence on which
to base historical reconstructions, so the processes of actual design must be extracted
from the gardens themselves.

When Miss Jekyll 'retired' to Munstead Wood she carried with her the inspiration of her first life. There was not only her technical experience of the uses of colour and texture to apply to her planting design, and the attuned hand and eye of a craftswoman who had made many beautiful things, there was also a cultural influence, the influence of 'good taste' as understood by her society. 'Good taste' implied a patina, it meant all things classical and of the Italian Renaissance; because of her travels Miss Jekyll extended this to the great old gardens of Italy and the Mediterranean, and at home it swept away the Kentish leapings and Brownian 'capabilities' of the eighteenth century to find a necessary 'sanity, serenity and sobriety' in a more distant time: 'Wherever I have seen the large formal gardens attached to important houses of the Palladian type ... throughout England, I have always been struck by their almost invariable lack of interest and want of any real beauty or power of giving happiness,' she wrote, thereby dismissing at a stroke the nineteenth-century attempts at a return to formalism.[5] Miss Jekyll's inspiration was fed by Francis Bacon, with whom she believed that the first purpose of a garden was to be 'a place of quiet beauty, delight for the eye and repose and replenishment for the mind'; and many of Bacon's favourite plants – primroses, rosemary, wallflowers, lilies, pinks, roses, honeysuckle, columbine, hollyhocks – are those from which her name has become inseparable.[6] And on to her taste for 'old' England was grafted her love of the Surrey vernacular, simply because it was hers, inspiring the further belief that all places were happiest when their local traditions were respected.

Lutyens very rarely alluded to his inspirations, and by the time he came to Munstead Wood in 1889 there were very few to be identified. His admiration for Philip Webb and Richard Norman Shaw as he had seen them building in Surrey (and he made a special visit to Chesters, Shaw's Northumberland house, when it was being completed in 1901[7]) must have led him to the Arts and Crafts movement, but it was very much entry by the side door. He later admitted that much of his use of timber was based on what he had seen at Stokesay Castle, a medieval castle with a perfectly preserved Elizabethan gatehouse in Shropshire, which he had visited during a walking tour with Herbert Baker during the short time they were in Ernest George's office together.[8] These two brief clues would seem to confirm that both the timing of the partners' meeting and what was in their minds at that time were peculiarly apt and well-matched. Miss Jekyll's need for an 'organic' house was just what the mainstream of architecture in London (a mainstream that Lutyens had not entered) was much concerned with. The embodiment of old principles in ever-new conditions, using a central theme, or motif, in the design, and staying close to nature – these were the theories of William Lethaby (who had been Shaw's chief draughtsman), given in a lecture to the Architectural Association in 1889, which Lutyens may have attended. There was another lecture that year which he might well have heard – the Scottish architect John Brydon on the value of seventeenth-century English architecture, and in particular, Christopher Wren. Wren was idolized by Lutyens later in his career, but at this time the appearance of his name gives an interesting clue to the mind behind the gardens – for it was Wren, working at Hampton Court for William III, who had planted trees *and* designed palaces. He had been, in fact, the last *compleat* architect in terms of masterminding the whole concept, the total visual effect of house and grounds as much as construction details. It is in this sense that Wren may well have attracted Lutyens as much as for the similarity of their commissions – the building of cathedrals and the rebuilding of cities.

In the 1880s and 90s an artificial battle between formalism and naturalism was raging in design circles. It was started by William Robinson, with his broadsides in *The English Flower Garden* in passionate defence of the flowers and the natural landscape, really a much-needed backlash at the Victorian carpet bedding traditions, but interpreted as quite something else. Miss Jekyll was to mourn that her old friend – 'our great champion of hardy flowers' – had regretfully put himself into an attitude of general condemnation of the system, including the denunciation of all architectural accessories, for Robinson's words were caught and used by those who, it seemed, wanted no architecture at all. Though Robinson was cited, it was really the *landscape naturalists* who were the target of Reginald Blomfield's *The Formal Garden in England*, which appeared in 1892; he took Henry E. Milner[9] to task for defining the art of landscape gardening as 'taking true cognisance of nature's means for the expression of beauty, and so disposing those means artistically as to co-operate for our delight in given conditions' by adding: 'This is a hard saying, put in plain English it seems to amount to this – "Fix upon certain passages that you like in natural scenery, and then reproduce them under artificial conditions."' With the example of water, of trying to understand why a natural lake is beautiful, Blomfield floors Milner at a stroke. 'The created character of a water feature must be consonant with the surrounding land, for fitness to surrounding conditions is a measure of beauty to both; a lake expresses spaciousness, but much of its charm is due to its outline,' says Milner. To which Blomfield replies: 'There is a curious irrelevance about these apothegms which reminds me of Ollendorf: "My aunt is beautiful, but have you seen my sister's cat?"'[10] Blomfield's book makes it quite clear that the battleground for formal versus natural was much larger than the garden (and the implications of this must wait for my last chapter), but that as far as the partners were concerned the way ahead was clear – they must have pored over the Blomfield-approved drawings by F. Inigo Thomas of the gazebos, terraces and sundials of Pitmedden, Canons Ashby and Brympton d'Evercy, for this was just what their combined belief in the values of old England called for; allied to Miss Jekyll's Robinson-inspired planting they would have an unbeatable combination, and their own, their very own, version of Arts and Crafts creation.

Perception

When Miss Jekyll first met Lutyens I am sure she saw no more in him than the architect of her house, but mutual respect and a cheerful affection soon followed. At that time, I am equally sure, she saw her future as devoted to her garden, to the ordering of planting relationships and the creating of pictures for different seasons of the year, to writing about this work for those who were interested, and to passing on her schemes for borders, or a rock or water garden, to those who asked for them. As it was her intention to submit most of the flora of the temperate world to this ordering, it would seem a large enough task. Her interest in old Surrey was really a 'folklore' interest, both because she loved the countryside and because she sought its peaceful way of life for her own; her interest in the buildings around her was her research for her dream house. In short, she had an acute understanding of everything in the small scale, the value of close details never escaped her, but that was as much, or as little, as she saw.

Except, that is, for her myopic perception, probably best illustrated by quoting a description of the Munstead woodland from her book *Home and Garden*:

The sun is away on my front and left, and the sharp shadows of the trees are thrown diagonally across the path, where the sunlight comes through a half-open place. Farther along, for some fifty yards or more, the path is in shade, with still more distant stretches of stem-barred glint of sunny space. Here the fir-trunks tell dark against the mist-coloured background. It is not mist for the day is quite clear, but I am on high ground, and the distance is of the tops of firs where the hillside falls steeply away to the north. Where the sun catches the edges of the nearer trunks it lights them in a sharp line, leaving the rest warmly dark; but where the trees stand in shade the trunks are of a cool grey that is almost blue, borrowing their colour, through the opening of the track behind me, from the hard blue cloudless sky. The trunks seen quite against the sunlight look a pale greenish-brown, lighter than the shadow they cast, and somewhat warmed by the sunlit dead bracken at their feet. When I move onward into the shade the blue look on the stems is gone, and I only see their true colour of warm purplish-grey, clouded with paler grey lichen.[11]

This is a particularly beautiful Impressionist painting; it is the intense perception of light and of what it does to colours by eyes that can see only details that the mind *knows* are there, and by a mind uncluttered with details which would only muddy the true vision. This is the perception of myopic eyes, eyes which have a sort of instinctive awareness of far more than they can actually see. In this way Miss Jekyll never missed the first snowdrops, and she managed the pony cart with dexterity, but she could *never* have imagined a large-scale design. She could never even have dreamed of the pattern of the Great Plat at Hestercombe laid out in space, because this is where the myopic mind is blind.

Then, of course, Ned Lutyens in this distant sense became her eyes.[12] As Robert Lutyens explained years later, 'She found in Father the ideal interpreter who eventually exalted her limited conception on to the plane of creative formal design.'[13] A new range of interest was opened to her with Lutyens's eyes – not only in the large-scale design of gardens but in a drawing together of all those distant themes she loved, both from the far-away Mediterranean gardens and from pre-eighteenth-century England.

For his part, Ned Lutyens was blessed with an almost photographic memory for details – he rarely sketched them, never made notes, but merely looked hard. When these details had been filed away in his brain the process of recalling them for a particular scheme was induced by much heavy pipe-smoking and, as he grew older, interminable games of patience. As with most great artists, this was a process he lived with – for the moment of enlightenment he was usually prepared with his 'virgins', small pads of paper ever handy, but as this was not always possible, the private collections of England and America are strewn with odd scraps, menu cards and the like, on to which the first sketches of some monumental design were made. As far as the gardens

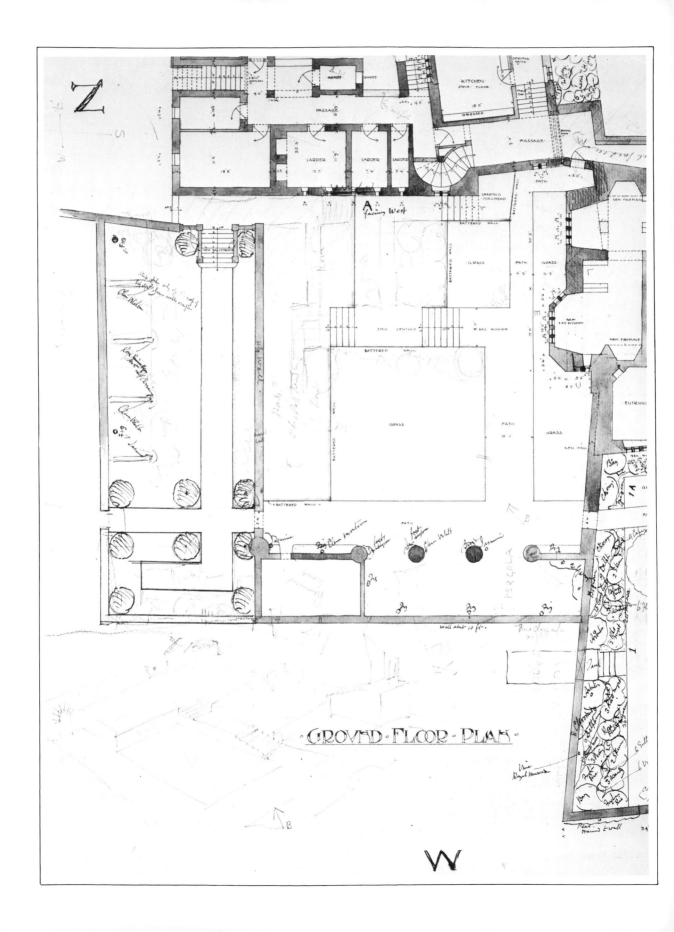

GROVND · FLOOR · PLAN

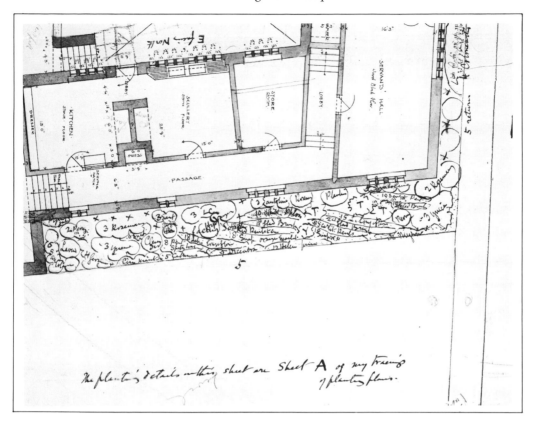

69. (*opposite*) Lambay: Lutyens's pencil sketch explaining the north court [see pl. 40].

70. (*above*) Lambay: a detail of the planting scheme for the east court [see pl. 40].

71. Edwin Lutyens: a photograph taken during an early wartime summer, probably 1915, in the garden at Lambay Castle, the home of his friends the Cecil Barings, with whom, Mary Lutyens remembers, he always seemed at his happiest.

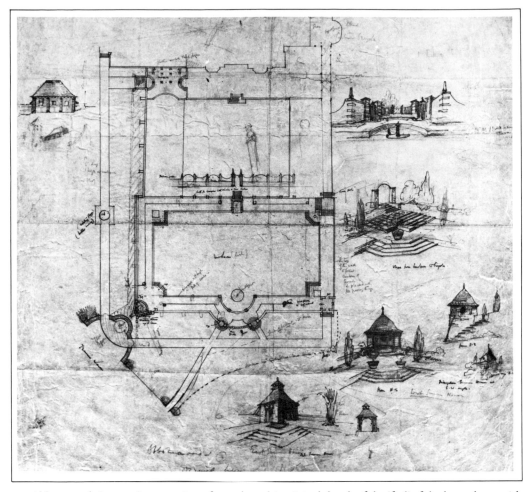

72. Abbotswood: Lutyens's conception of a garden – his original sketch of the 'feel' of the lower lawn with a garden house at one corner.

were concerned, the perception of the design in his mind was uncannily accurate and he usually put it on to paper right first time; designs were rarely altered, unless a client prevailed upon him to do so.

Creation

Partly because of his doubts about his own education and partly because of his distrust of 'the Lytton gift of the gab',[14] Lutyens hated theorizing and believed in doing things. Towards the end of his life his eminence in his profession demanded that certain papers and addresses be delivered, but then architecture was his theme; the dialogue with Thomas Mawson was his first attempt at public speaking – 'last night was horrible – my hand shook' he wrote to Emily afterwards – and indeed if the disorganized notes are anything to go by it seems clear that he and Mawson were not even speaking the same language and that the evening must have been a disaster.[15] Apart from the quote which opens this chapter, the reiteration of Lethaby's Arts and Crafts ideals and some clumsily reproduced Jekyllisms (notably a quip about Blomfield's delightful natural garden and Robinson's parterre at their respective homes) there are perhaps three points worth extracting.

First: 'In nature, I should say, there was no such thing as a free curve – every line obeying the laws and forces which produce it. It is not enough to allow the facile pencil to follow the dictates of hand and eye. There must be a reasoned conviction and will behind it.' Lutyens's reasoned convictions took geometrical expression, and he never abandoned them – in the garden designs the geometry of his schemes seems often to dominate unduly.

Secondly: 'The relation of a garden to the house as seen from various parts of the house is as important as is the house as seen from the garden.' Tortuous maybe, but the key to his belief in his right to total design. It is also the basis from which the partners worked – a complete investigation of the site and its sight lines which dominated the placing and arrangement of the house.

Finally, a tribute to the value of his partner: 'The true adornment of a garden lies surely in its flowers and plants. No artist has so wide a palette as the garden designer, no artist has greater need of discretion and reserve. The great lesson Nature tells us is how little we know, and the more we learn the less we seem to know.'

This last sentence in particular being pure Jekyll philosophy, I feel I need only add one footnote on the closeness of minds – regarding the divinity of hard work. Miss Jekyll from *Home and Garden* again: 'I only know that to my mind and conscience pure idleness seems to me to be akin to folly or even worse, and that in some form or another I must obey the Divine command "Work while ye have the light".'[16] Lutyens, in keeping, did not say how hard he worked, he did it – from the time he met Emily he worked desperately to build his practice and then ever harder to provide security for her and their growing family. This set him on a treadmill of labour from which he could never, or would never, escape: his only relaxation was dining out with people who were friends or clients, or both; he loved the rare opportunity of a day's fishing (hence his affection for Marsh Court), and he went to the theatre to see the plays of his friend James Barrie.[17] Music hardly entered his life – or at least not until he discovered a late rapport with Edward Elgar.[18] Reading his letters of these early years is exhausting – his daily letter to Emily was a sacred duty from the time of their engagement onwards (the total runs into thousands over the forty years of their marriage and indicates how much they were apart), usually giving a brief catalogue of his day's doings, but always full of faithful assurances of his love and that he would work ever harder for her sake. He seemed to be offering a complete home and garden service even in excess of the normal Arts and Crafts ideals: he looked for suitable sites, assessed them when found, designed the house and garden layout and arranged for Miss Jekyll either to visit the site or to be sent all the information, then he supervised the detail plans, always meticulously checking everything himself even if these were drawn by his office assistants, and then looking for fittings and furniture, if he did not actually design these himself. Most of the early houses had fitted kitchens and pantries completed to his designs – some effect of this can be seen at Lindisfarne and Castle Drogo and in the Queen's Dolls' House at Windsor Castle.

So much for ideals, motives and the pattern of work. The conditions of the time were exactly right to allow the genius of the partnership to find expression. The Edwardian Age was the last age when wealthy clients could afford to commission large country houses and gardens, and their work also encompassed the last years before the imposition of a jungle of planning and building regulations. Over half the houses and gardens were built on virgin sites, marvellous sites by any standards – hill tops, ridges, by the sea – sites which are just not available to architects today. But Lutyens knew how to treat them, and he examined them thoroughly, 'walking' large areas (this may seem an obvious necessity, but his thoroughness was exemplary). This freedom to act is well illustrated by the finding of the site for Castle Drogo, apparently fixed during a picnic with the Drewe family in the summer of 1910 – Ned prancing off through the heather with the younger members of the party and returning with a joyful 'Eureka!' Miss Jekyll was concerned with the on-site discussions only in the very early gardens, for in the years between 1900 and 1910 she gradually ceased travelling. Even in 1906, when she was sixty-three, very stout and very short-sighted, she probably went no farther than her pony cart would take her; she had seen Deanery Garden, Ammerdown, Hestercombe and Marsh Court, and even visited Lindisfarne, but after that she saw none of the gardens outside Surrey, relying on Lutyens for explanations of the site, soil and aspect, and on her own experience to provide suitable schemes. From this time onwards, the process of consultation was conducted by letter and a few flying visits to Munstead. The correspondence in 1906 about New Place at Shedfield in south-east Hampshire has survived to show the partnership at work. The handwritten note from Shedfield Lodge, Botley, home of the client Mrs Franklyn of Franklyn's Tobacco, who was building for her son, reads:

Toute suite. This is the only plan of the ground I have – will you let me have it back. Not enough? I have pencilled in the idea about the house, SE is a forecourt with (short) avenue to main road. Main gate in highway hedge. Avenue doubled continuing lines of court and terrace. Trees? Limes? Ilex?
NE by E space marked Orchard – will there be a better place for orchard? South? Say wood – Nuts in N axis of N dining room window
NE back road – lanes and turntable to coal and kitchen carts N side of lane did belong to Mrs Franklyn – squalid farm buildings NE by N kitchen garden
NW square garden determined by terrace for cutting? Drawing Room west window outlook bordered by belt of trees and underwood. Falling ground west of this belt – village allotments – hidden by aforesaid belt but belonging to Mrs F.
SE Terrace 30′ wide house grass walks poss parapet? finish of Terrace – steps? Summer house? or parapet?
Then big herbaceous borders – grass paths right and left – fruit trees – gooseberries – sort of fruit garden gradually into wild and away (?)

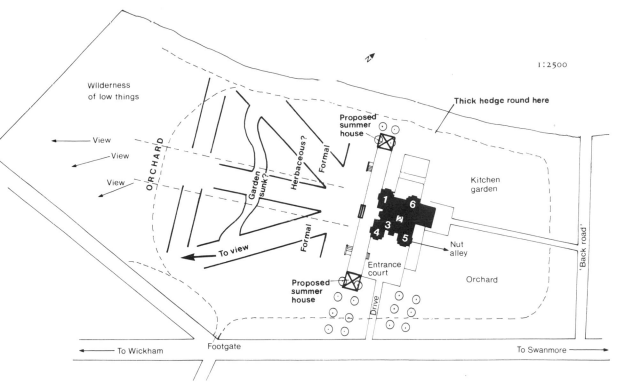

73. New Place: the sketch and discussion process at work. The basic plan and information in fine lines and print relates to Lutyens's letter; the heavy lines and print illustrate the outcome of a subsequent discussion. Though this is the best illustration of the partnership at work, the garden which survives is disappointing; I do not think either the summer houses or the formal garden were ever constructed and the rest of the layout is now much altered.
Key to house:
1. Drawing room   2. Court   3. Hall   4. Small sitting room   5. Dining room   6. Kitchen

The end of grounds SW to be planted wild and bring out the hedge row and tree screen so as it forms a wood selvedge
A way out for foot passengers at least in extreme SW corner or thereabouts NB axis of house. The house is 4 square and stands high up. Do you follow?

    Yrs very sincerely, Nedi.

    I have reproduced the sketch [73] to illustrate this exchange, and what decisions Miss Jekyll made. Lutyens must have visited Munstead to finish the scheme, for there is no record of further letters; the garden at New Place has been considerably altered, but the bones of these recommendations can be traced.[19] New Place had a comparatively level and straightforward site, and it is unfortunate that we cannot listen in this way to the discussions of more complicated plans.

The Backbones of Design

The ways of the landscape are not to be found in books or theories, but only in the landscape itself; Lutyens learned his rules 'out of doors' and he learned them well, and this is why I think he was an outstanding 'landscape architect' in the fullest meaning of both those words, even though, of the two professions this now embraces, one has largely chosen to forget this and the other has ceased to remember. I think Miss Jekyll taught him much about regard for the virtues of her beloved Surrey – or rather, in her he found the confirmation of his own affinity for this landscape and realized its validity for the designs of houses and gardens. But when it actually came to standing on a site and deciding what to do with it, she could not help him to see into the distance to conjure up the major elements of design, and the credit must largely be his. If we could ask him how he actually chose the site for Orchards or Little Thakeham (when he had acres to choose from), he would probably have quipped about a flag fluttering on a distant church tower or a particularly mournful and statuesque cow that had caught his eye (the flag flying is marked on the Deanery Garden survey), but what it really came down to was an ability to choose the optimum viewpoint from the site, fix that for his datum – usually placing it at the point of entry from the house into the garden – and then deploy the rest of the design as spaces, squares, rectangles, circles, which radiated from this axis conforming to the grain of the land. Because of this understanding of each site, it is difficult to generalize, but on virgin sites with views – Chinthurst Hill, Sullingstead, Fulbrook, Orchards, Marsh Court, Little Thakeham and Daneshill of the early houses – this is the very basic premise of the site, which I have tried to show in sketch plan [74]. The ultimate lesson – that no landscape can be designed in a vacuum – is thus emphasized by the adoption of his central ideas from the landscape itself. Perhaps where the natural limits were harshest, as at Heywood, or where the strongest historical limits were imposed, as at Ammerdown, then the central idea was most 'beautifully phrased' of all.

On to this basis he transposed his discovery of an age-old truth – which has a little to do with the wise virgins and something of Solomon's glory – namely that the human mind adores to be tantalized, and eventually surprised and rewarded. This was first explained to me (at a landscape lecture in the 1960s as I remember) by the tale of the Japanese Tea Master. The Master was old and revered, both humble and divine, and he had lived all his life in an equally humble abode in the midst of people who loved him. There was, outside the village which contained all their homes, a hill from which the most magical view spread down a green and pleasant valley to the distant snow-capped sacred mountains; it was a place that the Master visited to renew his spiritual strength and he most dearly wished to end his days within sight of that view. It came about that this was possible and he was given the land and money to build his heart's desire – the whole of the village were pleased for his sake and they longed to know what and how he would build. The house was finished and the elders of the village were duly invited for the tea ceremony; they entered the gate and climbed the hill through twisting paths and groves of oleanders, eventually reaching the small bungalow which seemed to have been stuck in the centre of a pinewood – where was this marvellous view they had heard so much about? They were ushered in, welcomed into the dark little house, and they fidgeted their way through the tea ceremony, held by the light of a single swaying lamp. If this was all they had come for they would have been better off in their comfortable

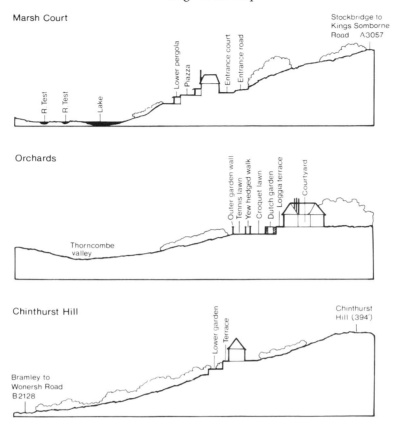

74. Elevations sketched to illustrate the placing of houses and their gardens on three sites.

homes. Finally, with his hand on the cord of the bamboo blind, the Master bade them rise and prepare themselves for his parting gift – he opened the blinds and the view was displayed in all its splendour, controlled and channelled between the flanking trees and revealed for an instant only. The blinds were drawn, the elders left the house and returned to the village, well satisfied. They had had a glimpse of heaven.

Thus Orchards and Marsh Court, as we have seen; the humble tea ceremony may have been expanded to an eight-course Edwardian luncheon and the view enlarged to the misty swellings of southern England – but it was heavenly all the same. However, the theme was tried even before Orchards, in a very early house, Chinthurst Hill, in 1894. The house was built on a 395-foot eminence above the valley of the Wey at Bramley (it could be seen rising from Munstead House), and the distant view over the Weald is completely hidden until one has zig-zagged up the hill and passed through the house on to the full-width terrace, softened, but not emblazoned, with planting. The same theme was exploited through Sullingstead at Hascombe in 1896, Fulbrook at Elstead, 1897, via Marsh Court to an eventual climax of enticement blended with medieval-style castle building at Castle Drogo (which though started in 1910 was not finished until twenty years later and so has to wait for the end of this story). But perhaps it was most skilfully accomplished in a town setting, in 1906 for Heathcote in King's Road, Ilkley, Yorkshire [75]. King's Road is one of the more select Ilkley roads, rising above the town, but the site is comparatively small (about 4 acres) and bounded by other houses and another road, Grove Road, which runs along the end of the garden at a lower level. Beyond Grove Road the houses stretch across the valley. The whole of the King's Road frontage is shuttered through high stone walls and the house is only revealed by entering the high, solid wooden gates; these give directly on to a walled entrance court with a circular granite sett paving pattern which clearly dictates the importance of the central front door. There are gateways right and left leading to garage and kitchen courts respectively, and beyond them the spaces between the house and its side boundaries are filled with enclosed gardens which were possibly both kitchen gardens. The only way for the 'upstairs' society to go was through the house, directed by the central axis through the symmetrical vestibule and hall and out on to the recessed terrace. From the windows of this south front, and from the terrace itself, the eyes are led upwards to the heights of Ilkley Moor – the circular lawn, the garden, and the rest of the houses of Ilkley fall away, clinging to the earth below. Having taken one's fill of the view, the house and garden reassert themselves. The house is incredibly rich – pantiled, of monumental stone, with fluted pillars, swags and stone-wreathed niches adorning the walls – and the terraces are even richer. Here slivers of slate and granite have replaced the soft brick and stone of the south, but the patterns – herring-bone, millstones – are repeated to carry across the terrace, down the grand steps each side to matching rectangular pools and parterres filled with lavender and roses on the level below. From all this pattern the smooth lawn rests the eyes – it has to be heavily buttressed to retain the level, and the retaining walls get larger as they get farther from the house; the borders, filled with clipped hollies, bays and green and golden yews, like so many plump chessmen out of line, cling to the true level of the land and fall away to culminate in central circular steps which lead via a short path to a footgate in Grove Road.

The Relationship of House and Garden

To Lutyens, house and site should, as in vernacular building, form an organic whole. Just as important was the relationship of house and garden – as Lutyens wrote, even 'the position of a staircase window may materially affect a garden plan.' His new west door at Woodside dictated the whole garden plan, after the site had inspired the concept, and we have seen how Folly Farm's several gardens spring from the doors and windows of the house. The final test, I feel, is that not only are the gardens dictated in this way, but also every photograph one wants to take of them, as I think many of the photographs in this book must show. In the end the photographer has simply to obey the architect's symmetrical dictates, for rarely will another 'angle' be so successful. In this process, windows were of very secondary importance to doors, and upper windows were of even less significance. The relationship was conducted very much on the basis of physical movement through the houses and gardens, and the casual glance, from a bedroom

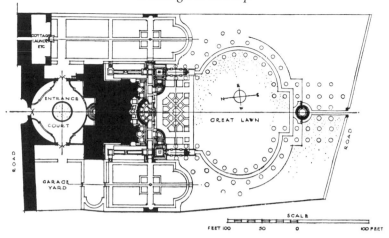

75. Heathcote: the epitome of a 'conceal and reveal' layout – the entrance was completely blinkered by high walled courts, with paths round the sides which were of no design significance at all and merely for practical use. The intention was to steer the visitor through the house and on to the terrace, where the choice was either the intricate patterning of the paving and planting and the experience of the garden, or lifting the eyes to the distant view of Ilkley Moor.

window or passing along a corridor, may have been rewarded with a 'pleasant' view but never a highly significant one. There was something slightly puritanical about this – the view was worth seeking, whether it be of distant landscape or close architectural garden, and the architect always imposed this opinion. Pictures from the upper windows of Lutyens's houses are rarely worth taking – I rest my case on the fact that the most stunning pictures of Hestercombe, Ammerdown (and later Amport House), where the houses were not his design, are to be taken from the roof!

Trying to divine the architect's intentions in the complex relationship of house and garden can become puzzling; eventually we must orientate ourselves as visitors, and begin with entrances and gateways. Both geometrically and in atmosphere, entrances were designed as an introduction to the house – fortunately Lutyens and Miss Jekyll saw exactly eye to eye on the necessity for a quiet introduction, and there are no flamboyant front gardens to be found. Lutyens's gates (or frequent lack of them) perhaps prove at the outset that there was no question of imposing purposeless grandeur on a setting, and this aspect of his blossoming organic philosophy would have been confirmed by Miss Jekyll. Munstead Wood, Orchards, Little Thakeham, Marsh Court, Chinthurst Hill – these country houses had only the simplest gate piers, matching the materials of the house, and gates; at Deanery Garden and Folly Farm, in quiet village settings, the most important entrances in the design were footgates, and the repeated attention to the careful detailing of these footgates is a constant expression of comforting human scale in the gardens [78, 79, 80]. Indeed, Lutyens's regard for foot-travellers in general is a very Edwardian aspect of his designs. Their convenience is always his primary consideration – as with the path and gate to the village he reminds Miss Jekyll of in the New Place design (page 105) – because he wasn't interested in motor cars and would

76. *(left)* The Salutation: the architect dictating the symmetry of the garden, beautifully illustrated in this recently restored garden which was designed by Lutyens, with the house, in 1911, but not planted by Miss Jekyll. The impact of the symmetry was to be revealed only by walking through the house and on to the terrace, and not by a casual glance from an upper window.

77. *(right)* The Salutation: the sundial which prevents the symmetrical view from upstairs, and relates the otherwise severe façade to its garden.

never have owned one had not Lady Sackville felt he should, and made him a present of 'a little grey Rolls' in 1923.[20] When a more urban site dictated the need for privacy (and perhaps occasionally the clients dictated a need to impress their neighbours), the gates become part of functional buildings and so keep their integrity – The Salutation in Sandwich and Great Maytham at Rolvenden (both in Kent) have entrances that architects love, and since they are introducing houses in the grandest Christopher Wren/Queen Anne style *and* giving the necessary privacy and seclusion they are enjoyable on all grounds.

Once past the entrance, either the natural landscape or the 'hard' landscape continues the theme. In the country Miss Jekyll liked to plant drive banks with versions of their natural flora. She suggested soapwort, eleagnus, rock pinks, valerian, and *Clematis vitalba* planted in long drifts in spaces to be cleared on the chalky banks at Marsh Court, and in the autumn of 1915, when Julius Drewe anxiously wrote that he was determined that the drive to his partly-built Castle Drogo should fit into the landscape, Miss Jekyll suggested holly, birch, Scots pine and rowan underplanted with dog rose, *Rosa polyantha, Cistus laurifolius,* tamarisk and blackthorn. Seven ilex were to stand beside the gates on the Chagford to Drewsteignton road – these were so frequently mentioned by Lutyens that they must have been his favourite trees – and they are there today. Drewe, however, felt this mixture a little too subtle for Devon and inclined towards heathers, bracken, broom, brambles and foxgloves. Miss Jekyll replied with a planting scheme that incorporated everything.[21]

In direct contrast to the lushly planted drives, forecourts were predominantly architectural features, with turning circles and footpaths marked by changes in the patterns of stone slabs or setts, and occasionally a grass centrepiece as at Marsh Court. Forecourts were only ever planted with the quietest evergreens, and though all Lutyens's houses, in the true Munstead tradition, did spring out of their briar bushes, the roses were usually on the garden side and entrances more formally marked with magnolias, *Garrya elliptica*, *Arbutus unedo*, viburnums, figs and vines. As these entrances and forecourts introduced the house, by implication they also introduced the garden 'proper' by introducing the materials and patterns that might be encountered later; however, their cool dignity was designed not only as Miss Jekyll's requisite for a calm respite from all the hurly-burly of the world without, but partly to compose one's mind for the recognition of the Architecture, which the house, in its entrance halls and principal rooms, would solemnly display. This was the architect's privilege, of course, and Miss Jekyll would have wholeheartedly concurred, for to her, also, the art was more than a little divine and mention of the word usually calls forth her most stentorian prose. Though Lutyens is well remembered for the jokes he played with his art, these jokes were seldom played in this sacred area but more usually kept decorously hidden from those who did not know a house very well – the 'crawling' windows which were inserted in the nursery wall and the peep-holes for older children to watch the dinner-guests arriving were very private jokes. For everyone else the mood would only be lightened on reaching that magic point where the house met the garden and the beguiling could begin. In stepping on to the terrace, the multi-dimensional, sensual world of the garden began to assert its power.

Millmead

All the design concepts I have mentioned so far were demonstrated in their simplest forms in a very special house and garden created by the partnership. Millmead is introduced here because the designer/site relationship was very close, the central idea is beautifully phrased within a very small space, 'every wall, path, stone and flower bed' can be seen in close relationship to the whole, and the entrance court is one of the most typical, and certainly the best preserved, of all. In the midst of all the great and impressive gardens, Miss Jekyll was pursuing schemes of her own; Lutyens designed Millmead especially for her, for she was the client and the planting designer, and it thus demonstrates the partnership working in a very pure light.

Miss Jekyll had long cherished the ideal that good design should not be the prerogative of large houses and gardens, and she longed to give the world – or Surrey at any rate – her perfected notion of a small house and garden. And where else should this be but in her beloved Bramley, which even her love of Munstead Wood had never quite dislodged from her heart. In *Gardens for Small Country Houses*, she describes with a charming

78. Hestercombe.

79. Ednaston Manor.

80. Castle Drogo.

Footgates, of which these are typical examples, are a major feature of all the houses and gardens, emphasizing the comforting human scale, and a respect for it, in an age without an infatuation for the motor car.

81. The Salutation.

82. Berrydowne Court.

Entrances which architects love, but purely functional for privacy, shelter or accommodation, never purely for 'show'.

anonymity how she found a plot of land in Snowdenham Lane in Bramley, where some cottages had been demolished and all was overgrown with docks and nettles: 'In 1904 an old former inhabitant went over it, and found that from halfway down it looked over the wooded grounds of the old home and the half-distant hilly woodland that had been the scene of childish primrose-picking rambles.'[22] The garden that was to be Millmead's does indeed look towards Bramley Park, and she could not resist it. It was only just over half an acre, and she bought it. That she had to pay her architect seems unlikely (excepting that she was a stickler for propriety), and Lutyens designed her 'small' house with a Dutch atmosphere to the garden front as the key to an intensively-designed garden.

The shape of Millmead's plot, as can be seen on the plan [83], is long and thin, bounded on both sides by other houses and back yards. The plot divides nicely into three equal parts – the entrance court and house, the rose garden and the second level garden, then the third level garden. The small section left over at the end is treated more elaborately than the rest, for it is the heart of the whole design – overlooking the woods full of childhood memories. In plan Millmead's layout may not look very inspiring to modern eyes because of this rather linear layout, for we have now spent so long trying to make the universal long thin plot of everyman's garden look anything but a long thin plot, and Millmead's garden does not disguise its shape; however, as a simple demonstration of the themes of the partnership, its direct concentration on that sacred spot at the end of the plot is the simplest of central ideas. The progress through the garden was sure and delightful, and here, especially, the 'true adornment' was the planting.

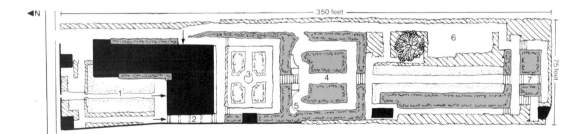

83. Millmead: sketch layout of the rectangular plot, which was completely bounded by other properties on the east and west. The foot entrance from the road (Snowdenham Lane) enters the court (1), through which a central path leads to the front door, with a secondary access to the garden via the pergola (2). On the garden front, the rose garden (3) consisted of four beds of hybrid tea roses of toning colours, a single variety in each bed (or they may have been divided with lavender into different varieties as at Putteridge Park [see pl. 107], with surrounding borders of varied greens, good textures and pale flowers [see pl. 88]). The second level of the garden (4) had a small dipping-well in the corner (5); the third level is the longest with a large old pear tree and the compost and rubbish areas (6) concealed behind hedges. The final level (7) has a third summer house, a sundial and another dipping-well, and overlooks the woods of Bramley Park. [See pl. 90 for the planting details.] The rather linear layout belies the softness of this garden, which was produced by luxuriant planting which spilled out from its allotted spaces; all the paths were of natural rolled sand, and there were no harsh edges.

84. (*left*) Millmead: the pergola of old ship's timbers squeezed in between the house and boundary wall.

85. (*right*) Millmead: the surviving 'quiet' Jekyll planting of the entrance court – clematis, laurustinus, bergenias, ferns, arbutus and box as she planted them.

Millmead is approached by a footgate with a small grille, in a high wall beside Snowdenham Lane. The photograph [85] shows a remarkable survival of Jekyll planting, for it is more or less as she intended it should be – green and quiet, with *Clematis montana* and *vitalba, Spiraea lindleyana,* laurustinus and arbutus against the wall, and bergenias, Lent hellebores, Solomon's seal and hardy ferns beneath them. The paved path directly to the front door is balanced by a waist-high box hedge, which carefully diminishes the importance of the side path leading to the narrow, pergola-covered passage which squeezes through between the western wall of the house and its boundary [84]. On the garden side the controlling axis is moved to the centre of the house, thus bringing the main length of the garden into perfect symmetrical balance after the rather low-key introduction of the entrance court. Millmead still has Miss Jekyll's vine over the pergola, and wisteria and escallonia on the garden wall of the house; originally choisya, lavender, rosemary and *Iris stylosa (unguicularis)* – traditionally planted at the house foot in Surrey sand so that it may find its necessary lime – filled the house border.

The gently sloping garden is controlled by short flights of rough sandstone steps; a rosemary hedge and three steps marked the boundary down to the first level, the rose garden – four beds in grass with a central sundial. If we assume that Millmead was planted in 1905, the year after Miss Jekyll found the site, she was still using her old

86. Millmead: the garden front, from the photograph in *Gardens for Small Country Houses*.

favourite roses (colour schemes with the hybrid tea bushes are of later dates – see page 142): the four beds were probably originally filled with Madame Plantier, a bush rose with small white pompom flowers, underplanted with lavender and nepeta, the scheme used in the Dutch garden at Orchards. To balance the frailty of the roses, the side borders were filled to bursting point with strong and textural planting in varied greens and muted colours, some of which can be identified in the plan [88].

At the head of the longer flight of steps, now centrally placed, which set the pattern for the rest of the garden, it is as though Lutyens almost said: 'You are on your own now – I have set the theme but the rest of the garden is for you to plant' – for from this point Millmead celebrates Miss Jekyll's favourite dry-wall planting, and the descending levels are achieved in clouds of the saxifrages, pinks and aubretias that she loved. Because of her travels she had always been a dedicated 'alpinist', and had experimented with several different rock gardens at Munstead Wood. She got much pleasure from the contrast between fragile flowers and rocks, and she knew there was no place for 'rockeries' in Lutyens's designs. The next best thing, and her own way of adapting a Surrey tradition, was the planting of sandstone walls with suitable trailing plants – and both the construction of the walls and the proportions of the planting were very important to the overall effect, so her directions for both these operations have been reproduced here [87, 89, 90]. Some of her early Surrey gardens, notably The Red House, Charterhouse, had given her some scope (though the real *tour de force*, Highmount in Fort Road, Guildford, was still to come, in 1909), but Millmead was special, her very own opportunity, and it survives whereas the others do not. The planting plans for Millmead were published in *Gardens for Small Country Houses*, so they also have survived to show exactly how it was done. The second level was filled with matching summer borders each side of the central path, and then a short flight of steps led to the third level, with a continuing summer border on the right-hand side. Here, what was supposed to be a tool shed was converted by her first tenant into another summerhouse – 'built of oak timber and brick with a tiled roof . . . [it] has the appearance of a miniature old Surrey cottage'[23] which is balanced by the old pear tree. At the end of the long walk by the border another four steps go down to a cross path, with a retaining wall planted with rock pinks, and dwarf, dark-flowered Munstead lavender backed by a hedge of hardy fuchsia. More steps lead down further to the lowest level, about five feet above the park, where the final planting is of low shrubs – a delicious mixture of pernettya, white rose, tree lupins, box, *Cotoneaster horizontalis*, sweet williams, pinks, gypsophila and saxifrages (see planting plan), which do nothing to obscure, but only decorate, the beloved prospect.

87. Dry-wall construction and planting details.

(a) Section of dry wall – 'A dry wall cannot be built against a scarp of hard sand or chalk. Enough must be taken out at the back to allow for fresh filling and ramming. It is upon firm and quite conscientious ramming that the stability of the wall depends.' 'As a good general rule [the wall] may batter back in the proportion of one foot in six of height. Every stone lying on its natural bed at right angles to the sloped back face has the back a little lower than the front. It follows that every drop of rain that falls on the face of the wall runs into the next joint to the benefit of the plants.'

(b) The elevation of the wall properly planted. '. . . it is well to place the plants in groups of a fair quantity of one thing at a time; and, in the case of small plants such as thrift or London Pride to put them fairly close together. It is well also to make careful combinations of colour . . . on a sunny wall there may be a colour scheme of grey with purple of various shades, white and pale pink, composed of dwarf lavender, nepeta, aubretia, cerastium, helianthemums of the kind that have grey leaves and white and pale pink bloom, rock pinks, stachys, dwarf artemesias and Achillea umbellata . . .'

(Sketches and quotes both from *Gardens for Small Country Houses*.)

(c) Sketches of the alternative arrangement for stones in the face of the wall.
(From *Wall and Water Gardens*.)

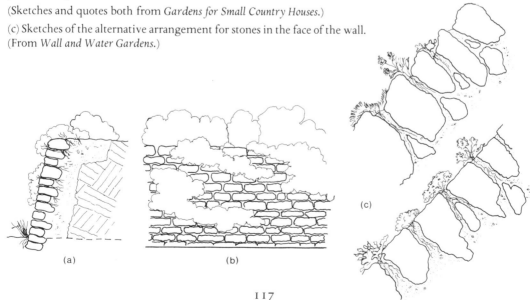

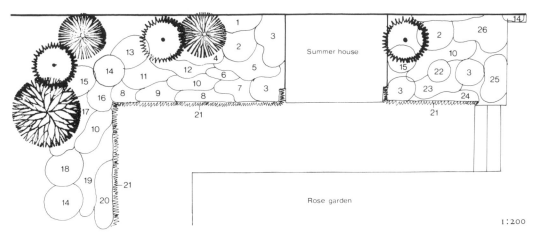

88. Millmead: the planting in the shade of the rose garden border – mainly greens with touches of yellow and purple with nothing to detract from the colours of the roses opposite.

Key to the planting:

1. *Viburnum opulus* (guelder rose)
2. Red cedar
3. Ferns
4. *Forsythia suspensa*
5. *Polygonatum multiflorum* (Solomon's seal)
6. Iris
7. *Geranium grandiflorum*
8. Pansy
9. *Geranium ibericum*
10. *Helleborus orientalis* (Lent hellebore)
11. *Echinops ritro*
12. White phlox
13. Lilac
14. *Viburnum tinus*
15. *Aucuba japonica*
16. *Galega officinalis*
17. Columbine (aquilegia)
18. *Arbutus unedo*
19. Polyanthus
20. *Bergenia cordifolia*
21. Box hedging
22. *Ruscus racemosus* (*Danae racemosa*)
23. Hemerocallis
24. *Tiarella cordifolia*
25. Rosemary
26. *Berberis aquifolium*

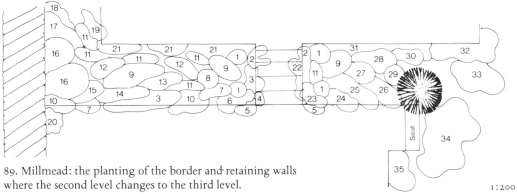

89. Millmead: the planting of the border and retaining walls where the second level changes to the third level.

Key to the planting:

1. *Buxus sempervirens*
2. Aubretia
3. *Cerastium tomentosum*
4. *Achillea umbellata*
5. *Iris stylosa*
6. *Veronica prostrata*
7. *Stachys lanata*
8. *Olearia phlogopappa*
9. *Rosa lucida*
10. *Nepeta mussinii*
11. Iris varieties
12. *Rosa* 'Madame Plantier'
13. *Echinops ritro*
14. *Sedum telephium*
15. *Helleborus orientalis* (Lent hellebore)
16. *Ilex aquifolium* (holly)
17. *Berberis darwinii*
18. *Campanula macrantha*
19. *Lysichmachia nummularia*
20. Fern
21. Pansies
22. *Campanula carpatica*
23. Hybrid rock pinks
24. *Arabis albida* 'Flore Pleno'
25. Dwarf lavender
26. *Centranthus ruber*
27. *Fuchsia magellanica gracilis*
28. *Chrysanthemum maximum*
29. Tree ivy
30. China rose
31. Polyanthus
32. *Berberis aquifolium*
33. Rambling rose trained into old damson tree
34. *Prunus lusitanica*
35. *Rosa alba*

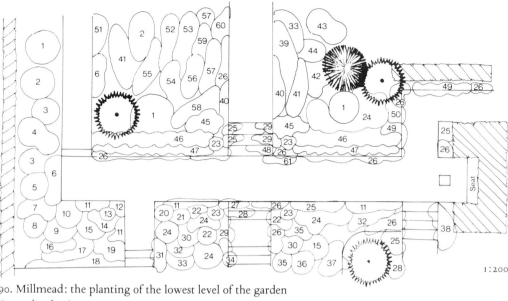

90. Millmead: the planting of the lowest level of the garden

Key to the planting:

1. *Viburnum opulus* (guelder rose)
2. *Sorbaria tomentosa* (*Spirea lindleyana*)
3. *Sambucus nigra*
4. *Spirea cerisifolia*
5. Lilac
6. *Bergenia cordifolia*
7. *Symphoricarpus albus* (snowberry)
8. Red cedar
9. Deutzia
10. *Calycanthus floridus* (allspice)
11. Sweet william
12. *Geranium ibericum*
13. *Kerria japonica*
14. *Campanula macrantha*
15. *Forsythia suspensa*
16. *Dropteris felix-mas* (male fern)
17. *Helleborus orientalis*
18. *Epimedium pinnatum*
19. Fern
20. *Pernettya mucronata*

21. White rose
22. *Gypsophila paniculata*
23. Box
24. Tree lupin
25. Pansy
26. Hybrid rock pink
27. Aubretia
28. *Saxifraga umbrosa*
29. *Campanula carpatica*
30. *Phlomis fruticosa*
31. *Cotoneaster horizontalis*
32. *Verbascum olympicum*
33. *Anchusa azurea italica*
34. Mossy saxifrage
35. *Papaver rupifragum*
36. *Spirea thunbergii*
37. White foxglove
38. *Veronica prostrata*
39. *Helenium pumilum*
40. *Stachys lanata*
41. Michaelmas daisy

42. *Helianthus multiflorus*
43. *Hebe brachysiphon*
44. Perennial lupin
45. *Berberis aquifolium*
46. Hardy fuchsia (*F. magellina*)
47. Dwarf lavender
48. *Sedum ewersii*
49. *Centranthus ruber*
50. *Cerastium tomentosum*
51. Iris
52. *Helenium striatum*
53. Delphinium
54. Pink phlox
55. White broom
56. Kniphofia
57. Oriental poppy
58. Rose
59. Hemerocallis
60. Peony
61. *Ceratostigma Willmottiana* (hardy plumbago)

Numbers (1–10) show the varied shrub planting that was used along the west garden boundary, and numbers (11–18) demonstrate the rather quiet planting with good contrasts in form and texture that Gertrude Jekyll regarded as basic to any scheme. The only bright patches here are provided by the sweet william on the edge of a predominantly green, yellow and blue scheme. On the opposite side of the path the dry-wall planting comes into its own with plenty of pretty pinks and blues in the alpine flowers overhanging the edges of the steps, and striking contrasts in form, e.g. the verbascum towering out of the creeping cotoneaster. Box (23) is used throughout the garden as an accent bush at the tops of the steps. The colours remain delicate through to (38), i.e. in all the lowest part of the garden. The same plants (pansies, campanula, rock pinks), with the addition of the miniature sedum, are repeated by the upper central steps, with long drifts of dwarf lavender and rock pinks (probably white) hanging beneath the hardy fuschia (46). Above these the fuchsia gives the key to a colour change to more vivid splashes of yellow, orange and red with the heleniums, poppies, day-lilies and centranthus.

Many people wish Miss Jekyll and Lutyens had built more Millmeads. It is the one house and garden which can fit happily into the concertina'd space of modern life; it shows Lutyens's geometrical sense working within fine limits to give just enough *finesse* to Miss Jekyll's practical and affectionate personality. Above all, he transformed her sense of place into a logical design, making a believable setting for some of her happiest planting. Millmead is the partnership working perfectly, in miniature. But it was virtually unique. Grander conceptions with more elaborate themes – special types of planting and a more frequent deployment of favourite architectural details – were much more the order of the day.

Terraces, Steps and Pavings

The recognition of the terrace as the prime feature in all Lutyens's gardens was partly technical, for in elevation the terrace 'settled' the house into its site, and partly social, for tea on the terrace was *de rigueur* for the new Edwardian ladies who wanted to prove themselves less likely to wilt in the sun than their aunts and mothers had been. (There were no conservatories for shade-lovers in these gardens – glass was a material that did not attract Lutyens, and Miss Jekyll felt that greenhouses were distinctly practical adjuncts to the kitchen garden.) The terraces progressed from simplest beginnings as quite flat or slightly raised terraces in rough sandstone slabs in most of the Surrey gardens, through to the giant three-decker at Hestercombe and bastion-like structures at Nashdom and Great Maytham. Their proportions do not follow any hard and fast rules, though they will always be found to have some geometrical connection with the house or the site; also they are never mean, or too narrow, which Blomfield identified as the most common fault with terraces in 1892, and which is often the case today. Lutyens's terraces had plenty of room for a tea party without obstructing their other main purpose – that of beginning the progress down into the garden. The height above the ground was dictated by the natural fall of the ground and the height of the house, and any hint of insecurity or the danger of falling over the edge was countered by wide flower borders or a solid and solidly traditional balustrade. For the sandstone houses the terraces were plain sandstone as well, but with the turn of the century and increased sophistication, finished limestone slabs and herring-bone brickwork, foreshadowed by Woodside and the Dutch garden at Orchards, became more usual. Folly Farm and Marsh Court are richer gardens largely because of the overall effect of the herring-bone brickwork for courts, terraces and paths, and it was always the old 2-inch narrow brick (sometimes called the Tudor brick because of a close association with Wolsey and Henry VIII at Hampton Court), which was the only size of brick that Lutyens really liked for visual effect.[24] His fondness for these narrow bricks sprang from both the Surrey and 'old English' traditions, but received a fillip in the early 1900s when he met Walter Hoare (a member of the banking family), who owned Daneshill brickworks just north of Basingstoke, which had been making bricks of many varieties and of very high quality for centuries. Daneshill House was built for Hoare, making the best use of his company's bricks for details on and in the house and in the garden, where there were

11. Little Thakeham, near Storrington, Sussex: the entrance court.
12. Little Thakeham: the vista through the west garden court.

13. (*above*) Folly Farm, Sulhamstead, Berkshire: a vista through the walls of the entrance and barn courts.

14. (*left*) Folly Farm: the formal canal garden and the 'Dutch' addition to the original farmhouse.

(*facing page*)

15. (*above*) Folly Farm: one of the 'platforms' raised at the four corners of the sunken rose garden. The interweaving of geometry and changing materials makes this the most ornate 'room' in the house out of doors, but all is softened with the simplest planting of roses and lavender.

16. (*below*) Folly Farm: the sunken rose garden and the final, 1912, addition to the house.

17. (*above*) The Hoo, Willingdon, Sussex:
Lutyens altered the house and designed the
garden in 1902. The main garden is simply a
large square lawn on the south side of the
house, but at the lawn's farthest extent the
land drops away and a high shoring wall of
flint and rubble stone was built to create a
lower walk. Two sets of steps lead down to the
walk, each guarded by a gazebo, very much in
the tradition of seventeenth-century gardens,
and certainly with reminders of Edzell and
Pitmedden.*

18. (*left*) The Hoo: the domed water-lily pool
beside the lower walk, a development of the
pool beneath the 'bridge' at Deanery Garden
but here a feature in its own right.

*Edzell Castle and Pitmedden House, both in
north-east Scotland. Edzell is owned by the Scottish
Office of Works and Pitmedden by the National
Trust for Scotland. Both are open all year.

tiers of brick terraces and attendant steps.[25] Hoare's bricks were also used for New Place at Shedfield, and the inspiration at least carried on to another good brick garden, with elaborate terraces, at Temple Dinsley near Hitchin in Hertfordshire.

Apart from the herring-bone, and the insertion of a millstone (real or made up of tiles and bricks) which was almost the partnership's trade-mark, started at Munstead Wood and followed through to Amport House over thirty years later, the terraces give an over-riding impression of function rather than decoration. Only in the north – at Heathcote in 1906 and again at Gledstone Hall in 1923 – did Lutyens feel it necessary to take one's mind off the cold wind blowing by the insertion of elaborate patterns. Terrace borders were planted to encourage relaxation, with clematis, choisya, vines, viburnums, jasmine, bay and myrtle, as well as roses, wafting their scents from the house walls. The delicate border planting, as planned for Deanery Garden [36], was a fairly standard scheme, bringing pinks and blues and white flowers out in May and June, with silvers and textural evergreens as a background for pots of lilies, fuchsias, pelargoniums or hydrangeas later on; in this way the terrace planting blessed the social calendar – pansies and mignonette for the first tea parties, lilies among the choisya and lavender after Ascot afternoons, and pink pelargoniums and hydrangeas for the Henley house party.

The style and materials of the terrace having set the key, the progress was assumed by means of steps and pavings. The steps that Lutyens designed are never merely functional – they are a celebration of the art of changing levels. They come in straight or angled flights, but the most often-repeated geometrical games are with circles. Various computations of materials were used, in accordance with their settings – it was unfinished stone for the early gardens, sometimes with tiles inserted for the risers, but with increasing formality this changed to finished stone for treads and copings, with bricks or tiles inserted for the risers. In all brick gardens the treads are made of bricks on their narrow sides. All the steps were designed to Miss Jekyll's expressed opinion that 'the decorative value of steps consists primarily in the alternation of horizontal bands of light and shade – shining treads and dark risers',[26] but while she may have been responsible for the innovative uses of materials, it was Lutyens who dictated the shapes – the strictly angled flights, as on the Deanery Garden terrace and at Great Maytham, being rather more formal than the concentric circles, the latter most often used in the transition to grass or another surface material. The other aspect that all the steps have in common is their sensuality – 18-inch wide treads with gentle 6-inch risers allowed for long, leisurely pacings, with the rule never broken so that the conversation need never be interrupted. Circular steps almost became another trademark – variations on themes of related radii, always with a relation to the width of the tread, with various proportions of the circles revealed, and always with the visual satisfaction of the completion of one circle as a landing, sometimes richly patterned, or perhaps in grass.

From the steps, the paths were never merely a means of keeping the feet dry, they were used to unify the whole garden design and state the relationship of every feature with the house. The path centres were fixed by the lines of secondary axes or cross axials from the terrace, thus determining the siting of other features; they were wide, always wide enough for two people to walk comfortably side by side, unless the scale of their

91. Hestercombe.

Steps: a celebration of the art of changing levels in various guises.

92. The Hoo.

93. Hestercombe.

94. Ashby St Ledgers.

95. Munstead Wood: the millstone outside the workshop door.

96. Amport House: millstone and paving thirty years on from Munstead Wood.

97. Pasturewood: millstone and brick-on-edge paving.

98. Pasturewood: millstone and tile-on-edge paving.

99. Marsh Court: the white stone necklace to the east lawn.

100. Munstead Wood: the craftsman's pride – many of the houses are carved with the names of their makers and the date.

setting would not allow this – as with the single-file herring-bone paths in the entrance and barn courts at Folly Farm. In the early countrified gardens the paths were equally carefully placed, but they followed Miss Jekyll's Munstead tradition of being just hard rolled sand, bordered with small slabs of sandstone cut into the ground; with increasing formality and the move away from sand, the need for hard surfaces was twofold and the traditional herring-bone brickwork, refined by Lutyens with an edging of rectangular limestone slabs, was the most distinctive result. Pavings also carried the decoration on to the lawns: several gardens, Heywood, Marsh Court, Heathcote among them, had lawns set with necklaces of white stones for the pure pleasure of the pattern. Whether to Miss Jekyll is due the credit for the invention of the 'mowing strip' I am not sure, but certainly the stone pavings around the borders on the Great Plat at Hestercombe are the most elegant mòwing strips ever devised. The fact that there were craftsmen of quality working for every building firm Lutyens employed adds just a little more of the sense of the vanished dream to these gardens, for when it comes to repairing these features today the cry most often heard is that the craftsmen cannot be found. No mortar was used; all the pavings, stones, bricks and setts were loose laid in sand – a more skilled technique. It was also convenient for planting: Miss Jekyll thought that most hard surfaces looked better with small plants in their crevices, though she bowed to her architect's pride in his design by saying that the plants must accentuate, and not obscure, the patterns of the materials.

The Garden as a House Out of Doors

When Miss Jekyll, on those early Munstead visits, showed Ned Lutyens the Spring garden and the Hidden garden in the making, she was showing him the traditions of the lady's bower and the sheltered courts of Moorish gardens (whether the shelter was needed from wind or sun was immaterial), combined with an answer to the practical needs of her society for a quiet retreat away from the domestic bustle and the to-ing and fro-ing of a dozen gardeners at work. That Lutyens in turn heard the echoings of 200-year-old conversations – Wren discussing with William of Orange's Queen Mary her plans for the Privy and Pond gardens at Hampton Court – resulted in the partnership becoming famous for their 'garden rooms'. The best-known – the rose garden at Folly Farm, the Italian garden at Ammerdown – have been seen as elaborate masterpieces on their own, but they are really best appreciated as part of their individual garden plans, and from these, as from most of the other gardens I have shown in plan, it will be seen that the partnership's attention to a sense of enclosure produced not only garden rooms, but in many cases a complete house out of doors. It is in the experience of this third dimension that the geometry so apparent in plan fades to the background, and the beguiling of the senses, with grand vistas, secret corridors, tunnelled pergolas and trysting places – all planted with a medley of colours and perfumes – takes over; in this aspect, more than any other, the gardens are Edwardian, representative of an age which delighted in the cultivation of the senses.

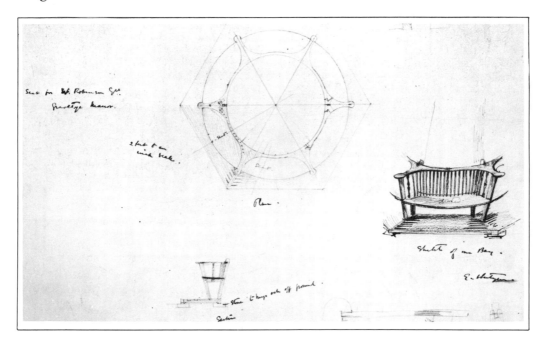

101. (*above*) Lutyens's sketch for a six-bay wooden seat round a tree at Gravetye Manor, William Robinson's garden in Sussex. Robinson had written: 'It is rare to see a garden seat that is not an eyesore,' before he met Lutyens.

102. (*below*) Lutyens's garden seat – the larger of his two designs. Miss Jekyll did not like white painted seats, which she thought 'too tyrannical', but here the white paint shows up the design immaculately against the dark yew. These seats are now being made to the original design for restored gardens.

103. Temple Dinsley.
104. Millmead.

Garden houses: the element of enclosure in the garden come full circle.

In gardens well stocked with gems of garden architecture the pergolas were the most outstanding features. Miss Jekyll acknowledged their Italian and Tudor origins and regarded them as excellent structures for showing off plants; Lutyens treated them, often physically, always materially, as extensions of their houses, and his pergolas are more substantial than any other structures which have borne that name in English gardens. As if in direct reply to Robinson's sneers about fragile rustic work whose chief merit was that it rotted away quickly and fell down, Lutyens's pergolas have piers of brick or stone, rarely under a foot square or in diameter (alternating square and round pillars are often used), covered with enormous cross-beams of oak. The high point of this design is the Adam's rib construction springing from the side of the house at Marsh Court [colour pl. 19], and perhaps the most impressive is Hestercombe's – 240 feet long and providing the grand finale to the garden pattern [57]. Pergolas planted with wisteria, vines and clematis were covered with fine slats to make a complete tunnel, smaller-scale structures were left open with climbing or rambler roses on the piers. (Miss Jekyll also liked pleached alleys of hornbeam, plane or beech, but as these could not involve architecture they somehow never appear in the gardens – perhaps the nearest conversion of the idea was a barrel-roofed covered walk at The Pleasaunce, Overstrand, Norfolk.)

The favourite material for enclosure was yew; with its omens of stability and eternity, it is the most symbolic of all garden plants. The patience to design in yew, and to wait for the due time and season when the intention would be achieved, adds a sense of repose to the gardens, and an intimation of innocent trust to the working partnership which sprang from Miss Jekyll, the countrywoman. That Lutyens had enough faith to design in yew is shown by his sketch of the topiary for the Dutch garden gate at Orchards [25], for those hedges are at that optimum height now, but he could not have done so without her; having so little experience of actually *growing* things (he never had a garden of his own) he was always surprised at how wonderfully his gardens grew – returning to Hestercombe in 1931 he found a 'hoary old age' far in excess of his own and could not believe he had conceived it at all.

The True Adornment of the Gardens

Though Lutyens confined this phrase to the planting, I have included the treatment of water here as well, for plants and water are often inseparable in the designed features of the gardens, and Miss Jekyll was responsible for the whole of the partnership's concept of water in the garden. From her earliest childhood she discovered the difference that a river – the Wey – could make to an otherwise waterless land, an understanding that was enhanced by moving up on to the arid Munstead Heath, so that (Lutyens already having come from an equally arid countryside) the seeds of their respect for water were sown, and led to Miss Jekyll's sympathetic feeling for it as the sacred element in the gardens of Spain. Left to herself, she was frugal with the precious substance – there was only one small tank in the garden at Munstead,[27] and an important aspect of the Millmead plan was the re-use of the old cottage well in the entrance court as a source of supply for the 'dipping wells' on the second level garden and at the very end of the garden overlooking the park, both for the comforting presence of the water itself and the practical purpose of watering the plants. It was certainly from her descriptions and pictures of Moorish gardens that the iris rills were introduced to cross Deanery Garden's lawn, and then elaborated to form such important features of the Hestercombe design. She was also aware that other designers allowed contorted shapes for pools and slightly disapproved of this; she managed to restrain Lutyens to the most simple shapes – rectangles or ovals are the best – and obviously she was happiest with those. The main purpose of still water was to provide reflection, usually of the architecture, as epitomized by the tank court at Folly Farm [68], but attention was also paid to the reflection of the shapes of suitable plants. For the most effective reflections the water must be kept to the brim, and where the pools were approached by steps, taking the steps into the water added to the sense of illusion. This also had practical purposes – steps going into the water were Miss Jekyll's approved safety feature to discourage accidents to children, and the lowest step provided the ideal position for water-lily baskets. As has already been explained with reference to Marsh Court (page 75), she felt that water-lilies and formal pools were inseparable, and all the garden pools were originally planted with them.

The respect for water was heavily underlined in their treatment of moving water – it was not for playing tricks with. Lutyens disapproved of elaborate fountains – 'hideous' was his description of the Paris-made model moved into the centre of his oval pool at

105. Hestercombe: the east rill garden.

Heywood in 1911[28] – and no fountain of his designing will be found in these gardens.[29] Water was always moved for a purpose – from pool to pool along the iris rills, nurturing the plants on the way – and never turned to profligate display. His very special contribution to the treatment of water in the garden – the domed and cavernous pools that both shelter it and enhance its value by the purity of their design – is one of the most constant demonstrations of his Jekyll-inspired respect for this element.

The use of water in the gardens is the first incomplete aspect of the partnership at work. Even though there is increasing sophistication to come with the canals of Tyringham and the water terraces of Amport House, the feeling that more could have been achieved by concentration on this aspect during the intense period of working together before the War is inescapable. That it was not so seems due to a misunderstanding. Miss Jekyll obviously regaled Lutyens with descriptions and photographs of the great Italian water-gardens, enough to inspire him to Hestercombe, but that is a high point from which they only retreated, probably because in 1909 he went to Italy for the first time and saw the Villa d'Este for himself:

Some of the work – the terrace balustrades – lovely; but more was horrible and ugly. It wants to be seen with great discrimination. Yet, there is real God-given loveliness, and oh, if I could have the chances. But you can see in the work where vulgarity prevailed over good taste and sense. The same then as now – if only people would see. Inside the palace the decoration was horrible, and outside a river is taken through the garden and played with *ad nauseam*. Over all is a great cloak of decay . . .[30]

106. Lutyens's ideal water garden with 'Emmie' and the children.

These words written home to Emily convey the shock that d'Este, in all her voluptuous decay, gave to Lutyens's eyes, schooled to Miss Jekyll's restraint and good taste which had guided him thus far (he also saw Hadrian's Villa, where the Canopus Canal was to be later reflected at Tyringham Park). If he had had a chance to get over the initial reaction, and the chances had come (but it would have meant *no* war intervening) while he was concentrating upon garden design, the treatment of water as an integral material of this English landscape might have resulted in outstanding gardens. But it was not to be, for he did not have the time.

The planting plans for the rill gardens at Hestercombe, finished in 1910 [105], show more than any others just how Miss Jekyll's knowledge and skill made it all look deceptively simple, how she abided by her rules for the best ways of subtly fitting plants to their settings, and how she never forgot that the work of the architect and the craftsmen must be enhanced but not obscured by her planting. This is why to have these

107. Putteridge Park: the plan for the rose garden.

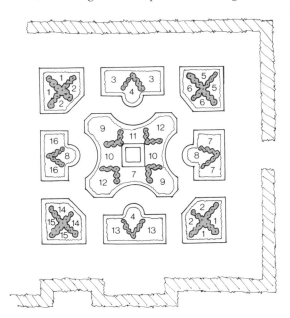

Key to the planting:
1. 'Madame Abel Chatenay' (deep pink with paler reverse)
2. 'Admiral Dewey' (flowers silvery pink, almost white)
3. 'Viscountess Folkestone' (creamy yellow)
4. 'Lyon-Rose' (warm yellow)
5. 'Killarney' (flesh shaded white, suffused pale pink with long pointed buds)
6. 'Irish Beauty' (a tea-scented rose, salmony pink)
7. 'Triumph'
8. 'Caroline Testout' (bright satin rose with brighter centre)
9. 'Captain Christy' (delicate fleshy white with centre richer in colour)
10. 'Marquise de Salisbury' (fine bright velvety red)
11. 'Liberty' (red)
12. 'Augustine Guinoisseau' (flowers white, slightly tinted with flesh colour)
13. 'Kaiserin Augusta Victoria' (free blooming, of pale primrose colour)
14. 'Antoine Rivoire' (rosy flesh on a cream ground)
15. 'Lady Ashtown' (pale rose pink, reflex of petals silvery)
16. 'Richmond' (crimson red)

The plan shows half of the yew-hedged rectangular rose garden; for the other half the planting pattern was the mirror image. All the beds were bordered with *Stachys lanata* and divided with bushes as shown, probably lavender, but unmarked on the original plan. Putteridge Park, like Temple Dinsley, was planted with roses from Messrs. R. Harkness & Co., the famous growers at Hitchin, and all these descriptions come from their 1912 catalogue, in which the prices ranged from 9d. to 2s. 6d. for a hybrid tea bush rose. ('12 good plants, our selection 10s. 6 – carriage paid'). It will be seen how the colours complemented each other; the pinks were kept in separate beds from yellowy or salmony colours, with the dramatic red and white contrasts in the centre. The important thing was that there was no magenta colouring. (Note: 'Triumph' is the only rose not in the Harkness 1912 catalogue, nor have I found it anywhere else, but it would seem, by both position and name, to have been red.)

gardens 'properly dressed' is so vital, for, as I hope every planting scheme described and illustrated will have conveyed by now, the green and quiet entrances, the 'restrained creepery' on the house walls, the delicate, early summer flowering terrace borders, the tumbling colours and textures on the dry walls, the simple perfumed rose gardens and the natural planting that complemented water features – all these schemes were faithfully produced, with variations, over and over again, for they were just as vital to the gardens as the wallcoverings and furniture are to the character of a room. In all these ways the partnership managed what could well be called perfection, but as the water never went any farther, neither did the planting, and though Lutyens was interested in mastering the transition from formal garden into landscape, this too was never achieved.

The footnote to these best years of the working partnership is illustrated by Marsh Court, where by early 1915 the faithful Johnsons wanted to organize the wilder parts of their garden. They had apparently asked the nurserymen, Cheals of Crawley, to think up some planting schemes for the extensive slopes north of the east lawn, where they had had a tennis court installed on the top level, and for the long drive. Lutyens wrote to Miss Jekyll on 29 April 1915: 'Mr and Mrs Johnson would much rather that you should do the planting. The gardener (Epps) is very pleased with your method of making planting plans as he knows exactly where to put the plants; he says that Cheal's plans are much too vague and that he feels entirely at the mercy of a nurseryman! Epps also says that your plants are better than anyone else's, and that Mrs Johnson would like your plants . . .'[31] These hasty compliments were apparently dictated by Lutyens and sent by an assistant in the office; the plans were for the drive, which was planted with drifts of rock pinks, valerian, eleagnus and *Clematis vitalba*, and a large two-part plan [45] showing the paved east lawn with surrounding yews and a straight walk to the north of it leading to a circular area, from which paths radiated across the slope, one to the new tennis court. This was the land that Lutyens said 'wanted treating'; there was also a fourth plan for an informal water garden on the marshy land 100 feet below the house, beside the Test. Lutyens's note concludes: 'I'm afraid this is all too vague for you, but when I come down, which I hope will be soon, I can explain it all to you. I hope that there will be a garden (on chalk) for you to do at Middlefield.'[32] It was not signed. There is no further correspondence and the plans are vague and incomplete, with Miss Jekyll's planting suggestions scrawled on, as I have noted them on my plan. What I feel is more telling is the manner of the note, and the manner of its sending. There seems great doubt that he ever made the promised visit, nor was there to be a Jekyll garden at Middlefield, his house at Great Shelford in Cambridgeshire. The vagueness and incompleteness of it all illustrates what was in fact the case – that the partners were losing touch.

THE WAR AND AFTERWARDS

The battlefields [are] the obliteration of all human endeavour, achievement
. . . and the human achievement of destruction is bettered by the poppies and
wild flowers – that are as friendly to an unexploded shell as they are to the leg
of a garden seat in Surrey.

Edwin Lutyens from France, 1917[1]

I N 1910, at the age of forty-one, Edwin Lutyens traded in his reputation as a builder
of delightful country houses for that of international architect. He stepped beyond
the confines of the cosily related, like-minded and very English society that he had
served, on to the harshly-lit stage of monumental classicism. There were to be more
gardens, but they seem a refuge from long hours spent wrestling with building
commissions, government committees and travelling, and because of a growing, strong,
classical influence, they were to be quite different from what had gone before.

In 1910 King Edward died; this, coming shortly on Lloyd George's taxes on incomes,
land and death, and followed by a constitutional crisis at home and troubles abroad, had
a saddening and disillusioning effect on the society which provided Lutyens with his
clients. Suddenly, it appeared that everything was falling apart. Perhaps the sharpest
blow was the closest, for 1910 was also the year that Lutyens's wife Emily became a
theosophist. It appears that Ned and Emily's marriage had at first been blissfully happy,
even though they soon discovered their differences: there is an often repeated story that
on honeymoon they sat on the beach at Scheveningen side by side, hand in hand, but
facing opposite ways – for she loved to look at the sea and he could not bear it.[2] By 1908
their family was complete, with one son, Robert, and four daughters, Barbara, Ursula,
Elisabeth and Mary ('I suppose,' Mary Lutyens has recently written, 'we were lucky in
that none of us was called Gertrude').[3] Ned's dream of a little white house to share in
peace with Emily and the children did not materialize. They lived at 29 Bloomsbury
Square, over the office,[4] and even the comparatively small amount of time he seemed to
spend there, between endless excursions to clients, houses and sites, was spent working
at his drawing board. It was the old, old tale of neglect in the face of the search for
success, and though neither of them wanted it that way, Emily did not help. After a
brief early effort she found architecture boring, and absolutely refused to entertain any
of his clients or to modify her aristocratic attitude of mind which refused to understand
the driving force of vocation within him. Sadly, it was her 'not of this world' aura which
had attracted him and inspired him so in the beginning – it was what he loved most in
her and continued to adore always. Perhaps, like most men of achievement of his age,
he needed a comforting and domesticated wife to soak up the frustrations of his career,
as well as a woman to inspire him; in many marriages it was the lot of the woman to try

to be both, but Emily would not try. Her great belief in spiritual attainment as more important than anything social or practical (or indeed, even artistic) was to take her off on the long pilgrimage after the star of theosophy – a twenty-year search which she has described with disarming frankness in her book *Candles in the Sun*. She left him spiritually, and physically as well, often dragging the children off behind her. Throughout this period Lutyens worked even harder, and became ever more tolerant and also more guilt-ridden and miserable about losing her, despite the flow of daily (sometimes twice daily) letters which neither of them could, or would, stop writing. Today it is commonplace to mix Eastern mysticism with Western traditions, but then, seventy years ago, to the apostle of Edwardian sensuality, to the gentle architect of an age learning to express its desires with a new honesty, Emily's need for theosophy must have been an especially bitter blow. 'The new attitude of dedicated holiness now inculcated in us inclined us to consider him an "outsider" – a vulgar, meat-eating, ordinary being, too insensitive to have received the call,' was Elisabeth Lutyens's memory from that time.[5]

Outside his home there were, of course, many who were only too pleased to receive him, to whom he showed none of his sadness. (Indeed, it must have been that the more delightful and lighthearted he appeared to those who met him over the years, the more lonely he became inside.) He was wined and dined all over London and wherever he went; his jokes and good humour, his unabashed frankness which sometimes got him into trouble, made him an exciting, if unpredictable, dinner guest. One place where his eccentricities were matched was at Renishaw, the Sitwell home in Derbyshire, where he was a frequent visitor prior to the outbreak of the War. They were working visits (he made slight alterations to the house), and one imagines that he and Sir George talked endlessly about gardens, but there are no Lutyens touches to the Renishaw garden. Buried in the Renishaw archives, however, is a plan for a little garden, with much stonework and water, which he designed for Sir George's amusement and which was attached to a cottage at the park gates – The Green at Eckington (no. 87 in the Survey, page 172). Lutyens also tried to convert Sir George to Jekyll planting – Miss Jekyll was asked to do a late summer border of pinks and blues and a scheme for a green alley, both of which were rejected, altered with many crossings-out, and never materialized.[6] However, in *Great Morning*, that evocative book of the dying moments of the Edwardian age, Osbert Sitwell has left this legendary description:

One had never seen before, and will never see again, anyone who resembled this singular and delightful man. An expression of mischievous benevolence was his most distinguishing mark, as it was that of his work. He would sit, with his bald, dome-like head lowered at a particular angle of reflection, as his very large, blue, reflective eyes contemplated a view, a work of art, or something peculiarly outrageous that he intended shortly to say. Meanwhile, he held in his mouth, rather than smoked, a small pipe . . . and when he spoke his speech tumbled from his mouth, like that of an impetuous schoolboy.[7]

The commission for the Imperial capital of India at New Delhi marked the end of the great years of garden designing; what had started with Lutyens's disillusionment at the

108. Edwin Lutyens: portrait by Augustus John (1917).

Villa d'Este, seen on a visit to Italy as designer of the British pavilion for the Rome International Exhibition of 1911, followed by trips to South Africa and India,[8] all leading to more commitments than one hard-working human frame could cope with, meant that it was the gardens that had to go. Miss Jekyll, in her turn, had been chiefly occupied with Lutyens's gardens and with growing and selling her own plants from Munstead Wood, as well as with her books,[9] but now she turned to other clients as Lutyens's work tailed off. In 1911 her private commissions jumped to ten, including her best surviving water garden, planted in a tree-shaded dell at Vann near Hambledon in south-west Surrey. Most of her other gardens were small, some just border plans, as they were in 1912 when her commissions included the small formal garden in Godalming which still survives in good condition as a memorial to the radio officer of the *Titanic*, John George Phillips, who would not leave his post. In 1913 she did eleven commissions, mostly in Surrey and Sussex, and during the war years she added another thirty clients

109. Gertrude Jekyll: portrait by William Nicholson (1920).

to her long list.[10] In 1917 she planted the borders at Barrington Court in Somerset, the only survivor of her planting schemes before the restoration of Hestercombe.

As a farewell to all that the country houses had stood for, Lutyens designed Ednaston Manor near Brailsford in Derbyshire for William Player in 1912. Building started in 1913, but was stopped by the War, and the house was not finished until 1919; however, Ednaston belongs firmly to all that had gone before. It is the most elegant, cool and finely balanced symmetrical house of them all. The formal garden is small – a walled terrace parterre with herring-bone brick paths on the south front and open to the fields on the south side [colour pl. 22], and a more intricate double terrace with brick retaining walls dropping to a level lawn and orchard on the east; these gardens were not planted by Miss Jekyll but have been lovingly tended by the Player family. Planting in the Jekyll tradition has been retained; on the south terrace parterre are found some of the rarer plants and plant relationships that once bloomed at Munstead Wood – *Carpentaria californica*, with large single white flowers, with cistus and potentillas, and *Clematis* 'Nellie Moser' twining with a Banksian rose; blue Himalayan poppies, *Meconopsis betonicifolius* (*M. baileyi*), naturalized beneath the azaleas and the Himalayan rose which has flourished so well at Ednaston that it has grown up and over a large holly tree, and moss roses grown on tripods with clematis growing with them.[11]

War

In March 1912 Lutyens set out on the first of an incredible eighteen voyages to India, which were to occupy most of the winter months of every year until 1930, the last visit being in the autumn of 1938, and to dominate the rest of his life's work. In August of 1914, with the outbreak of war, Emily and the children were sent out of London and he worked long days, and into the nights, alone. Delhi became more difficult and politically involved; perhaps the only spark of pleasure was the summer of 1916, the summer of the Somme, which the whole family spent at Folly Farm – almost the only time that he lived in one of his own houses, or in the country with a beautiful garden.

The following year he was asked by Fabian Ware of the Imperial War Graves Commission to go to France and see the battlefields so that he could give his recommendations for the design of cemeteries and memorials. For one who felt unable to express himself in words, the letters to Emily from France at this time offer a profound description of the pity of war: after the lines that preface this chapter, he continued:

The graveyards, haphazard from the needs of much to do and little time for thought – and then a ribbon of isolated graves like a milky way across miles of country, where men were tucked in where they fell – ribbons of little crosses, each touching each across a cemetery – set in a wilderness of annuals, and where one sort of flower has grown the effect is charming, easy, and oh, so pathetic, that one thinks no other monument is needed. Evanescent – but for the moment almost perfect . . .[12]

Lutyens and Herbert Baker were appointed principal architects to the Commission in 1918 (at a salary of £400 per annum, and expected to devote half their time to the work), and their combined influence formed the Commission's 'style' which is still adhered to today.[13] Lutyens was responsible for the design of 128 cemeteries, together with the great Thiepval Arch on the Somme, the Arras Memorial, the Australian National Memorial at Villers Bretonneux, and at home, in Whitehall, the Cenotaph, named from his memory of a long-vanished Olympian stone seat beneath a silver birch tree – the Cenotaph of Sigismunda – in the garden at Munstead Wood.[14]

In his report to the War Graves Commission, Lutyens had noted that while it was 'important to secure the qualities of repose and dignity there is no need for the cemeteries to be gloomy or even sad-looking places'.[15] He advocated that good use should be made of the best and most beautiful flowering plants, and for advice on this aspect he naturally turned to Miss Jekyll. It seems that she designed detailed plans for some cemeteries, and from then on her ideas were adapted to form the continuing policy of the Commission, so that the lovingly tended gardens which we can still see today are in fact closely related

110. (*above*) War Graves: Warlincourt Halte British Cemetery at Saulty. This was the first cemetery for which Lutyens asked Miss Jekyll's advice; it was undoubtedly his determination that the cemeteries should not be 'gloomy', and her desire to bring the flowers of home to the foreign fields, which set the pattern for all the cemeteries of the Commonwealth War Graves Commission.

111. Warlincourt Halte British Cemetery at Saulty, near the Arras–Doullens road: sketch plan for entrance layout and planting, with two pyramid oaks and a carpet of *Berberis aquifolium* (which was kept down to 2 inches) around the Great Stone. The photograph [pl. 110] shows that the oaks have been replaced by columnar evergreens, and there is grass in place of the berberis.

1:100

to Miss Jekyll's original designs. The War Graves Commission have no surviving records of this planting, but the Reef Point Gardens Collection contains the complete planting plans for five cemeteries which were Lutyens's responsibility – Warlincourt Halte British Cemetery at Saulty [110, 111], Hersin Communal Cemetery, Gezaincourt, Daours and La Neuville British Cemetery at Corbie. The layout plans for each were sent to Miss Jekyll from Lutyens's Queen Anne's Gate office, with his notes on the surroundings and the soil conditions. The over-riding impression in these plans is her concern to bring the flowers of home to these foreign fields, and her sensitive acknowledgement of the nationality of those who rest there.

The planting details in the five sets of drawings vary slightly, but in general her recommendations were for surrounding the cemetery with a holly or yew hedge with native trees planted for shelter, while the fastigiate oak or Lombardy poplar were chosen as symbolic trees for focus planting. Borders and spare pieces of land were planted with shrubs, the workaday shrubs of the English country lanes – blackthorn, whitethorn, hazel, guelder rose and honeysuckle. The ground was scattered with spring flowers – daffodils, Lenten roses, fritillaries, forget-me-nots; and the borders where the headstones stand were to contain the most familiar flowers of English gardens – foxgloves, columbines, London pride, bergenias, nepeta, and, of course, plenty of roses.

For Lutyens the years from 1918 to 1922, apart from the winter trips to Delhi, were almost entirely taken up with memorials. The long lists of those he designed recalled his haunts of happier times, for he built the war memorials of many towns and villages where he was known for his houses and gardens – Southampton, Leicester, Stockbridge, Shere, Stow-on-the-Wold, Rolvenden, Busbridge near Munstead, and Abinger in Surrey amongst them.[16] The war itself, his visits to the battlefields where he saw the full horror of what those at home could only dimly understand, long hours working on never-ending streams of memorials for little pay and with the prospect of more remunerative commissions faint indeed – all this had a deep and lasting effect on this vulnerable and ingenuous man. Part of his vulnerability, and equally part of his lively genius, was due to his childish delight in the fun that was to be had out of life; he believed that architecture was a game, to be played with gusto, and that one must never become too solemn or too full of pretensions to play games. However, his faith in his fellow players, and perhaps in his own ideas, was severely shaken at this time. With the coming of peace he soon regained his outward aplomb, but the gardens, where his inner self had found expression in the real joy of creation, were never to be quite the same.

Gardens Again

At Gledstone Hall in Yorkshire and Tyringham Park in Buckinghamshire, Lutyens returned to garden designing, but in a severely classical style which was now applied to the gardens for the first time.

He had met Amos Nelson, a Lancashire mill-owner, on one of the interminable passages to India. Nelson had recently acquired a 5,000-acre estate near the Yorkshire borders at Skipton, with a rather 'unwieldy' Georgian mansion by John Carr of York. The first intention had been to alter this mansion, but that was probably before the meeting with Lutyens, who now had the reputation and charm to be very persuasive – and Amos Nelson was convinced that he would be better off with a new Gledstone Hall. The result is usually recognized as one of Lutyens's best classical houses, but I find it very cold, and from the garden Gledstone is the product of a mind that has seen too

112. Gledstone Hall: an original *Country Life* photograph of the canal garden.

many memorials. Even more than the house, the garden architecture has a massive, pristine solidity against which mere plants do not stand a chance – part of the trouble being that the design is of the warm south, whilst the planting has to contend with the bleak wind that blows across these Yorkshire moors. The same garden concepts are there – the steps come down from the south front of the house to a long tank garden, with a sheet of water, beautifully levelled, to lead one's eyes to the hills, flanked by huge retaining walls with double-bordered walks on the top level [112]. The refinement of the geometry and the finish of the stonework make Hestercombe seem cottagey, and the symmetry is devastating, but somehow it isn't a game any more. And it isn't a garden for pleasure, either; even if those great walls offer shelter, walking beneath them makes you feel like a dwarf, out of scale, and there is no kind path to lead – one is left to pick a way around the beds stuffed with bergenias, iris and *Rhus cotinus* (for quick effect). Miss Jekyll never saw this garden, and down in gentle Munstead Wood she could have no idea of how harsh and dour Yorkshire could be; she noted the need for the plants to be *strong*, and the clumps of bergenias – which were her special solution to this need – are quite effective. She packed the top borders with yuccas, lupins and great clumps of grasses, and the terrace parterres with roses, but without success. Such institutional severity could not easily be softened.

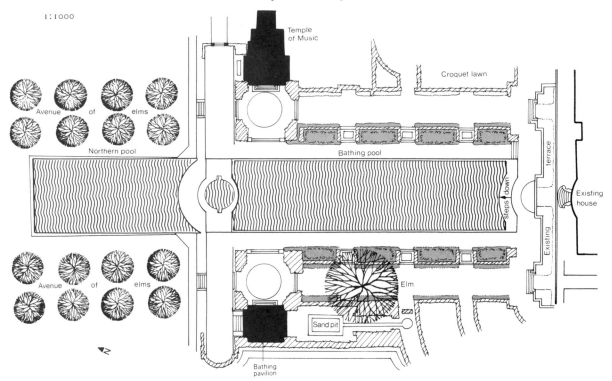

1:1000

113. Tyringham Park: sketch plan of Lutyens's garden added to Soane's house. The layout is governed by the axes from the house and its surrounding terrace, and the bathing pool is 60 feet wide, flanked by Lutyens's Temple of Music and the bathing pavilion.

In a Buckinghamshire setting at Tyringham the classical theme was played with much greater reward. Here the key was the house by Sir John Soane, built in 1792 – a small squarish house of three white bays, the central one bowed and rising to a dome which had been added since the original building of the house. It is set in a park originally landscaped by Humphry Repton. It was an unusual situation for Lutyens because the garden side faced north, to a distant but low-key view over fields [113]. His central axis was extended 450 feet from the central door, and a strip 60 feet wide was, in the manner of a magician, turned to a sheet of water; on a centre 290 feet from the door he crossed the canal with a wide grass walk which extended the full width of the garden area, ending in a semi-circular enclosure at one end and passing through a field gate at the other. Where the grass crossed the canal it was widened to accommodate a central circular pool where two Doric columns were raised – rather reminiscent of the Canopus Canal at Hadrian's Villa – with a lead spouting leopard by William McMillan clinging to the top of each one. The larger canal was in fact a swimming pool with full-width and luxurious semi-circular steps into the water at each end; the pool was flanked by gravel walks (centred on secondary axes from the existing terrace steps) and enormous box enclosures. The farther pool was architecturally much more simple. It was for pleasing the eye only, it was less emphatically framed in white stone, and it made an effective transition to the gentle fields and trees beyond. In the southern angles of the crossing Lutyens sited two classical temples, four-square with enormous pediments and plain domes, which faced each other across the water. One is a temple, the Temple of Music dedicated to 'The Supreme Spirit Author and Guide of the Universe'. Lutyens built this garden for a Silesian banker and his wife, the Konigs, for whom music was a passion – but somehow the spirit of this temple expresses exactly his own ideas of where his God was to be found.[17] To underline the theme that is Tyringham's – that a healthy mind and healthy body are equally divine – the other 'temple' is skilfully divided into changing pavilions. Tyringham was finished in the mid 1920s, a peculiarly apt expression of the mood of its time far removed from any relationship with the previous gardens of the partnership, a mood to which the beautiful people of the Konigs' week-end parties, sporting in their undress, added the necessary decoration. The planting was confined to the box borders, and though these would make very suitable settings for single-colour themes *à la* Jekyll, there is no indication that it either would have, or did, appeal to her at the time. She was over eighty, and much of her time was occupied with schemes for 'natural' planting for Ursula Ridley at Blagdon and Edward Hudson at Plumpton Place – Lutyens, it seems, tactfully declined to involve her in this alien situation.

For all it may be hard to appreciate (some may find it refreshing) after the Edwardian gardens, Tyringham has been elaborately praised as a garden suited to the reputation of the great architect Lutyens had now become (the Tyringham temple domes not only complement the house dome, they remind us that Viceroy's House at Delhi was nearly finished), and as a 'classical' garden it is undeniably beautiful.

Tyringham is contemporary with a little-known and very different garden at Amport House near Andover in north Hampshire. Here Lutyens returned to his old trick of upstaging an ugly house – gauntly Victorian again, built for the 14th Marquess of Winchester in 1857, and now owned by old clients of his, the Sofer-Whitburns, for whom he designed the garden. He designed it for Miss Jekyll, too, for it exploits delightfully all the themes she most enjoyed, and her planting schemes are clearly the result of considerable work and much pleasure. The garden consists chiefly of an expansive water terrace, or terraces, on two levels above the rolling chalk of the Hampshire downs [114; colour pls. 23, 24]; the centrepiece of the first level is a large oval pool, with double edgings forming an oval iris rill, filled (as at Deanery Garden over twenty years before) with *Caltha palustris*, golden club and water plantain in alternate clumps. The water is taken from each end of the pool via iris rills to square pools on the right angles, and then proceeds down to the next level and two more square pools before flowing to the sides of the terrace to be collected for re-circulation. The design is symmetrical and it ends suddenly, above the fields, with a ha-ha and double borders which were to be decorated with twin garden houses, but these were never built.

Apart from the planting of the iris rills and water-lilies in the pools, Miss Jekyll went to considerable trouble in choosing roses for the beds around the square pools, and the

114. Amport House: one of the symmetrical sets of lily pools and rills on the lower terrace level. Some of the rose beds can be seen on the upper level.

result represents hcr association with the famous rose breeders, Dickson's of Newtownards, County Down, with whom she had a close business relationship at the time. All the roses chosen for Amport House come from their 1927 Hawlmark Catalogue, and reflect her appreciation of the blush and salmon shades of hybrid teas which they were developing. The Amport planting was for eight bushes of each variety, a single variety in each bed, carefully shaded in their juxtaposition: Betty, coppery splashed golden yellow, was next to Joseph Hill, pink-salmon with copper on the outside petals; Château de Clos Vougeout (a Pernet-Ducher rose), velvety scarlet shaded fiery red, was a neighbour to Emma Wright (McGredy), a pure orange, and Los Angelos (Howard Smith), salmon shaded apricot. Another relationship was formed with beds of her much-used favourites; K of K, semi-double scarlet, Red Letter Day, velvety scarlet, cooled with Mrs David McKee, dreamy warm yellow, and Ethel Malcolm, a creamy ivory white. A final delicate group included her old friend Dean Hole, silvery carmine shaded salmon, Madame Abel Chatenay, carmine rose shaded salmon, and the pale rose-coloured Lady Ashtown.

Miss Jekyll's other indulgence at Amport was the rock garden, an enclosed layout of raised rectangular beds (possibly raised for the convenience of an ageing Mrs Sofer-

142

Whitburn) off the east end of the terrace, containing lavender, hyssop, santolina, iberis, nepetas, rock pinks, ferns, sedums and yuccas. I have reproduced the plan of this rock garden as she obviously enjoyed it so much [115, 116].[18]

Amport's water terraces, with their intricate horizontal pattern but minimal sculptural effect of either architecture or planting and complete avoidance of any integration with the surrounding landscape, are a unique, and untypical, work of the partnership. The garden is completed by a parterre with the Winchester coat of arms on the west side of the house – mid-Victorian – and an 'orchard' of cordon limes, now in a splendid condition, which is also thought to pre-date the water garden. (There is no record of Miss Jekyll suggesting the limes.) But everything comes to an abrupt stop at the field boundary, where the field falls away gradually to the valley below – and perhaps with more time, and more time to be interested, the partnership would not have allowed this to be so (though of course the land is highly valuable agriculturally, which is not the case in Surrey). Nonetheless the sureness and simplicity of the design is impressive.

The partnership was again in harness on a unique and charming commission. In the early 1920s Lutyens was asked to design a dolls' house, which would be the gift of the nation to Queen Mary as a token of affection, a means of raising money for her favourite charities, and a record of a disappearing lifestyle. Many of the best-known artists and designers of the day (Russell Flint, Edmund Dulac, William Nicholson, John Nash and Paul Nash) were among the artists who did miniature paintings; Belloc, Chesterton, Housman, Hardy and Kipling were included in the long list of writers of special texts for the library books; craftsmen and household names (Hoover, Colman's Mustard, Rolls-Royce) were contributors to fitting out the house down to the smallest details, and Miss Jekyll was asked to design the garden. 'The grass is of green velvet . . . On each side of the paved central path are two groups of flower beds, planted with clumps of blue and purple iris, with a standard rose at each angle, and a filling of summer flowers, lilies and orange tiger-lilies, carnations, sweet peas, poppies, marigolds, gentians and fuchsias.'[19] There are terracotta pots of agapanthus, hydrangeas and rhododendrons in tubs, and miniatures of Lutyens's garden seats. The flowers are all of painted metal – though not done by Miss Jekyll herself because her eyesight was too bad by this time – and the whole garden is planted in a drawer with the yew trees fixed to fold down over the rest of the planting. She also included a fairy ring of toadstools, butterflies, snails and a thrush's nest full of eggs.

The Partnership Fades

In the 1920s Lutyens was at the peak of his reputation and career, and at the point when his peripatetic existence was at its farthest from the ordered pacing of the seasons which governed life at Munstead Wood. His daughter Elisabeth had tried to take her missing mother's place – she visited clients with him and acted as hostess for luncheon parties at the Garrick. She writes: 'After years of loneliness he was slow to realize that it was

1:200

115. (*opposite*) Amport House: Miss Jekyll's plan for the raised-bed rock garden – patience will reveal the beds to have been complementary. Bed A was probably in the shade of large trees, beds B and C are a variation on the same theme, beds F and G look complicated but are basically *Senecio greyii* surrounded by groups of iris and purple sage, with santolina and catmint on the outer rings for further contrast. Bed H is mainly statuesque crinums and yuccas, with carpeting to provide an impressive view from the steps. The dotted lines indicate elevations.

Key to the planting:

1. *Yucca filamentosa*
2. *Yucca gloriosa*
3. *Santolina chamaecyparissus*
4. Rock pinks
5. Iris 'Purple King'
6. Hyssop
7. 'Ver. tobar', which I can neither trace nor identify as a hebe
8. Dwarf lavender
9. Nepeta (catmint)
10. Iris (early yellow)
11. *Stachys lanata*
12. *Campanula carpatica*
13. Phlox (*amoena*), rosy pink rock variety (*subulata?*)
14. *Lithospermum prostratum* (*diffusum*)
15. *Armeria maritima alba* (white thrift)
16. *Iberis sempervirens* (candytuft)
17. *Ophiopogon Jaburan*! (described in the Munstead catalogue as 'neat plant, with sword-shaped leaves and spikes of purple flowers in late autumn')
18. Iris 'Purple Shadow'
19. *Sedum spectabile*
20. *Sedum telephium* 'Munstead Dark Red'
21. *Skimmia japonica*
22. Hartstongue fern
23. Male fern
24. Helianthemum (sun rose) (rose pink variety with dark green foliage)
25. *Veronica traversii* (now *Hebe brachysiphon*)
26. *Sedum spurium* (dark red variety)
27. *Othonopsis cheirifolia* (in the Munstead catalogue as a plant for sunny aspect with thick glaucous leaves and deep yellow daisy flowers)
28. *Sisyrinchium bermudianum* (blue flowers)
29. *Pterocephalus parnassii* (grey cushion, pink flowers, scabious-like)
30. Mossy saxifrage (pink-flowered)
31. *Polygonum affine*
32. *Phlox stellaris* (a rock phlox with lilac-white flowers)
33. *Helianthemum* 'Hanbury' (probably a yellow variety)
34. *Asarum europeum*
35. *Asphodelus luteus*
36. *Hebe buxifolia*
37. *Papaver rupifragum* (now *alpinum?*) (dwarf perennial poppy with apricot flowers)
38. Helianthemum (with coppery flowers)
39. *Bergenia ligulata*
40. *Saxifraga decipiens* (red-flowered)
41. *Silene alpestris* (neat variety with clear white flowers)
42. Dwarf ivy (green and gold leaves)
43. Golden thyme
44. *Iris foetidissima*
45. *Senecio greyii*
46. *Iris florentina*
47. *Iris pallida dalmatica*
48. Purple sage
49. *Cistus formosus* (now *Halimium lasianthum*) (low spreading shrub with greyish leaves, golden yellow flowers)
50. Teucrium (cream-flowered variety)
51. 5 white crinums
52. *Aster corymbosis* (late-flowering, dwarf and white)
53. *Fuchsia magellanica gracilis*
54. Centranthus (red valerian)
55. *Yucca recurva*
56. 5 purple crinums
57. Lady fern
58. *Cerastium tomentosum*
59. *Cineraria maritima*
60. *Veronica prostrata* (*rupestris*)

Note: The plant list reveals the Amport rock garden to be one of Miss Jekyll's feats of alpine expertise – however, most of the plants are still available from an alpine and rock garden specialist such as W. E. Th. Ingwersen Ltd, Birch Farm Nursery, Gravetye, East Grinstead, W. Sussex RH19 4LE.

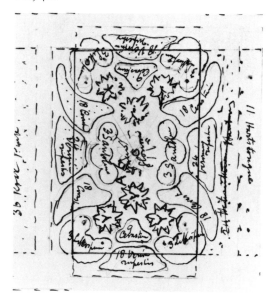

116. (*above*) Amport House: part of Miss Jekyll's original planting plan for the rock garden.

possible for one of his family to need him and respect him as a great artist, but gradually he began to take me into his confidence.'[20] A frequent guest at the luncheons was E. V. Lucas, who has sketched the public face:

His eyes grow merrier, his spectacles ever rounder, his head loses a hair here and there, but he is still undefeated, still an eternal child, an apostle of beauty and thoroughness, a minister of elvish nonsense. He builds a New Delhi, eighty square miles of palaces and avenues, he builds a Queen's Dolls' House, an affair of inches but such that Japanese cherry stone carvers could not excel. His friends are legion; his mind electrically instant to respond to any sympathetic suggestion; he never broke his word, he never let you know if he was tired, and with it all he was out for fun.[21]

This view, from the lunch table at the Garrick, is almost the last we shall have of Lutyens, for he remained like this for the rest of his life; perhaps most of the aspects of this complex genius have been captured in the portrait by Augustus John, painted in 1920 [108].

At Munstead Wood, which Lutyens rarely saw now but heard of through friends and letters, life had slowed down at last. Miss Jekyll had been eighty in 1923, but her days were still full of interest and variety. She had returned to recording the ways of the simple country life which was disappearing around her, and *Old English Household Life* was published in 1925. Throughout the 1920s she still planned about ten gardens a year, but never saw any of them, and her correspondence about these and other gardening queries kept her busy. Although the last of her gardening books was published during the war (*Garden Ornament*, 1918), she still wrote articles based on her notes of progress and experience at Munstead, and some of these were published as *A Gardener's Testament* after her death. Both she and her garden were now very famous, and she frequently pleaded for peace; by 1925 she was forced to rest in the afternoons, which cut into her precious day.

In 1930, after twenty years' building, Lutyens's answer to the medieval builders, Castle Drogo on the edge of Dartmoor, was at last finished. When Julius Drewe started the castle he was given a glowing recommendation to Miss Jekyll: 'a great designer, an artist, old and experienced in the ways of plants and a lover of the wilderness and moorland'[22] was how Lutyens referred to her in a letter, and Drewe was duly sent to see her at Munstead. His first consideration had been the approach to the building then starting, which was to be a dramatic demonstration of the art of concealment, for the traveller along the narrow, high-hedged lanes from Drewsteignton village is given no glimpse of his destination. The drive to the castle leaves the road via a semi-circular clearing marked with *Quercus ilex* and twists and turns up the slope, heightening the expectation to fever pitch, only revealing the castle itself at the last possible moment. Drewe was very anxious that this approach should retain its moorland character, and Miss Jekyll had responded with a sympathetic planting of holly, birch, Scots pine and rowan, with drifts of dog roses, *Rosa polyantha*, *Cistus laurifolius*, tamarisk and blackthorn to which Drewe added heather, bracken, broom and foxgloves. This seems to have been the extent of Miss Jekyll's involvement; perhaps Drewe found the leafiness of Munstead too unsympathetic to his Dartmoor home, and perhaps she refused to argue with a man with whom she could have had little in common. There are no further records of Miss Jekyll's dealings with Drewe, and Lutyens was left to struggle on alone; though the two men built up a firm friendship on the basis of their strongly held, and differing, opinions regarding the building of the castle itself, they never reconciled their differences over the garden. In October 1915 Lutyens produced an isometric sketch of his ideas for a garden on the south-east front of the castle, which entailed much buttressing and intricate level-changing to cope with the steep fall of the ground. He also planned a lodged entrance into a formal courtyard on the north side, which was never built. By 1920 the design had been reduced in scale but intensified and made more formal, with the inclusion of features which most of the other gardens show – herbaceous borders, a fig court garden with domed circular pools recessed under the walls, and a large circular garden with tiers of grass and borders focusing on a central pool, very much in the style of the Italian oval at Heywood. Here we seem to come to the crux of the Drogo problem – Lutyens, schooled in Miss Jekyll's Mediterranean tastes, had envisaged a castle of the South, with its courts and bowers elaborated by his geometrical games, whereas Julius Drewe's illusion of himself was as a latter-day lord of the North, whose castle must look like a stronghold.

As a result of this impasse, Drogo has no garden near the castle. Some time in the 1920s Drewe brought in George Dillistone, a garden designer from Tunbridge Wells who had worked for him at previous houses in Sussex and Torquay, and Dillistone appears to have transferred the bones of Lutyens's 1920 design to the spacious sloping hillside north-east of the castle. It has thus become a retreat garden, which may be a feasible idea for a castle, but in divorcing Lutyens's axial design from the source of its axes, the doors and windows of the castle, Dillistone made a nonsense of the orderly format which had been the partnership's abiding rule – that formality must flow from the house and fade as it meets the natural landscape. Drogo's garden perhaps represents the mood of the 1920s, the new bravado which saw the old rules as there only to be broken.

In 1927 Lutyens designed a house known as 3100 Massachusetts Avenue, Washington D.C., which is the British Embassy in the United States. The garden, also designed by him and possibly after discussions with Miss Jekyll, is ultimately suited to its purpose, for diplomatic parties in the grand style, and for the private amusement of the Ambassador and his family and staff. There is an elaborate raised rose parterre on the south front, with wide steps leading down to a spacious lawn. On the west side the scale is more intimate, with a sheltered walk to the swimming pool and enclosed tennis courts – which, here, being an accepted part of the image of diplomatic life and purely functionally sited, are acceptable, where they seem oddly unsuited to an English garden. Both the Embassy and Tyringham remind us how the sporting of lightly-dressed bodies in healthy recreation was very much the motivation of the 1920s *beau monde*, and it was something with which the partnership's ideal of a garden could not really contend. Even Lutyens's inventive mind could only cope with a swimming pool when it was on

117. (*above*) Plumpton Place: the rose borders planted between Lutyens's clapboarded entrance lodges.

118. (*opposite above*) Plumpton Place: an old *Country Life* photograph of the border by the lake.

119. (*opposite below*) Plumpton Place: Miss Jekyll's last fling – a striking gathering of astilbe and gladiolus.

Tyringham's Olympian scale, and his tennis courts were always hidden behind walled enclosures. This failing (though to be fair, it is a failing which no one has yet overcome) produced the final irony of the Drogo garden, a sad postscript to the fading partnership. When Dillistone re-used Lutyens's design he stretched it, as on a rack, on to the hillside, with the yew-walled rectangle filled with flower borders on the lower level; the approach to the garden from the castle enters here and climbs the slope, through an informal planting of azaleas, maples, magnolias and spring flowers – a charming but incongruous woodland interlude – to the climax of both the design and the hillside, a great formal yew circle set on a 900-foot height. As the climax of the design the yew circle contained, of all things, a tennis court.[23]

It was also in the late 1920s that Edward Hudson found his last house, a moated manor called Plumpton Place, north-east of Brighton, which Lutyens altered for him as well as modifying a near-by mill house and building a clapboarded range of entrance lodges. The garden planning and planting was the subject of a long correspondence between Hudson and Miss Jekyll, both now considerably mellowed with age. Her enjoyment of natural planting, which became so evident in these final years, was encouraged by Hudson – 'I don't want what I call the *swagger* sort of gardening,' he told her. Along with his letters he plied her with snapshots of the areas to be planted, and

though Plumpton has been much altered and no coherent picture can be obtained, there are some delightful vignettes to be imagined. From the rose garden between the lodges [117], Lutyens bridged the moat to a footpath crossing the parterre in front of the house. A spring scheme for this parterre is mentioned – orange and brown wallflowers with Pride of Haarlem and Clara Butt tulips. On the west side of the house is the large lake, and the lakeside walk was flanked with a herbaceous border in the best Munstead tradition – bergamot, *Helenium pumilum* and orange African marigolds giving a splash of colour in the centre, with echinops, shrub roses, iris, Japanese anemones, all shading to pink at one end and purple at the other [118, 119]. The Mill House garden was planted profusely, but naturally, with nut and fruit trees – medlars, quince, crab-apples – and drifts of daffodils, primulas, Solomon's seal and hellebores with bergenias and acanthus for emphasis. The mind that had made Munstead Wood was still very active. For Christmas 1929 Hudson sent Miss Jekyll a card with a photograph of the Plumpton garden, 'from one who has been honoured by your kindness and friendship for so many years', with a note to the effect that the planting was being carried out as she suggested; later he sent more photographs for her to see the progress.[24]

Besides these last efforts on behalf of Edward Hudson, Miss Jekyll was working hard for Lutyens's daughter Ursula, who having married Viscount Ridley in 1924 found the grey skies and cold winds of his ancestral Blagdon in Northumberland very discouraging. The magnificent yew-framed border planned has been described in Chapter 2, but Ursula had also had the brilliant idea of turning an old stone quarry near the house – where the cold winds could not reach – into a garden. Miss Jekyll was planning the quarry garden, of which part of her plan is reproduced [120], in the spring of 1928, and though Ursula grew impatient for the old lady to complete her task, her letter to Ursula of 7 June shows how, though she was nearly blind and very frail, her mind's eye for beautiful garden pictures never failed: of the mass of rock rubble in the quarry she said, 'They should look as if it was a sort of moraine of debris and pieces of rock fallen from the cliff to be planted with gentians . . . saxifrages and alpine campanulas . . . and so on.' As will be seen from the plan, the quarry was turned into a dell of daffodils, followed by peonies and iris beneath perfumed and flowering shrubs; Ursula complained that Miss Jekyll's liking for holly would make the place too dark, but in the end she was delighted with the results of the planting.[25]

The grand finale for the partnership must of course be Delhi – the making of a garden for Viceroy's House, New Delhi, which Nikolaus Pevsner called 'the greatest folly in the world'.[26] The garden on the west front of Viceroy's House (now Rashtrapati Bhavan) is like no other in the Lutyens canon. It is called a formal Indian garden – it is 700 feet wide and the walk from the loggia exit of the house (though it is more aptly described as a palace) to the potting sheds at the farthest end is almost a quarter of a mile, a walk which only the garden boys would have been expected to take very often. Eight tennis courts take up but a fraction of the space, and the major part is an utterly fantastic parterre where water is the dominant theme, though hardly on the scale of its treasured use in traditional gardens of the East. Here the life-giving liquid is proffered flagrantly to the absorbing sun in a series of magnificent pools and canals and tiered fountains,

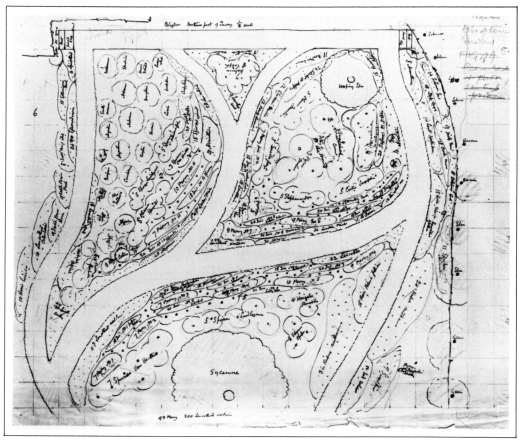

120. Blagdon: the quarry garden. Miss Jekyll's planting plan for the north part of the quarry, with drifts of peonies and iris among *Olearia haasti*, amelanchier, cistus, and *Sorbaria tomentosa* (*Spirea lindleyana*).

designed to represent the leaves of the giant *Victoria Regia* water-lily. The planting between the pools is of rose gardens and stone boxes of shrubs, and in the centre of the garden a raised green lawn stands both as a symbolic triumph for the English way of gardening, and as a carpet intended for the vice-regal garden party tent. Beyond the parterre an Indian version of a pergola, which seems to have borrowed the horns of a dozen sacred cows, arches between the walls which hide the tennis courts, leading to a walled circular garden with tiers of planting and a central pool – Heywood again, but on an enormous scale reminiscent of a Roman amphitheatre. And that is just where this garden belongs, as the eighth wonder of the world, to rank with other miracles of empires that have gone.

Curtain Fall

At the end of her book *Candles in the Sun* Lady Emily Lutyens tells how, in 1930, she gave up following her theosophical star and returned to her husband, and how their last years together were among their most settled and happy.

At Munstead Wood the light was fading, and the average of ten gardens a year – all by correspondence – slipped to five in 1929, two in 1931 and one in 1932; Miss Jekyll's efforts for Ursula Ridley and Edward Hudson had been her last performances, and with the ending of the year she died peacefully. She would have been most happy to know that Lutyens and his family enjoyed her house the following summer: 'We adored it. It was dark and cool, specially designed for her dimming sight, with long galleries overlooking the wonderful garden, large rooms and quiet corners, the whole house redolent of wood-burning, pot-pourri and furniture polish. Outside there were flower borders for each month of the year and grass paths stretching from the house, past beds of lilies of all kinds, to coppices of trees on a bed of wild flowers'.[27] At the end of the summer they left Munstead for always – Lutyens did not see it again, and the garden did not long outlive its mistress.[28]

Miss Jekyll's death was followed by a particularly unhappy footnote to the partnership. In 1933, somewhat belatedly and after many arguments, the Irish government decided that there should be a memorial to the 49,000 Irishmen who had died fighting in the First World War, and though it may have been obvious at the time that Lutyens was the architect to choose, the choice cannot have helped to smooth the path of history. He designed the elaborate Park of Remembrance at Islandbridge by the Liffey in 1936 – ten acres laid out with a stone of remembrance flanked by fountains, they in turn flanked by the four classical book rooms and two circular, tiered sunken gardens with central pools. It was somehow the monumental simplicity of all those other memorials, overlaid with the grandeur of Delhi and yet tinged with the delight of the tiered oval at Heywood and memories of so many other happier gardens, gathered into a fatefully sensitive whole. The projected bridge over the Liffey was never built, and the Park of Remembrance lies isolated, neglected, and largely forgotten.

In 1929 Lutyens had received the commission for his cathedral at last – the Roman Catholic Cathedral of Christ the King in Liverpool was to be the homage of his art to his much-neglected God, and its design completely occupied the last years and thoughts of his life. He was elected President of the Royal Academy in 1938, and in 1940 he started work with the Academy's committee for the rebuilding of London which it was hoped would take place after the War. In 1943 he was given an honorary fellowship of the Institute of Landscape Architects, though this was for his work on the London Plan and not connected with garden design. It seemed that the cathedral and his dream of the new London had, by the mystical echoings of fate, brought him to stand beside his spiritual mentor, Christopher Wren, at last. But he was too late, and neither were to be. Sir Edwin Lutyens died, with his wife and his unfinished cathedral drawings by his bed, on New Year's morning of 1944.

6

A RECKONING

Architects find in gardens a just sphere for design, but they cannot be expected to have a wide knowledge of horticulture. Miss Jekyll added to this knowledge an intimate sense of design and Sir Edwin's association with her in the joint labour of design and planting led not only to the splendid results in individual gardens, but also to the widening of his outlook on the whole question. It was an ideal partnership.

Sir Lawrence Weaver, 1925[1]

In common with the best stories, circumstance and fate here played their part; if Miss Jekyll had not met Ned Lutyens in that Surrey garden in May 1889 then it seems certain that neither these gardens, nor many of the country houses, would have been designed.[2] The circumstances of the meeting would not have borne much alteration, for Lutyens's strong sense of his own vocation would have brooked no competition from a younger partner, and yet it was just this spark, of what may so easily be called genius, that Miss Jckyll needed. She did planting schemes for many other architects – Robert Lorimer, Herbert Baker, Hugh Baillie-Scott and later Oliver Hill among them[3] – but always only on a distantly polite professional basis; in 1901 Emily Lutyens wrote that 'Bumps' had told her sister Betty Balfour (for whom she would have been planting Fisher's Hill garden at the time) that 'the difference between working with Ned and Lorimer was as between quicksilver and suet'.[4]

Though the pooling of skills which Lawrence Weaver describes might seem obviously desirable, it has rarely been achieved on the terms in which Lutyens and Miss Jekyll understood their partnership, that is to say, on *equal* terms, with an equal contribution to both the conception and the creation of the design. In the history of landscape design only the brief partnership between John Nash and Humphry Repton in the 1790s, of which Luscombe Castle in Devon is the most notable survivor, would seem comparable.

The partnership was, therefore, both uniquely fortuitous *and* unusual, and while these two aspects have inspired nostalgic affection for these gardens, they must also govern any assessments which may be made. If the gardens beckon our hearts from beyond an abyss of war, industrial depression and national decline, then the judgements of our minds must also be tempered by these changing circumstances. The judgements of the years since the partners' deaths have, however, been far from understanding.

The Commentary of Hindsight

It is clear from the quotation at the beginning of this chapter that Lawrence Weaver valued the partnership. His appreciation was also reflected by their friends and contemporaries after first Miss Jekyll and then Sir Edwin died. In *Architecture and Personalities*, Sir Herbert Baker, one of their oldest friends (with whom they had both had their differences), added his view of the relationship: 'This intimate friendship was, I think, the most valuable influence on his early career. She had a great personality and rare gifts; she was a skilled craftswoman and not only an expert gardener, a planter of flowers, but she had a painter's sense for arrangement in colour harmonies. But her outstanding possession was her power to see, as a poet, the art and creation of home-making as a whole in relation to life; the best simple English country life of her day, frugal yet rich in beauty and comfort . . .'5

There were many other fittingly elegiac appreciations, which effectively drew the curtain on a vanishing world but did little to recommend the value of the partners' work to the newcomers, those in architecture and landscape, who were taking on the challenge of the sprawling suburbs and expanding towns of between-the-wars Britain. Even by the time of Miss Jekyll's death in 1932, garden design was being seen as a somewhat trivial art, for the decline of the partnership had coincided with the rise of the new profession of landscape architecture, and if close and equal partnership between an architect and a gardener had been unusual before, it was now thought undesirable: both an architect with a feeling for landscape, such as Lutyens had, and a gardener with artistic vision, as Miss Jekyll was, were encroaching on the role which the new profession saw as its own. It will be remembered that Miss Jekyll had come to her gardening as a plantswoman; her childhood interest in wild and garden flowers had developed into a considerable knowledge from her travels and her visits to country house gardens all over Britain. She had joined the ranks of the Royal Horticultural Society and taken her place with ease in a company devoted to the breeding, nurture and glorification of all garden plants. If she had not met Lutyens, she would probably have stayed a plantswoman, and remained in our memories beside Ellen Willmott and Dean Hole primarily because of the flowers she grew and loved; but by working with Lutyens she stepped across the very thin, but very definite, dividing line between gardener and garden designer. She was probably aware that this was a dangerous step, for in her books on garden design – *Gardens for Small Country Houses* and *Garden Ornament* – she carefully clung to an architectural co-author, first Lawrence Weaver and later Christopher Hussey, so as to be fore-armed. In both these books, and especially *Gardens for Small Country Houses*, first published in 1912, she represents an England covered with gardens of a uniform charm and order, all with straight lines and convenient enclosures, with fine brick and stonework and lush planting, all speaking of the good sense and propriety that she regarded as English virtues. She illustrates the work of the sixteenth and seventeenth centuries and of contemporary designers – C. E. Mallows, Inigo Triggs, Walter Cave, and of course Lutyens – and she comments on the design of 'hard' features in the garden – walls and pavings, pools and pergolas. Though, as far as I am aware, she never actually designed any of these formal features herself, and her own garden layouts always seem to have been governed by the rule that what was best for the plants was best for the garden, she was seen as an advocate of the architect as playing a lead in garden design, something the new men no longer wanted to see. The re-issue of *Garden Ornament* and *Gardens for Small*

Country Houses during the 1920s enshrined these formal tastes as hers to an audience of plantsmen who felt she was guilty of defection, to a rising number of small garden owners who could no longer afford such luxuries, and to a new breed of garden architects who were facing a dilemma of their own.

This dilemma concerned the state of garden design in Britain, where the modified formalism of the partnership and its contemporaries was meeting a new wave of natural and free-flowing design ideas. Concern for the resultant disarray had been countered by the formation of the British Association of Garden Architects in 1928, but it soon became clear that it was not simply the old formal versus natural argument all over again, but that B.A.G.A. consisted of two definite factions – those who wanted to design gardens on one hand, and those with rather larger spatial ambitions on the other. The struggle was short-lived, the garden connotations were hastily buried, and the Institute of Landscape Architects was born in 1929. The new Institute set out to take up the challenge of the open landscape outside garden walls, and its first President was none other than Thomas Mawson, who had had his non-discussion with Lutyens as far back as 1908 and had come a long way since, but by quite a different path and without much sympathy from either of the partners.[6] Garden design was left to the few élite, who had the charisma to draw clients who could afford the luxury of a professionally designed garden, but without Lutyens's adventurous spirit they achieved only tasteful imitations. As gardens grew smaller, the partnership's gentle progression from house into landscape became less and less relevant, but as there was nothing to take its place the translation of garden design into modern terms was achieved elsewhere – in the Europe of the Bauhaus, under the Californian sun, and then with influence from Japan and finally from South America, where Burle Marx has turned form and planting to abstract art.

The only English visionary who did influence garden and landscape design was Christopher Tunnard, and it was Tunnard who looked at Miss Jekyll and saw only that she had failed. Though he went to America because he saw that his ideas would have little relevance in war-torn Europe, Tunnard's *Gardens in the Modern Landscape*, published in 1938, was a product of his English experience. In it he compared and contrasted Miss Jekyll with Claude Monet: having called her 'the most outstanding planter since the eighteenth century', and noted how Monet's lifelong struggle to capture colour, form and light on canvas was unfinished, yet his achievement an encouragement to others, he continued to compare them:

Both had an almost primitive love of the soil, a passion for gathering from Nature the nourishment to sustain burning convictions and long-cherished beliefs. Both preferred an existence withdrawn from civilization, surrounded by familiar, daily-renewed contacts with the lesser animate things. Both suffered from failing eyesight and both achieved greatness through work and the love of the tools and methods they employed ... BUT there is one fundamental difference in their achievements. Monet, in his later years, planned and made an inspired garden, a painter's garden indeed, but an achievement acknowledged to be equal of some of his work on canvas. Jekyll, the amateur artist, on the other hand, though accomplished enough as a technician was not of the calibre of Jekyll the planter. If she had been able to express herself as well with the brush as with the planter's hand, the problems of light and colour which she constantly disregarded might have been recognized and solved. As it was, in upsetting the crude Victorian paintpot, she failed to provide an alternative large enough to serve as a source of inspiration to posterity.[7]

Tunnard's criticism was based on Miss Jekyll's long perpetuated reputation as a 'great artist', but it would seem that the interpretation of the word 'artist' has been misleading. For her reputation as a *painter* we have only contradictions: her desires and her education were for painting, she knew (and presumably benefited from knowing) many great painters, and she worked and studied hard, especially at copying the masters – and surely copying a Turner demands more than average talent? However, of all this work the only certain evidences are 'Cheeky', the portrait of her brother's dog exhibited at the Royal Academy, and some paintings of bulls, which remain with her family – neither being the expected legacy of an embryo Impressionist. She often wrote that her failing eyesight had forced her to surrender her artistic ambitions when she was in her thirties, yet it never stopped her working on intricate planting plans and writing long letters right up until the end of her long life. And those many planting plans, now in the Reef Point Gardens Collection, may be models of efficiency, and even the forerunners of all planting plans that have followed, but they are always only efficiently drawn and sometimes the draughtsmanship is rather pedestrian – especially compared with the brilliant and inventive sketches by Lutyens which often cover both his plans and her own. (The only solution to these contradictions is that, having painted 'in the shadow' of Brabazon since she was about twenty-four, and then having seen what the world of art did to his reputation and life's work in the 1920s, her paintings were consigned to a ritual pyre at Munstead Wood.[8]) It would thus seem that Herbert Baker was using his words carefully and exactly when he described her as having the power to see 'as a poet, the *art* and creation of home-making as a whole in relation to life' – and this was indeed her art, being no more of a painter than a poet, as the often Herculean prose of her books well shows. Therefore, Tunnard was unjust to liken her to someone with whose talents hers were not comparable, and the tale of her early life would seem to force the conclusion that though hers was rather more than an average drawing-room talent, it was not of the brilliance or endurance that a professional reputation demands.

The essence of all these contradictions was that Tunnard's criticism was read where it would have most effect, among the rising ranks of professional landscape designers, and Miss Jekyll was accordingly dismissed by the profession which should have guarded her legacy. It was a very elevated dismissal, for she was swept on to a pedestal, along with the legends of Munstead Wood, the supposed mystique of the colour rules, and her close association with a great architect. Landscape designers, looking for a professional aura of their own, avidly adopted the architectural themes of contrasting form and texture, and of spatial composition (much to the continuing amusement of architects), to govern the concepts of good planting design, but Jekyll planting itself was consigned to history as being too complicated, too labour-intensive and too expensive for modern use, and the adaptations were usually to someone else's credit. No one acknowledged that she had felt her demonstrations of colour and of the magic of light to be better achieved in reality, and in words, than on canvas. The nature of her writing and her extensive and extensively-displayed knowledge make each of her books something of a pursuit course in Latin nomenclature, and this, combined with the fact that the books have been out of print for so long and are now both rare and expensive, means that they have become prized by enthusiasts of garden history rather than as working manuals. But, most tragically of all, the reality has been allowed to fade; if by some miracle the gardens had survived intact, who knows what inspiration would have come from the sun-spattered 'flowery incidents' of the Munstead woodland, from the tapestried richness of the piazza at Marsh Court or the magical dell of Blagdon quarry? If her books were not enough, then these and a hundred delightful garden pictures were her legacy, and if they have failed to inspire us, it is our fault, but not hers.

The turmoil in the world of landscape design in the 1920s and 1930s was, of course, only a shadow of what was happening to architecture. Lutyens, with his country houses and their gardens to all intents and purposes hidden by his great city buildings, Delhi rising and the war memorials, found himself a paradoxical figure, occupying a position 'of splendid if puzzling isolation in national architecture' in the 1920s.[9] His belief in architecture for art's sake found no sympathy in the schools of rising architects being processed to strain after functionalism, Le Corbusier and concrete. Even though in 1932 he warned a group hopefully entitled the 'Tomorrow Club' that they would have to fight for their profession because 'the Architect is shelved like a bottle of flavouring on a kitchen dresser, to be used in small quantities as taste demands', he was not heard.[10] Though he told them that the only way to make the public appreciate architecture was to observe the rules of unity, method, scale, rhythm, time *and* tradition, and so blast apathetic eyes open to beauty, they would not listen. When he died, surrounded by the cathedral drawings and great London plans, with his funeral taking place in Westminster Abbey and his ashes placed in the crypt of St Paul's, the paradox turned to legend. The publication of the Lutyens *Memorial* in 1950 – long announced, massive, 115 pages of analysis and praise, 338 pages of perfect drawings (to call them *working* is hardly appropriate), and 1,000 pristine, statuesque and unreal photographs, a tribute such as no one but Wren had been accorded – just removed him farther into the realms of the divine. In his review of these tomes, Nikolaus Pevsner had to come to the conclusion that Lutyens was, 'without doubt, the greatest folly builder England has ever seen. Castle Drogo beats Fonthill, the Drum Inn at Cockington beats Blaise Castle and the Viceroy's House at Delhi beats any other folly in the world.'[11]

The Present Position

So, with the reputations of their makers elevated beyond practical use, what happened to the beautiful houses and gardens that they had made? They were launched into the unsympathetic air of the mid-twentieth century and the perils of the open market, into an age in which architecture had indeed become a little-used flavouring, occasionally desirable for prestige purposes but very rarely understood. In the final analysis, the making of the gardens at the last possible moment in history turned out to be too late.

The partnership was really too late in a purely personal sense. Just as Miss Jekyll's experience was so necessary, her increasing age limited the scope of the achievements. In 1893, when Woodside's sculptured vista was cut into a Buckinghamshire field, she was fifty; during the next ten years she and Lutyens worked closely together to transform Surrey traditions into beautiful houses and gardens, and they discussed and made over forty gardens during this time. But just as they were, professionally, moving beyond the Surrey confines, Miss Jekyll 'retired' to Munstead Wood and more or less ceased travelling. For another nine years their rapport carried them through another twenty houses and gardens, most of which Miss Jekyll never saw, and it was just when this rapport was wearing thin that Lutyens became 'imperial' architect. The higher and farther he flew, the more she – now very stout and painfully short-sighted – retreated into her Munstead burrow; the War came , and only out of its dire circumstances came another spark of collaboration, when Lutyens remembered the comforting flowers of her gardens and decreed their presence in the war cemeteries, to the eternal gratitude of the mourning relatives of that, and another, war. The gardens which came afterwards show two minds diverging, and while Lutyens wins the approval of those who tend his architectural reputation for the classical beauty of Tyringham's canal and temples, it was a garden where the site and planting did not count. Miss Jekyll, in her turn, was clearly more interested in natural planting, but without Lutyens to extend her vision the physical as well as the visual connection between the garden and the landscape was not made with the mastery the partnership had once used to fit the houses and gardens into their sites. It must also be regretted that their treatment of water never had the chance to develop beyond the high point of formality in the tank cloister at Folly Farm – if only she had been ten years younger, who knows what ingenuity we would have seen?

More than ever, though, it has become a matter of money and changing values, and the gardens have been catapulted into an age in which their costs, and the costs of their maintenance, are unbelievable. Tales of how Lutyens 'broke' his clients are legion, but he certainly did not do it to make his own fortune, and his buildings and gardens were expensive because the materials and the craftsmanship that he demanded, even in those days, exacted a high price. Allusions to costs are rare, and have to be multiplied at least twenty times to reach a comparative understanding in today's terms. Money first really entered Lutyens's life (much to his annoyance) when the Countess of Lytton stipulated that he must earn £1,000 a year to keep Emily in anywhere near the manner to which she was accustomed. When they were looking for their first home, and he fell in love with 29 Bloomsbury Square, he worked out that to live there (rent, taxes, insurance, living and staff) would cost him £1,450 a year, and to clear this he would need to get £29,000 'of work in a year', thus he was taking 5 per cent.[12] He was to be dogged by money troubles all his life, worried about tax when fees came in large lumps, never able to afford to build a house for himself, always aware of the need for economies with fuel, lighting, etc., and in general he hated talking about and dealing with money. On this basis, however, and remembering that a man with £1,000 a year at the turn of the century was very comfortably off, Lutyens's few references to costs show just how more than comfortably off his clients needed to be. The early Surrey houses and gardens probably cost their owners (including Miss Jekyll) between £6,000 and £10,000 (i.e. between £120,000 and £200,000); in 1905 Lutyens wrote about Nashdom at Taplow: 'Princess Dolgorouki wants for £6,000 what I can do for £20,000', and an estimate of £15,000 was eventually settled on. He felt he had found wealthy clients in the Fenwick family, for whom he altered Temple Dinsley in Hertfordshire in 1911 (and built Abbotswood), and he hoped they would spend £20,000, which seems to have been his 'ideal' sum. For Heathcote at Ilkley the lowest estimate was £16,300 for the house only, though £10,000 had been the limit set by the client, with another £10,000 allocated for the 'garden and finishing'. The eventual contract sum for Heathcote was £17,500. Against these comparatively modest houses, Castle Drogo was estimated in 1910 at a cost of £60,000![13]

After the war, with the consequent spiralling in costs, such patronage required even greater wealth. Sir Amos Nelson, who is reputed never to have quite understood what he was letting himself in for with Gledstone Hall, is quoted as saying in 1927: 'Gledstone did not cost half a million, it has not cost a quarter of a million, but beyond that I do not care to say.'[14] Sir Amos must have been one of Lutyens's wealthiest clients, yet even he had to stop the bills: the main entrance drive and half the garden at Gledstone were never completed – at these rates, even for a place in the history of architecture, the price was obviously just too high.

The Survey

It is in these contexts that the surviving state of the gardens must be seen, and the following pages contain my survey of the gardens of the partnership made between the years 1891 and 1937. I have interpreted the word 'partnership' in the broadest sense, and entered all the gardens where there is documentary or visual evidence of both partners having been involved. Gardens made after Miss Jekyll's death in 1932 are included because they were still 'her' gardens in influence, as were all the garden works which Lutyens did; however, the gardens which she planned exclusively for her own clients, in the main 'natural' gardens which have not survived well, and in which Lutyens played no part, are listed separately as Appendix A (page 188).

My Survey numbers the 112 gardens, and lists them in order of the date of design, though in many cases construction was a protracted process. The names of the original clients, with their connection with the pattern of partnership if this is known, are also given. The whereabouts of significant design information is included, as are indications as to the present use and ownership of the garden. I have made some comments on the present state of gardens where this is relevant, but in the main this is indicated by a 'star' rating, for which the key is as follows:

  †   indicates the death of a garden
  *   garden just about revivable at considerable effort and expense
  **   garden still existing but with original design altered
  ***   original design surviving but showing its age
  ****   original design surviving in good condition

Further key reference

R.P.G.   Reef Point Gardens Collection at the Documents Collection,
          College of Environmental Design, University of California, Berkeley 94720, U.S.A.
R.I.B.A.D. Royal Institute of British Architects, Drawings Collection,
          The Heinz Gallery, Portman Square, London w1
C.L.   *Country Life* Library, I.P.C. Magazines Limited,
          Kings Reach Tower, Stamford Street, London se1
L.W.   Lawrence Weaver, *Sir Edwin Lutyens' Houses and Gardens*,
          Country Life, 1921 (see also Note 3 to Introduction)

1891

1. THE RED HOUSE, Effingham, Surrey (now Corpus Domini Convent) †
   Client: Miss Susan Muir Mackenzie.
   Miss Mackenzie was a friend of Miss Jekyll; The Red House is now greatly altered and only faint Jekyll touches to the garden remain. Afterwards, Miss Mackenzie moved to another house in Effingham called The Hermitage, which was not designed by Lutyens but for which Miss Jekyll did a garden plan with some planting details (R.P.G. Folder 3).

2. EATON HALL, Cheshire (house largely demolished but gardens remain) ★★
   Client: The Duke of Westminster.
   Plan for a parterre garden by Lutyens (R.I.B.A.D.). There is nothing to indicate that Miss Jekyll did the planting, but this small (and prestigious) job for Lutyens undoubtedly came via her connection with the Duke, for whom she had designed embroideries and interior decorations (see F. Jekyll, *Gertrude Jekyll: A Memoir*, p. 100).

1891–1902

3. CROOKSBURY HOUSE, near Farnham, Surrey ★
   Client: A. W. Chapman.
   Some planting sketches (R.P.G. Folder 5); photographs (C.L.).
   This was the first Lutyens/Jekyll garden of any size, but very little of the original design survives. Arthur Chapman was married to Agnes Mangles, Harry's sister; Agnes was thought to be rather beautiful and had been painted by Charles Lutyens, Ned's father – thus, out of this connection both Ned's career and the partnership with Miss Jekyll were born.
   Private house, in split ownership.

1892

4. WOOD END, Witley, Surrey (now Orchards) ★★★
   Client: Lady Stewart.
   Lutyens altered the house and it is a Jekyll-only garden of dry walls and flower beds.
   Private house.

1893

5. WOODSIDE, Chenies, Buckinghamshire (now Chenies Place) ★★★★
   Client: Adeline, Duchess of Bedford.
   Garden layout plan published (L.W.); no planting plans; photographs (C.L.).
   The first garden of the formal partnership which has survived very well; it has been

fortunate in a succession of careful owners and is structurally sound. The original house (not designed by Lutyens) has been split into two, but the whole of the garden design is with one half.

6. CHINTHURST HILL, Bramley, Surrey ★★★★
   Client: Miss Aemillia Guthrie.
   Jekyll terrace and border planting plans (R.P.G. Folder 4).
   The house, the terraces and lower garden are in very good order, and restoration of the planting would complete a fine partnership work. The R.P.G. Collection plans are for a 'grey border', for which the plants cost £6 14s. 0d., and a double herbaceous border, 180 feet long.
   Private house.

   1894

7. RUCKMANS, Okewood Hill, Surrey
   Client: Miss Lyall, the sister of Mrs Robert Webb of Milford Manor.
   No plans have been found.
   Lutyens converted the house from a traditional Surrey cottage, and there is a 'cottagey' garden which has Jekyll touches, but has been much altered in recent years.
   Private house.

   1895

8. LASCOMBE, Puttenham, Surrey
   Client: Colonel Spencer.
   No plans have been found.
   Another Jekyll 'cottagey' garden.
   Private house.

9. MUNSTEAD CORNER, Godalming, Surrey (now Munstead Place)
   No plans have been found.
   A Jekyll natural garden across the lane from her own house.
   Private house.

   1894/6

10. MUNSTEAD WOOD, Godalming, Surrey ★
    Client: Miss Gertrude Jekyll.
    Layout plans and planting plans published in Jekyll & Weaver, *Gardens for Small Country Houses*; Jekyll, *Colour in the Flower Garden* and other books; also articles and photographs (C.L.). R.P.G. (Folder 1) has some Jekyll sketch plans, Lutyens's details and the original survey of the site by Peak, Lunn and Peak, dated 1883.
    Private house (see also Nos 11, 12, and 13).

    c. 1896

11. THE HUT, Munstead, Godalming, Surrey ★★
    Client: Miss Gertrude Jekyll.
    The Hut (built by Lutyens, 1894) was surrounded by the June garden, the plan for which is published in *Colour in the Flower Garden*, Ch. 5.
    Now a separate private house.

12. THE QUADRANGLE, Munstead, Godalming, Surrey (originally Munstead Wood's stables and workshops.)
The garden of The Quadrangle occupies what was most of Miss Jekyll's kitchen garden and nursery ground.
Private house.

13. MUNSTEAD ORCHARD, Godalming, Surrey (originally the head gardener's cottage at Munstead Wood)
The garden of Munstead Orchard was probably always separate from the main garden, but now contains the Thunder House, which Lutyens designed for Miss Jekyll to watch the storms over the Wey valley.

1896

14. SULLINGSTEAD, Hascombe, Surrey (now High Hascombe) ⋆⋆
Client: C. A. Cook.
No plans have been found, but the shape of the garden layout remains, and Jekyll planting is now being restored.
Private house.

15. HEADMASTER'S HOUSE, Charterhouse, Godalming, Surrey ⋆⋆
(See Note 37 to Chapter 2.)
(R.P.G. Folder 8) contains some Jekyll sketches for the Headmaster's Garden; part of this has been built over.

1897

16. FULBROOK, Elstead, Surrey ⋆⋆
Clients: Mr and Mrs Gerard Streatfield.
No garden plans have been found, but old photographs (some C.L.) show a terraced garden with rose beds and a rose pergola which was largely the work of Mrs Streatfield, with possibly a little advice from Miss Jekyll. The garden is in good condition but Lutyens's pergola has been demolished.
Private house.

17. BERRYDOWNE COURT, Ashe, Overton, Hampshire ⋆⋆
Client: Mr Archibald Grove.
No garden plans have been found. Probably built by Musselwhite's of Basingstoke. Fine walled entrance court survives, as does the walled kitchen garden, both definitely Lutyens's designs, but the flower garden is nondescript.
Private house.

1898

18. HAZELHATCH, Burrows Cross, Shere, Surrey ⋆⋆⋆
Client: The Hon. Emily Lawless.
Lutyens built this small house, which was surrounded by a Jekyll-inspired woodland garden at Miss Lawless's request – she was a great naturalist. The essential spirit of the woodland survives.
Private house.

19. THE RED HOUSE, Charterhouse, Godalming, Surrey ⋆
    Client: The Rev. H. J. Evans (see also Note 37 to Chapter 2).
    Lutyens built this house for the retiring Chaplain of Charterhouse School. The garden is on a steep slope, and was tiered with dry stone retaining walls falling to a woodland dell – it was a real Jekyll *tour de force* and of her many vanished dry walls it is probably the one most worth restoring, though it would take effort and expense beyond the abilities of a private owner. Ample similar planting information survives in *Wall and Water Gardens* and *Gardens for Small Country Houses.*
    Private house.

20. ORCHARDS, Munstead, Godalming, Surrey ⋆⋆⋆
    Clients: Sir William and Lady Chance.
    House and garden layout plan published (L.W.), but no planting plans have been found; photographs (C.L.)
    Orchards represents the single most important house and garden of the partnership for the period before 1900, and it is certainly one of the most important 'heritage' houses of Surrey of any age – and yet it has been allowed to slip from our grasp and is now being converted to split ownership. This development is especially tragic as Orchards had been maintained in a style to which it was accustomed until a very short time ago; for the sake of Lutyens's reputation it would have been much more appropriate if circumstances had brought Orchards into the care of the National Trust, rather than either Lindisfarne or Castle Drogo.

21. WITWOOD, Park Road, Camberley, Surrey †
    This small Lutyens house survives but its garden does not. No plans have been found.

    1898–1904

22. LES BOIS DES MOUTIERS, Varengeville, Seine Inférieure, France ⋆⋆⋆⋆
    Client: M. Guillaume Mallet.
    The Mallets introduced Emily Lutyens to theosophy.
    Some Jekyll planting plans (R.P.G. Folder 36). The form and layout of the garden is in splendid condition and still in the ownership of the Mallet family.
    Private house, but garden frequently open.

    1899

23. LITTLE TANGLEY, Wonersh, Surrey ⋆⋆
    Client: Mr Cowley Lambert.
    Some planting plans survive (R.P.G. Folder 11) for early Jekyll borders and an altered layout (1912) by Miss Jekyll which was not carried out.
    Now in split ownership as private houses.

24. OVERSTRAND HALL, near Cromer, Norfolk
    Client: Lord Hillingdon.
    No plans survive, and there is no evidence that Miss Jekyll did the garden; however, immaculate borders and lawns provide a fine setting for the Lutyens house, beautifully cared for.
    Now The Leicester Home.

25. THE PLEASAUNCE, Overstrand, near Cromer, Norfolk ***
    Client: Lord Battersea.
    No plans have been found, though the garden, with its superb barrel-vaulted 'pergola', was obviously Lutyens's design; there is again no evidence of Miss Jekyll's involvement, but the sunken parterre garden would be much improved with Jekyll-style planting.
    Now The Christian Endeavour Holiday House.

26. TIGBOURNE COURT, Witley, Surrey ***
    Client: Sir Edgar Horne.
    No plans have been found, but a Lutyens/Jekyll country garden with flat terrace, pergola, rose and shrub borders survives.
    Private house.

27. STOKE COLLEGE, Stoke by Clare, Suffolk **
    Client: Lord Loch, the Countess of Lytton's brother-in-law, who advised her that Ned should be earning £1,000 a year before he could marry Emily and that the couple's feelings should be tested by a year without communication while Ned made the effort! Lord Loch obviously felt that, after they were safely married, a little commission would help – Lutyens altered this house slightly, but his influence on the garden is vague.
    Now a school.

28. LITTLECROFT, Guildown, Guildford, Surrey †
    No plans have been found; another tiered hillside garden which has gone.

29. GODDARDS, Abinger Common, Surrey ****
    Client: Sir Frederick Mirrielees.
    Garden layout plan published (L.W.), but no planting plans have been found. Photographs (C.L.).
    Private house.

30. PASTUREWOOD HOUSE, Holmbury St Mary, Surrey (now Beatrice Webb House) ****
    Client: Sir Frederick Mirrielees.
    No plans have been found.
    Lutyens built a small extension to this Flockhart house, with a large pergola. Miss Jekyll planted a large hillside rock garden.
    Now the Fabian Society Conference Centre.

    1900

31. WINKWORTH FARM, Hascombe, Surrey **
    No plans have been found.
    Lutyens visited the house in 1900 and there are fragmentary alterations by him; also good Jekyll features in the garden – dry walls, a dipping well and wisteria growing over cherry trees – and it is almost certain that she knew the garden, which was latterly the home of Dr Wilfrid Fox, the maker of near-by Winkworth Arboretum (National Trust), who also must have influenced the present planting.

32. FISHER'S HILL, Hook Heath, Woking, Surrey *
    Client: The Rt Hon. Gerald Balfour, M.P. (Emily Lutyens's brother-in-law).
    No plans have been found, but a list of plans with names of garden borders survives (R.P.G. Folder 15).
    Private house in split ownership.

33. GREY WALLS, Gullane, Lothian, Scotland ★★★
    Client: The Rt Hon. Alfred Lyttelton, M.P.
    Garden layout plan published (*The Memorial*, Vol. 1); photos (C.L.); no planting plans and probably not Jekyll planting, though still influenced by her.
    Now the Grey Walls Hotel.

1901

34. THE DEN, Pershore, Worcestershire
    Client: Mr H. Avery, who wrote to *Country Life* (c. 15 April 1901) asking for the name of an architect to do a garden sloping down to the river. Apparently Lutyens was recommended.

35. DEANERY GARDEN (now The Deanery), Sonning, Berkshire ★★★★
    Client: Mr Edward Hudson.
    Garden layout plan and some planting plans with photographs in *Gardens for Small Country Houses*; some plans for house and garden (R.I.B.A.D.); some plans and sketches (R.P.G. Folder 19); photographs (C.L.). Regrettable addition of a swimming pool.
    Private house, but garden occasionally open for charity.

36. ABBOTSWOOD, Stow-on-the-Wold, Gloucestershire ★★★★
    Client: Mr Mark Fenwick.
    Lutyens sketch layout for part of the garden (R.I.B.A.D.); photographs (C.L.). Built by Cubitt & Company.
    Private house, now owned by the Dikler Farming Company; the garden is open during the spring and summer for charity.

37. MARSH COURT, Stockbridge, Hampshire ★★★
    Client: Mr Herbert Johnson.
    Garden layout plan published (L.W.); photographs (C.L.); some Jekyll planting plans for later work on the garden (R.P.G. Folder 44).
    Now a boys' preparatory school.

38. HOMEWOOD, Knebworth, Hertfordshire
    Client: The Dowager Countess of Lytton.
    No plans have been found, and it is not known whether Miss Jekyll did the garden.
    Private house.

39. ST PETER'S HOME, Woolverstone, near Ipswich, Suffolk ★★
    Client: Mr C. H. Berners.
    No plans have been found.
    Nice paved rose garden, borders on south garden front and long walk with Lutyens's *clair voyée*.

1901 onwards

40. FOLLY FARM, Sulhamstead, Berkshire ★★★★
    Clients: Mr H. Cochrane/Mr Z. Merton.
    Garden layout plan published (L.W.); photographs (C.L.); some Jekyll planting plans (R.P.G. Folder 52).
    Private house, but garden frequently open during the summer.

1902

41. THE HOO, Willingdon, Sussex ★★★★
Client: Alexander Wedderburn, Q.C.
No plans have been found; photographs (C.L.).
The house is privately owned and now turned into flats, but the garden is a model of fine conservation.

42. LITTLE THAKEHAM, near Pulborough, Sussex ★★★
Client: Mr Ernest Blackburn.
Garden layout plan published (L.W.); not Jekyll planting.
Now Little Thakeham Hotel.

43. MONKTON HOUSE, Singleton, Sussex ★★
Client: Mr William James.
No plans have been found; photographs (C.L.); the house is still in the same family ownership, but the garden has been altered by Mr Edward James, who is quoted as disliking Lutyens's 'cottagey' gardens.
Private house owned by The Edward James Foundation.

44. AMMERDOWN PARK, Radstock, Somerset ★★★★
Client: Lord Hylton.
Complete plans of the garden have been published (*The Memorial*, Vol. 2); photographs (C.L.); not Jekyll planting though she knew the garden.
Private house.

45. THE MANOR HOUSE, Mells, Somerset ★★★★
Client: Sir John and Lady Horner (his ancestor was the original Little Jack Horner, and the 'plum' he pulled from the pile of monastic deeds he was sending to the King was Mells Manor).
No plans have been found, but both Lutyens and Miss Jekyll were frequent visitors to Mells Manor (Miss Jekyll was related to the Horners by the marriage of her brother Herbert to Lady Horner's sister, Agnes Graham) and contributed to the garden.
Private house.

1903

46. WARREN LODGE, Thursley, Surrey †
Client: Mr Robert Webb.
Lutyens was working on alterations to this house at the time of his marriage and spent part of his honeymoon there; his sketch layout plan for the garden survives (R.P.G. Folder 31), but bears no resemblance to what is now there. A pity.
Private house.

47. BUCKHURST PARK, Withyham, Sussex
Client: Mr R. H. Benson.
There are Lutyens's plans for this garden (R.I.B.A.D.) and many features remain.
Private house.

48. PAPILLON HALL, Lubenham, Leicestershire †
Client: Mr Frank Belleville.

Part of the garden layout is published (*The Memorial*, Vol. 1); photographs (C.L.).

The 'butterfly' plan was popular at that time but no architect had a better excuse than Lutyens: Papillon Hall was built on the site of a seventeenth-century house which belonged to a Huguenot refugee, David Papillon, whose Spanish wife was reputedly murdered, leaving a curse on her home to the effect that tragedy would befall anyone who removed her slippers from a hiding place within the walls. The slippers were carefully preserved in the house Lutyens built, but were stolen by an American serviceman during the Second World War – after that the Belleville family and their house were haunted by the dreaded ill-luck, and both house and garden were razed to the ground in 1950. Only a few hummocks in a field survive of the white, roughcast house, with formal courts and terraces within the 'wings' of the plan which once looked out over the misty Leicestershire countryside.

49. LINDISFARNE CASTLE, Holy Island, Northumberland ★★★★
Client: Mr Edward Hudson.
Miss Jekyll planned the planting of flowers and vegetables for a small walled garden (R.P.G. Folder 91), which is now being restored.
The Castle is owned by the National Trust and open as advertised.

50. DANESHILL, Basingstoke, Hampshire †
Client: Mr Walter Hoare.
No plans have been found. The house has been converted to office use and the garden completely altered.

51. POLLARDS, Nightingales Lane, Chalfont St Giles, Buckinghamshire
Client: Mr Archibald Grove (he bought this after selling Berrydowne Court).
Some planting information (R.P.G. Folder 41); it seems that Archibald Grove asked Miss Jekyll about the garden, but, after disagreements over Berrydowne, he wouldn't let Lutyens near the house!
Private house.

1904 onwards

52. ASHBY ST LEDGERS, Northamptonshire ★★★★
Client: The Rt Hon. Ivor Guest, M.P. (later Lord Wimborne).
Complete layout plans and some planting plans for this garden survive (R.P.G. Folder 47); photographs (C.L.).
Private house.

1904

53. MILLMEAD, Bramley, Surrey ★★
Client: Miss Gertrude Jekyll.
Complete garden layout plan and most planting plans published (*Gardens for Small Country Houses*); photographs (C.L.); some plans and sketches, mostly duplicates of those published, survive (R.P.G. Folder 35). For many years Miss Jekyll owned this house and it was let to a 'suitable' tenant, but it was eventually sold.
Private house.

54. LAMBAY CASTLE, Lambay Island, Rush County, Dublin, Eire ★★
Clients: The Hon. Cecil Baring (later Lord Revelstoke), a close friend of Lutyens; Mary Lutyens has written: 'Father always seemed at his happiest with the Barings' (Mary Lutyens, *Edwin Lutyens*, p. 67).
Layout plan published (*The Memorial*, Vol. 1), and good planting plans survive (R.P.G. Folder 56); photographs (C.L.).
Private house.

1905

55. NASHDOM, Taplow, Buckinghamshire (now Nashdom Abbey) ★★
Client: H.H. Prince Alexis Dolgorouki.
No plans have been found, and possibly not originally Jekyll planting, but there is a lovely round pergola'd rose garden (revivable) by Lutyens. He thought it a 'really lovely site' when he saw it in July 1905, 'but quite unsuited to the house' that the Princess Dolgorouki insisted on building. The great bastion terrace necessitated by the site originally led down to a tennis lawn and flower borders, which have now been replaced by vegetables, carefully tended by the Brothers of the Anglican Benedictine Order whose monastery it is.

56. GARDEN AT ESHOLT, Sheffield
Client: Mr A. J. Hobson
No plans have been found. Lutyens priced the work for a small garden at £500.
I have not traced this garden, but I hear from Dr Michael Tooley of Durham University that he has, though nothing significant survives. (Dr Tooley is restoring the Lindisfarne Castle garden; see also his article 'Gardens designed by Miss Gertrude Jekyll in Northern England', *Garden History*, Vol. 8, no. 3, 1980.)

57. KNEBWORTH HOUSE, Hertfordshire
Client: The Earl of Lytton.
A plan for a five-circle herb garden for Knebworth by Miss Jekyll survives (R.P.G. Folder 61); see also Note 5 to Chapter 3.
Knebworth House garden and country park are open all the year.

58. ESHER PLACE, Esher, Surrey ★
Client: Lady Helen Vincent.
No plans have been found. Lutyens wrote on 11 August 1903 (Lutyens Family Papers) of Esher: 'a rotten place for a home – all garden facing N – nothing south.' His first plans were vetoed (for garden features only, the house being a French Château of 1895–8 by Robinson and Duchene), but an amphitheatre and small formal garden, both with Lutyens characteristics, remain. Part of the formal garden now belongs to 7 The Gardens.
Now the Electrical and Plumbers' Trade Union Training College.

1906 onwards

59. HESTERCOMBE, Kington, Somerset ★★★★
Client: The Hon. E. W. Portman (later Lord Portman).
Complete garden layout published (*The Memorial*, Vol. 2); photographs (C.L.); some Jekyll planting plans owned by Somerset County Council and kept at the house; others (R.P.G. Folder 77).
Now owned by Somerset County Council as Fire Brigade Headquarters. The garden is open regularly during the summer months.

19. (*above*) Marsh Court, Stockbridge, Hampshire: the pergola which springs from the house walls.

20. (*below left*) Marsh Court: looking out from the entrance porch across the forecourt to where the drive emerges from the trees; the emphasis is on a quiet, almost blinkered approach, in preparation for the differing glories of the house and garden to come.

21. (*below right*) Marsh Court: the entrance to the garden – the vivid white chalk and red brick patterning the loggia ceiling introduces the richly-textured garden. (This is a recent photograph and the colours have remained inexplicably vivid, even after nearly eighty years' exposure to the weather.)

22. Ednaston Manor, Brailsford, Derbyshire: the south terrace.

23, 24. *(previous page and left).* Amport House, near Andover, Hampshire: the water terraces.

1906

60. BARTON ST MARY, East Grinstead, Sussex ★★
Client: Sir G. Munro Miller.
The best set of layout and planting plans for any Lutyens/Jekyll garden is represented by the set for Barton St Mary (R.P.G. Folder 51). The bones of the garden survive, but the planting has been much altered.
Private house.

61. HEATHCOTE, Kings Road, Ilkley, Yorkshire ★★★★
Client: Mr Ernest Hemingway.
A small layout plan is published (*The Memorial*, Vol. 1), and the complete layout survives.
Now the offices of N. G. Bailey & Co. Ltd, Electrical and Instrumentation Engineers.

62. THE DORMY HOUSE, Walton Heath, Surrey ★
Client: Mr G. A. Riddell.
Complete layout of this small garden with planting details is published (*Gardens for Small Country Houses*), but the house has been turned into flats and part of the garden has been built on; all the pleasurable garden features have been wilfully removed – this is a great pity.
Private house in split ownership, adjacent to Walton Heath Golf Clubhouse.

63. HEYWOOD HOUSE, Ballinakill, Port Laois, Eire ★★★
Client: Sir E. Hucheson Poe.
Garden layout plan published (*The Memorial*, Vol. 2); photographs (C.L.); no planting plans.
The house (not Lutyens) has been destroyed by fire and reduced to a heap of rubble under grass. The garden survives as part of the grounds of the Salesian Fathers' Missionary College and is frequently open to the public.

64. NEW PLACE, Shedfield, Hampshire ★★
Client: Mrs Franklyn of Franklyn's Tobacco Ltd.
Complete layout sketch plans of the garden with Lutyens/Jekyll notes and correspondence survive (R.P.G. Folder 49) but the garden is much altered; the house was built by Lutyens around part of a seventeenth-century merchant's house brought from Bristol.
Now Simpact Systems Ltd Conference Centre.

65. EARTHAM HOUSE, near Chichester, Sussex
Client: Sir William Bird.
No plans have been found.
This garden has only vague connections with the partners, and a good atmosphere, but no special features survive.
Now a boys' preparatory school.

1907

66. WITTERSHAM HOUSE, Wittersham, Kent ★★★★
Client: The Rt Hon. Alfred Lyttelton, M.P. (he bought this after selling Grey Walls).
No plans have been found; photographs (C.L.).
There is a definite 'partnership atmosphere' to this fine garden but no positive proof; Lutyens made alterations to the existing house.
Private house.

1908

67. WHALTON MANOR, Northumberland
Client: Mrs Eustace Smith.
No plans of the garden have been found.
Lutyens converted practically the whole of one side of the village street to make this house, but I do not know if there is a significant garden.

68. TEMPLE DINSLEY, near Hitchin, Hertfordshire ***
Client: Mr H. G. Fenwick (see Abbotswood, No. 36 above).
No plans have been found; photographs (C.L.).
Complete formal garden, mostly in brick, with a large rose garden still planted (as it originally was) by Harkness of Hitchin.
Now Princess Helena College for Girls.

69. CHUSSEX, Walton Heath, Surrey **
Client: Mr W. H. Fowler.
No plans have been found; garden description (L.W.).
Part of the garden has been built on and it has been divided, but much of the original character remains with this (quite) small Lutyens house.
Private house.

70. MIDDLEFIELD, Great Shelford, Cambridgeshire (sometimes known as Great Blow)
Client: Mr Henry Bond.
No plans for layout or planting have been found. *The Memorial*, Vol. 1, shows the house just after completion with a formal garden laid out; though Lutyens promised Miss Jekyll in a note that the garden was ready for her attention there is no evidence that she ever prepared plans.
Now a private house/offices Acushnet Ltd.

1909

71. GREAT MAYTHAM, Rolvenden, Kent ****
Client: Mr H. J. Tennant (brother of Alfred Lyttelton's first wife, Laura).
No planting plans have been found, and possibly not a Jekyll garden.
Lutyens built on the site of an older house, adjacent to the old walled garden which is *The Secret Garden* of Frances Hodgson Burnett's book. He added paths, and steps to extend the formal layout beyond the walls, but his main feature is the majestic terrace, which has recently been rebuilt.
Now owned by Mutual Households' Association Ltd; the garden is usually open on some days during the summer.

72. RENISHAW, Chesterfield, Derbyshire
Client: Sir George Sitwell, Bart.
Lutyens was a frequent visitor to Renishaw (see Note 6 to Chapter 5), and he probably suggested that Sir George and Miss Jekyll would enjoy corresponding over planting schemes for his famous garden; the fragmentary plans, crossings-out, substitutions etc. on her plans (R.P.G. Folder 88) suggest that perhaps this was not the case. Miss Jekyll's planting apparently did not last long in the Renishaw garden. (See also M. J. Tooley, *Garden History*, Vol. 8, No. 3, 1980, p. 39 ff., and No. 87 below.)

1910

73. HOWTH CASTLE, Dublin, Eire
Client: Mr J. Gaisford St Lawrence.
No plans have been found; photographs (C.L.).
Lutyens altered the castle, which he thought 'a funny old place with the makings of a wonderful garden' (Lutyens Family Papers, 31 July 1909), and formal borders and walks are shown in the photographs.
Private house.

74. GREAT DIXTER, Northiam, Sussex ★★★★
Client: Nathaniel Lloyd Esq.
I have not seen the plans, but Lutyens did the layout for the garden for this house which he extended for Nathaniel Lloyd; the Lloyd family have always done the planting, and it is, of course, now Christopher Lloyd's garden.
Both house and garden are frequently open.

75. 100 CHEYNE WALK, London SW3 ★★★
Client: Sir Hugh Lane.
Simple formal layout of lawn with surrounding paving and a central pool overhung by a mulberry tree.
Private house.

76. ANGERTON HALL, Morpeth, Northumberland
Client: Mrs F. Straker.
Lutyens apparently altered this garden, but Dr Tooley thinks there is no evidence that Miss Jekyll was involved. (See also M. J. Tooley, *Garden History*, Vol. 8, No. 3, 1980, p. 66.)

1910 onwards

77. CASTLE DROGO, Drewsteignton, Devon
Client: Mr Julius Drewe.
Lutyens recommended Miss Jekyll to Julius Drewe, and she did natural planting for the drive (R.P.G. Folder 128). Lutyens suggested several formal garden layouts for the castle (R.I.B.A.D./Drewe Papers), but these were all rejected and the existing garden is by George Dillistone.
The Castle is owned by the National Trust and open as advertised.

1911

78. THE SALUTATION, Sandwich, Kent ★★★★
Clients: Gaspard and Henry Farrer.
No plans have been found and it is probably not a Jekyll garden, though full of her inspiration. The garden layout is almost certainly Lutyens.
Private house.

79. HILL END, Hitchin, Hertfordshire (now Langley End)
Clients: Mr H. G. Fenwick of Temple Dinsley (No. 68 above).
No plans have been found.
Small house built as a dower house for Temple Dinsley with a natural garden.
Private house.

80. PUTTERIDGE PARK, Luton, Bedfordshire ✴✴✴✴
Client: Sir Ernest Cassel.
Lutyens layout plan for this garden around an existing house, together with Jekyll planting details, survive (R.P.G. Folder 92). Especially fine rose garden.
Now Luton College of Education.

1912

81. BARHAM COURT, Canterbury, Kent
Client: Mr E. Stainton.
No plans have been found. Lutyens renovated and extended an existing house and added a stone paving-girded lawn with borders, steps and paths.
Private house.

82. EDNASTON MANOR, Brailsford, Derbyshire ✴✴✴✴
Client: Mr W. G. Player (Player's Cigarettes).
No plans have been found, but Lutyens designed the formal garden around his house. The planting has always been by the Player family, especially Mrs Stephen Player.
Private house.

1912 onwards

83. VICEROY'S HOUSE, New Delhi, India ✴✴✴✴
The main feature of Viceroy's House garden was the formal Indian garden, for which the complete layout plan is published (*The Memorial*, Vol. 2). I do not know whether Miss Jekyll actually drew planting plans for the enormous flower borders (R.P.G. has nothing), but they are certainly planted – and immaculately maintained to this day – according to her tastes and rules of colour. (See Note 26 to Chapter 5.)
Now Rashtrapati Bhavan.

1913

84. ABBEY HOUSE, Barrow in Furness, Lancashire (now Cumbria)
Clients: Messrs. Vickers Ltd.
Cumbria County Council Archives Department have the Lutyens plans for this house, but there is no evidence of a significant garden that I know of.
Now owned by Cumbria County Council as a home for elderly people.

85. FROG'S ISLAND, Walton Heath, Surrey (now The Island)
Client: The Countess of Londesborough.
Lutyens added a wing to this house, and a small formal garden.
Private house.

86. ADDINGTON PARK, Kent †
Client: Mrs Sofer-Whitburn (see also No. 96 below).
There are Lutyens sketches for this garden (R.I.B.A.D.), but the house (not his) has been demolished and no trace of the garden remains.

1916

87. THE GREEN, Eckington, Renishaw, Derbyshire ✴✴
Client: Sir George Sitwell, Bart.

The Renishaw Estate Office has Lutyens's plan for this small garden with much stonework, which Sir George apparently built for his own amusement.
Still owned by Renishaw Estate but let as a private house.

1917

88. FELBRIDGE PLACE, East Grinstead, Sussex
Client: Mr H. Rudd.
Lutyens corresponded with Miss Jekyll over plans (R.P.G. Folder 127) for an enormous and elaborate formal garden around an equally impressive house (which he hoped to build), but none of the commission was ever carried out.
Site now owned by Whittington College.

1918

89. 34 HILL STREET, London W1
Client: Lady Sackville.
Lutyens altered this house but nothing is known about the garden.

90. 40 SUSSEX SQUARE, Brighton, Sussex ★★
Client: Lady Sackville.
Lutyens made three houses into one for Lady Sackville, with terraces leading to a tunnel beneath the side road connecting to the main walled garden.
Private houses.

91. 182 EBURY STREET, London SW1
Client: Lady Sackville.
Lutyens garden plan (R.I.B.A.D.) for this garden.
Note: Mr Nigel Nicolson says that Lutyens also designed a garden for Lady Sackville's house in Crown End Lane, Streatham, the last of her trail of houses, which she eventually sold in 1932 (letter to the author, 16 March 1981).

1919

92. CLIFFORD MANOR, Stratford upon Avon, Warwickshire ★★★
Client: Mrs Rees-Mogg.
No plans have been found, but this is an interesting garden with many partnership features.
Private house.

1920

93. PENHEALE MANOR, Egloskerry, Launceston, Cornwall
Client: Captain P. Colville.
Some Lutyens/Jekyll plans survive (R.P.G. Folder 142) concerning this garden, but they only made a small part of the existing garden.
Private house.

94. HEATH HOUSE, Headley, near Epsom, Surrey
Client: Edward Hudson.
Plans and correspondence (R.P.G. Folder 140) relating to a new design for the garden of this house which Hudson proposed buying. The commission was not carried out.

1921

95. THE QUEEN'S DOLLS' HOUSE (at Windsor Castle)
There are some Lutyens sketches (R.P.G. Folder 226) with which he explained the garden layout and scale to Miss Jekyll.
The Dolls' House is frequently on view to the public when Windsor Castle is open.

1923

96. AMPORT HOUSE, near Andover, Hampshire ★★★★
Client: Mrs Sofer-Whitburn.
Lutyens layout plans and Jekyll planting plans survive (R.P.G. Folder 173).
The house was built for the 14th Marquess of Winchester in 1857, requisitioned in 1939 and bought by the Royal Air Force in 1957. The rock garden Miss Jekyll planned has gone, but the water terraces survive and are well cared for.
Now the Royal Air Force Chaplains' College.

97. WHITE HOUSE ON THE CLIFF, Roedean, Sussex (now No. 40 The Cliff)
Client: Lady Sackville.
I know of no plans, but I am indebted to Mr Nigel Nicolson for the following notes: 'The main Lutyens feature was a long sunk garden, with terraces at different levels, and a central parterre patterned with slates like stacked cards ... apart from that, Lutyens made an outdoor loggia where Lady S had her meals, even in winter ...' (letter to the author, 16 March 1981).
Private house.

98. GLEDSTONE HALL, Skipton, Yorkshire ★★★★
Client: Sir Amos Nelson.
Lutyens garden layout published (*The Memorial*, Vol. 1); Jekyll planting plans survive (R.P.G. Folder 195); photographs (C.L.).
Private house.

99. MELLS PARK HOUSE, Mells, Somerset †
Client: The Rt Hon. Reginald McKenna, M.P.
Small formal garden by Lutyens/Jekyll (R.P.G. Folder 201), now destroyed.
Private house.

100. ASHWELL BURY HOUSE, Ashwell, Hertfordshire ★★
Client: Mrs H. Fordham.
Miss Jekyll's layout and planting plans survive (R.P.G. Folder 70) but seemingly Lutyens had nothing to do with the garden, though he altered the house.

1924

101. TYRINGHAM PARK, Buckinghamshire ★★★★
Client: Mr F. A. Konig.
Lutyens's complete layout plan published (*The Memorial*, Vol. 2); photographs (C.L.); no evidence of Jekyll planting.
Because this garden is relatively young it is in good structural condition; it has seemingly found an appropriate new use as the garden of a clinic for naturopathic healing, dedicated to the undoing of the damage that our stressful daily lives inflict upon our bodies (exactly

the ideals for which Lutyens designed the garden in the 'health and beauty' mood of the 1920s), but even so, this is a garden spoiled by misunderstanding.
Now the Tyringham Clinic.

1925

102. LONG BARN, Sevenoaks, Kent
Clients: The Hon. Harold Nicolson and the Hon. Vita Sackville-West.
It is now known that Lutyens helped to design this garden, the forerunner to Sissinghurst. Mr Nigel Nicolson writes: 'Lutyens came with her [Lady Sackville] to spend the weekend of 16–17 May 1925 at Long Barn. My father's diary for 17 May reads: "Ned Lutyens comes and on Sunday we design the new garden on the lower terrace." Lady Sackville's reads: "Ned has designed for Vita and Harold their new Dutch garden." On 14 July 1925 her diary records that she paid for its construction, a gift of £600.' (Letter from Nigel Nicolson to the author, 8 March 1981.)
Private house.

1927

103. THE MARCHES, Willowbrook, Eton, Buckinghamshire †
Client: Mr E. L. Vaughan.
Complete formal layout plan (Lutyens's office) with Jekyll planting details survives (R.P.G. Folder 199).
Private house in split ownership.

104. THE BRITISH EMBASSY, Washington, U.S.A. ★★★★
Lutyens's layout plans published (*The Memorial*, Vol. 2), but no planting plans found.

105. THE PRIORY, Seaview, Isle of Wight
Client: Unknown.
Complete Lutyens layout plan survives (R.P.G. Folder 220), with coloured elevations and sketches for extensive alterations to an existing house with an elaborate garden added; however the present garden bears little resemblance to the plan and the house is certainly not Lutyens. Seemingly the commission was never carried out; maybe it was for friends of Miss Jekyll (who used to spend holidays at Seaview) and she was too old to cope?

1928

106. PLUMPTON PLACE, Sussex ★★
Client: Mr Edward Hudson.
Correspondence between Edward Hudson and Miss Jekyll concerning natural planting for the Mill House and flower borders for the main house survives (R.P.G. Folder 222); Lutyens did the layout for the formal garden around the house which he altered.
Private house.

107. BLAGDON, Seaton Burn, Northumberland ★★
Clients: Viscount and Viscountess Ridley (Lutyens's daughter, Ursula).
Some Lutyens plans (R.I.B.A.D.) and considerable Jekyll plans and correspondence with Lady Ridley (R.P.G. Folder 221) survive, but the main Jekyll features – the quarry garden and the new garden borders – have gone.
Private house, still in the same family ownership.

1934

108. MIDDLETON PARK, Bicester, Oxfordshire
Client: Lord Jersey.
No plans have been found for this uninspired garden layout around one of Lutyens's last houses, which was more famed for Lady Jersey's exotic bathroom than for its garden! Private house, split into several flats.

1935

109. HALNAKER PARK, Chichester, Sussex
Client: The Rt Hon. Reginald McKenna, M.P.
No plans have been found, but a nice pergola and terraces survive.
Private house.

110. 36 HILL STREET, London W1
Client: Baroness Porcelli.
No plans have been found, but a photograph (*The Memorial*, Vol. 3) shows a beautiful paved courtyard made by Lutyens when he altered the house.

1936

111. THE IRISH NATIONAL WAR MEMORIAL, Islandbridge, Dublin, Eire ★★★
Lutyens's design and working drawings for the whole layout are in the Office of Public Works, Dublin; the work was actually carried out under the supervision of J. T. Byrne of the Board of Works.
The Memorial commemorates (in two languages) over 49,000 men who died in the First World War; it was finally dedicated on Armistice Day 1940, and is now in pitiable decline.

1937

112. PASSENHAM MANOR, Stony Stratford, Buckinghamshire
Client: Mr George Ansley.
No plans have been found, but Lutyens touches exist in the garden of this house which he altered.
Private house.

Note: Details of war cemeteries are in Note 13 to Chapter 5; some unsolved mysteries, with plans for overseas gardens and landscape layouts, are listed as Appendix B, page 192.

The conclusions from the Survey have to be seen, at first, with an open mind, and the multifarious problems of garden conservation will come later. They also have to be drawn with a regard for what is possible, and there are only a very few below the 4-star classification which can be singled out for attention; even the 4-star gardens, beautiful as many of them still are in general terms (as the modern photographs in this book show), are somehow at the point of decision. In a world where values and financial priorities have changed so much, the survival of all of them into a significantly distant future must be in question. The question whether they, or at least a representative selection, *should* be kept is one which I think public opinion should be given the chance to decide *before* (but it is only just before) it is too late – and this is my final reason for writing this book.

The Survey shows that from the twenty-eight gardens before 1900, the achievement of Woodside shines like an early primrose peeping from a heap of tumbled stones; most of these gardens are just too old to have survived time and changing ownership, and, as with the majority of gardens Miss Jekyll did on her own, it was their naturalness and the ultra-suitability of her planting which has been their downfall. In southern Surrey and northern Sussex in particular, almost every garden has candytuft and saxifrages creeping over dry stone walls, hostas and ferns gathering in the shade, and a yucca somewhere – a sort of county-wide watered-down Jekyll planting which has become indigenous, so that it is impossible to know now if the genuine article was ever there at all. Also, as the Survey notes, hardly any planting plans survive from these early years. Woodside, however, is a very important and precious garden, showing how understanding of the site can create an artistic and sculptural garden, and demonstrating decoration with brick and stone in ways that were to be refined in the gardens to follow. Also, it has been lucky (and it can never be more than luck) with careful owners, and the present owner is carrying out gentle restoration. The fact that there are no planting plans presents a temptation to experiment: the yew-enclosed borders would make ideal settings for the one-colour gardens – grey or blue, gold or green – for which there was no room at Munstead Wood, and it is equally tempting to 'jump' thirty years and suggest replanting the hexagonal beds in the pond court as miniatures of the hexagonals in red or white at Blagdon; but all this would be doubtfully correct, for Woodside is so early that it must be closely associated with the earliest themes at Munstead, with planting suggestions in line with old photographs, which show the walks and pond garden planted with spring flowers [21]. This is the key to the value of Woodside, for here Miss Jekyll was teaching the sequence of a garden – the spring flowers and the shelter of the pond court made a welcome for the first warm days, and the borders of the river garden, the water garden and then the rose garden over the bridge were encountered in due time with the advance of the summer.

Five other gardens of this period are important. Chinthurst Hill at Bramley needs only the restoration of its border planting, from plans which do exist, to be properly dressed, and then the house and its garden and garden view would be a complete demonstration of the early partnership at work. The Red House at Charterhouse near Godalming – a small house of great ingenuity in which it is possible to see the beginnings of Castle Drogo – would make an ideal foil for the restoration of at least one of Miss Jekyll's virtuoso dry-wall gardens, and plenty of planting information is available from the plans for Millmead, and in *Gardens for Small Country Houses*. Goddards at Abinger Common is beautifully preserved in a village which appreciates and recognizes the value of its presence, a 'favoured' village in estate agents' terms, surrounded by National Trust property and the equally secure Evelyn estate, which would seem to assure (if anything can) that Goddards will survive.

But, ironically, it is the single most important house and garden of this period, and arguably one of the most important houses and gardens in Surrey of any age, which is most at risk. Orchards symbolizes the theme of leisurely progress through the house and into the garden, an indivisible combination which demonstrates, with a delightfully immature charm, all that Lutyens's ingenuity could display about the art of living elegantly in the country. To split up this house is so against its designed nature that it cannot but harm it, possibly beyond recall, and if Crooksbury and Fisher's Hill are any precedent, division of the spoils is death to a garden.

After 1900, no less than twenty-three gardens from the next ten years, the peak years of the partnership, must be considered. The loss of Fisher's Hill's garden is especially sad when we think of Miss Jekyll's carefully planned borders, but nature has reclaimed her own in the woodland dell around the house in a way that cannot be called less beautiful. However, nature should not be allowed to repossess the next eight gardens of note in this section, and equally the fact that they are famous should not be allowed to harm them. Grey Walls and its garden geometry seem eminently suited as a golfing hotel at Muirfield, and prestige assures its maintenance; the hotel community cannot be so very different from the extended Edwardian family for which it was designed, and surely Alfred Lyttelton, the legendary amateur sportsman who had the house built, would be happy to know that some of the most lauded heroes of these latter days enjoy his house. Grey Walls, built to withstand bitter winds from the northern seas, is well able to stand up to the demands of the modern sporting life.

In the gardens of the soft south, though, the atmosphere is more fragile; Deanery Garden at Sonning and Abbotswood at Stow-on-the-Wold are 'prestige' houses too, but care needs to be taken about the siting of swimming pools and the harsh paraphernalia of modern patios lest they breach the peace, and peace of mind, of the golden afternoon. (At Miss Jekyll's Munstead Wood a swimming pool has replaced the nut walk and all its related borders.) At the multi-coloured Marsh Court, where house and garden are inseparable and must be retained together, and at the only slightly less valuable Temple Dinsley, the priorities and pressures of running a school are obviously a full-time job which allows only limited time and money for the heavy maintenance of elaborate gardens. Pergolas are rotting (where do you find 12 × 12-inch curved beams of slow-seasoned oak now anyway?); pavings and steps are crumbling; at Marsh Court the soft chalk has proved too much of a temptation to little boys' penknives, and childish efforts at lettuces and carrots have taken over from Miss Jekyll's border planting. Folly Farm at Sulhamstead and The Hoo at Willingdon, on the other hand, have ideal owners, who consider that the welfare of the garden as its designers intended should have priority over modern fancies. Folly Farm, for many years owned by the Hon. Hugh Astor and his family, has been constantly restored and tended and opened to visitors, and the Astors have made a new garden, reflecting their own tastes, well away from Lutyens's design – which they realize is what the visitors want to see. However, even for this family, whose name is synonymous with wealth, the mounting expenses of this elaborate garden are a cause for concern. Ammerdown, the giant yew-hedged parterre near Radstock, has fewer materials to crumble, but its whole merit rests on the proportions and health of those yew hedges – the maintenance of which the present Lord Hylton regards as his personal task – but no one is apprenticed to the management

121. Great Maytham: the terrace, rebuilt in 1977–8 for a contract sum of £35,000.

of hedges any more. Alongside such giant problems, the National Trust's lavish care for the little walled garden at Lindisfarne, just another of the castle's curiosities, seems even more banal.

With the exception of Ashby St Ledgers in Northamptonshire, still in fine condition, and Hestercombe and Great Maytham, whose restorations are illustrated [58, 121; colour pl. 8], the remainder of the roll-call of these most important gardens is a sorry tale. Daneshill [122], misunderstood and neglected in the charge of Hampshire County Council, is a disaster; farther south in the county, New Place at Shedfield is now offices, with some reprieve for parts of the garden, most of which suffered irreparable damage during years as a school, and where all the meaning of Lutyens's careful site arrangement (see page 105) has been lost. The Salesian Fathers at Heywood in Southern Ireland, and the Benedictine Anglican monks at Nashdom near Taplow, dedicate as much care to their gardens as they can, but it cannot be enough and they acknowledge the need of both financial and practical help. In Dublin Bay, Lambay Castle has for years been the retreat of the present Lord Revelstoke and a private nature reserve, but the planting of the courtyards was sacrificed years ago. At Barton St Mary much of the garden has been built on – the flower-filled kitchen garden is an empty court, though the rose hoops remain; the raised flower bed outside the garden door (see page 92) has been severed by a central path to make access to the garden more instant, and the delicate transition to the woodland wild has been over-clipped and gardenized. Again, northern ebullience has prospered, and Heathcote's valuable lessons in games with both site and materials remain intact.

From the decline or change in direction after 1910, six gardens tell the story. The Salutation at Sandwich and Ednaston Manor in Derbyshire were neither of them Miss Jekyll's gardens, but both gardens are a vital part of the symmetry of the houses, and both are in good order. Putteridge Park's rose garden is a neat tribute to Miss Jekyll's love of roses, and it can be planted in accordance with surviving plans. Equally, Amport House's water terraces are Lutyens's tribute to his partner and should be retained; at the moment they are in fairly good condition, but they are on the brink of needing expensive, careful restoration. Gledstone Hall is a bit of a folly garden, but magnificent; however, if the cost of its building bears any relation to the cost of its maintenance and restoration, any work (which must soon become necessary) will be out of the question. Finally, Tyringham Park, Lutyens's major classical garden, must be saved.

To Preserve or Not to Preserve?

It is easy to arouse affection for these gardens as nostalgic works of art and to say that they must be kept, but are there stronger reasons for their preservation? And is the indefinite preservation of a living garden possible at all? To answer the first question, I would like to present three of what I believe are important aspects of the case for keeping at least some of these gardens.

Firstly – and it is the reason for keeping most buildings and landscapes from the past – for the lessons they hold for us now and in the future. These gardens have a lot to teach about the technical aspects of garden and landscape design, especially in the use of scale, texture, pattern and organization within given spaces, and the satisfaction that can be gained from the experience of those spaces. These lessons still have a relevance in the gardens we make for ourselves today – for instance, many thousands of ordinary gardens would be infinitely more satisfying if that vital point of contact between house and garden was identified and adhered to, if the layout of the garden answered both the needs of the house and the influences from around the site, if the front aspect was green and calm, and all surprises were saved for the private world of the back garden, and if the gentle sequence of the blossoming year was allowed to govern the progress from the house. The adherence to just the spirit of these rules could restore peace and order to many gardens, which are our only haven from a landscape increasingly in disorder and chaotic disarray.

For all their aristocratic connections, the gardens of the partnership (especially in the light of their place in history after the English landscape garden, the Picturesque and the Victorian formal revival) exhibit a refreshing return to a human scale. They were not designed to impress or intimidate (except perhaps Gledstone and Tyringham), or for great social functions, but they were family gardens; the extended Edwardian family it may have been, but nevertheless they are full of details which are sympathetic to our human form. The pergolas are just right for two people to walk side by side; the steps and paths encourage a leisurely measure, the steps scaling the levels with just enough pace and space to allow the conversation to continue undeterred. There are no formidable expanses of bare lawn to be crossed, but everywhere flowers, details, commentary and symbols of shelter and repose, to entertain the eye and refresh the mind. And, lest all this narration from the unseen architect should prove oppressive, there are always cool vistas back to the house, or out into the world, to restore confidence. The rich textures of stone, brick, tile and wood, the basic materials of our earth, used to such overwhelming effect in the gardens, may be reminiscent of a luxury that has vanished, but, as the changing fashions in architectural practice are witness, we have found no other sources for the sense of stability and satisfaction that they give.

The subtler aspects of the garden's experience, the gentle assertion of beguiling mastery over the visitor, and the satisfaction of his need for delight, shelter and peace were the special gifts of Miss Jekyll's experiences and of the society that made her. They may be typically Edwardian, but surely they are the most essential gifts of the English garden of any time? Architecture and planting were united into faultless organization which exerted a firm sense of direction, giving a choice but never allowing hesitation or doubt. The preservation of these aspects is the most difficult task of all, and it has been disrupted or diverted in many gardens already. All the plans have illustrated the sense of progress and purpose in their individual designs; on the ground this was emphasized by pattern, changes of level, provision of enclosures, and changes in planting, which have been further described and illustrated in some of the gardens. If one was too tired, or too preoccupied, to choose a course, the garden would take control and lead effortlessly onwards with a depth of understanding of the human state that has little to do with petty arguments about formal versus natural and the inordinate cost of the specially

122. Daneshill: how not to treat a Lutyens house with a Jekyll garden!

123. (*left*) The Dormy House, Walton Heath: a photograph from *Gardens for Small Country Houses*, of the approach from the golf club. Miss Jekyll planned a minimal maintenance garden – a rose-covered pergola, small lawn and planted pavement.

124. (*right*) The Dormy House today – minus its Jekyll garden, planted pavement, rose pergola and chimney, though more care is lavished on the golf greens than ever.

made narrow bricks. But in our obsession with the eighteenth century and its landscape of intimidation, and our need to transmute this, quickly, into our corporate twentieth-century playgrounds for giants, the gentle cajoling of the human spirit which was the greatest lesson of these gardens has gone unlearned.

A second important reason for preserving these gardens is to remind us that gardening was once a gentle art. The gardens, no less than their houses, are a tremendous tribute to the high standards of the quiet craftsmen who were to be found working for country building firms in the days before the war to end all wars. Many of the firms who worked for Lutyens, such as Thomas Underwood who built most of the early Surrey houses, have long gone out of existence, and others that remain have not kept their records back so far.[15] The main house-building and garden-making period has now gone beyond living memory, and so it is now only the supreme workmanship, which shows up well in many of the photographs, which remains as their memorial. To restore the Jekyll planting would also be to remember a more peaceful time; to many eyes such childhood favourites as London pride and columbines would make a welcome return after years of absence,[16] and we – who are so ready to accuse the Victorians of having garish flowers – are surely ready for a respite for our own eyes from the ever bigger and brighter blooms that fashion has decreed. Rich and beautiful paving bordered by generous sweeps of gentle, perfumed flowers is one of our abiding dreams of an English garden, and it is in the Lutyens/Jekyll gardens that this dream, to perfection, can be found.

Of course, it can also be found in other gardens as well, and this brings me to the third reason for preservation – to set the scene for twentieth-century gardening. Gardening is such a personal art that its history has lately tended to leap from one rootless masterpiece to another without acknowledgement, but so many gardens that we love have been influenced by the partnership, and in particular I would cite three of the most universally admired gardens of all – Sissinghurst Castle, Hidcote Manor and Dartington Hall.

Harold Nicolson and Vita Sackville-West's garden at Sissinghurst was made in the 1930s without consciously recognizing the partners' lead, but Lutyens was a frequent visitor, and a visitor who gave advice, at their previous home, Long Barn at Sevenoaks, which was the workshop for the Sissinghurst garden. Vita repeatedly rejected any Jekyll influence on her planting, though Lutyens had taken her to Munstead Wood (which she found not looking its best) with Lady Sackville in August 1917, and the same favourites, the same luxuriance and at the same time restraint in colours are there at Sissinghurst, gloriously for us all to see. Nigel Nicolson feels that the Lutyens influence in his mother's garden *is* pervasive, and to anyone who has visited both Sissinghurst and Folly Farm, the same conclusion is inescapable.[17]

At Hidcote Manor garden, made by Major Lawrence Johnstone after he bought the house in 1905, the sense of *déjà vu* is also strong; there is no definite connection this time, but just to see so many plants which Miss Jekyll loved – the red dahlias and cannas, the old fragrant sweet peas, hemerocallis, Japanese anemones, lupins and peonies in the abundant kitchen borders, and many other planting relationships seen only in her plans becoming reality – is to realize that Hidcote garden was made by someone who must have read Miss Jekyll's early books and articles and seen Munstead Wood and Orchards illustrated in *Country Life*.[18]

At Dartington Hall, Leonard and Dorothy Elmhirst started making the garden in 1925 and employed three very pro-partnership designers: H. Avray Tipping, the editor of *Country Life*, Beatrix Farrand and Percy Cane. Beatrix Farrand planted the woodland garden at Dartington in the 1930s, fresh from her visits to the aged Miss Jekyll, and the careful colour grouping of the rhododendrons, camellias and magnolias, undercarpeted with wild flowers, must be her tribute to the Munstead woodland. There are many other tributes at Dartington also – the sunny border of yellows, purples, silvers and greys, verbascums, rue, salvia, thalictrum, phlomis, delphiniums, anchusas, artemisias, nepetas and santolina, is a particular joy.

The last irony is, of course, that these gardens *are* there to be enjoyed, with Sissinghurst and Hidcote carefully nurtured by the National Trust into a possible eternity beyond even the dreams of their makers, while Munstead Wood has gone, and no other major garden of the partnership remains in anything like comparable glory.

Apart from her tributes at Dartington and rescuing the Jekyll drawings for posterity, Beatrix Farrand helped spread the Jekyll influence to America, where Miss Jekyll's books were already popular. A transatlantic friendship through correspondence had developed between Miss Jekyll and Louisa King, who was a respected gardener, maker of a well-known garden at Orchard House, Alma, Michigan, and founder and vice-president of the Garden Club of America.[19] Beatrix Farrand and Louisa King, and also Florence Bell Robinson, were mainly responsible for the adoption of 'English gardening' as typified by Miss Jekyll, with special reference to herbaceous borders, particularly in the climatically suitable Southern and Eastern states, and it is an influence which has not died. In April 1978, *Southern Living*, a magazine in the *Sunset* tradition[20] which reaches the whole of the southern half of the U.S.A., advocated in a major article the creation of a 'classic' border in the Jekyll tradition, with a simple explanation of the rules, plans and examples to be followed. Somehow this article's breezy manner represents the most hopeful approach of all, for it strips away many of the difficulties in Jekyll planting that we have made so much of, and defines in a few straightforward paragraphs the essence of all she was trying to convey: by keeping smaller and more finely textured plants to the fore, stronger and taller plants behind, by contrasting spiky and cushion forms, and placing the flowers according to the colour rules, by planting in generous drifts, with interlocking shapes of contrasting texture, and species and colours repeated along the borders to achieve harmony, the essence of properly dressing the Lutyens gardens becomes a game, an enjoyable adventure, rather than the impossible task that so many of her critics have made it seem.

Even given the will and good reasons, preservation of these gardens is still an expensive and difficult undertaking; restorations like Hestercombe [58] and Great Maytham [121], let alone the annual upkeep of such gardens as Folly Farm or Ammerdown, demand tremendous resources in this unsympathetic age. Any actual means of preservation has to be seen within the context of the general preservation of gardens and historic landscapes, and at present there is a sense of urgency in conservation circles, which feel that something must be done soon or we shall have little left to preserve. In theory there has been a welcome realization that a building of merit (and all Lutyens's houses are listed buildings) depends very much on its setting, and everything within the curtilage of the property should be carefully conserved. In practice this depends very much on the county council or the local district council concerned, and finally it comes down to the personalities involved. A pro-Lutyens owner who finds he has a like-minded conservation officer might well succeed in getting his main garden features – terrace, pergola, garden house, pool – listed along with the house, and if he is

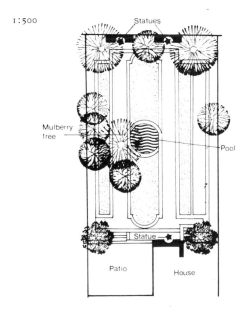

1:500

125. The original plan for 100 Cheyne Walk, London, is a classical plan for a restful town garden, which was an extension of Gertrude Jekyll's ideal for the forecourt as a refuge from the busy world. The sense of repose comes from the elegant proportions of the paths and grass, the serene central pool, the classical statues, and the wide border of plants on the right.

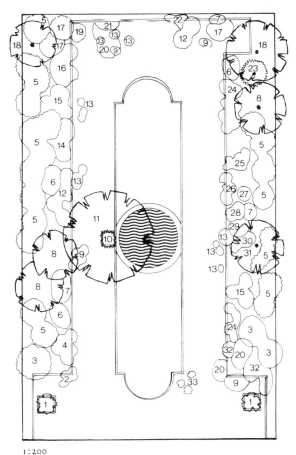

Key to the planting:
1. *Laurus nobilis*
2. *Ajuga reptans atropurpurea*
3. *Mahonia bealei*
4. *Geranium sylvaticum album*
5. *Rhododendron ponticum*
6. *Polygonatum x hybridum*
7. *Lilium regale*
8. *Acer japonicum*
9. *Stachys lanata* 'Silver carpet'
10. *Bergenia cordifolia*
11. *Fagus sylvatica pendula*
12. *Euphorbia wulfenii*
13. *Alchemilla mollis*
14. *Phalaris arundinacea picta*
15. *Verbascum hybridum*
16. *Hydrangea macrophylla* 'Madame Emile Mouillière'
17. *Fatsia japonica*
18. *Sorbus aucuparia*
19. *Passiflora caerulea*
20. *Yucca gloriosa*
21. x *Fatshedera lizei*
22. *Hedera canariensis* 'Gloire de Marengo'
23. *Taxus baccata fastigiata*
24. *Bergenia purpurascens*
25. *Iris germanica* 'Golden Alps'
26. *Dianthus* 'White ladies'
27. *Avena candida*
28. *Salvia officinalis purpurascens*
29. *Verbascum bombyciferium*
30. *Santolina chamaecyparissus*
31. *Rhus typhina laciniata*
32. *Anthemis cupaniana*
33. *Sisyrinchium striatum*

1:200

126. John Brookes's 'revival' of Jekyll planting for the design of 100 Cheyne Walk adapted as a Chelsea Flower Show garden. John Brookes is probably the most successful designer of garden planting at work in Britain today. He has used his knowledge of Jekyll planting, and combined it with his skill in the use of modern and old-fashioned planting, to produce a sophisticated and luxuriant town garden based on the proportions and the classical atmosphere of the original garden.

It must be remembered that this garden was created for show conditions – though they are conditions not so very different from those governing the appearance of the main flower border at Munstead Wood, constantly attended and in its prime from July till October. The basis of the planting of the show garden was the *Rhododendron ponticum* – stripped of its flowers to enhance the white, pale yellow and green composition in the foreground. With a greater variety of shrubs substituted for the rhododendron, or even, in my opinion, as it stands, this garden would provide all the lushness of planting and variation in texture that is so much in demand for small town gardens today.

persuasive enough, get a grant towards their repair. However, this is often not the case: the local authority may be too overburdened to consider anything outside the house, the officer in question *may not like* Lutyens's work, and though the Historic Buildings Council would like to grant money for garden restorations, they have no money with which to do so. It is sad that in official circles the buildings are regarded as having priority always, but fragile gardens are dispensable because in theory they can be restored. In practice they almost never are.

It is also generally thought that the best person to look after a garden is an 'understanding private owner', but experience has proved the need for this to be doubly qualified – he or she must be a hard-working, self-effacing owner, willing to devote time, energy and money to a garden which will be credited to someone else; also, he or she should be a tax-assisted private owner with reimbursements against maintenance costs given in return for opening the garden to the public. Some of the gilt rubs off this apparent solution when it is realized that opening a garden to the public, especially a small and intensively designed garden, involves so much effort, expense and, in the end, damage, that the whole operation becomes self-defeating. Undeterred, the Garden History Society, the Gardens Committee of the Historic Buildings Council and the U.K. Committee of I.C.O.M.O.S. (the International Council on Monuments and Sites) are working for the millennium when a Secretary of State demands evidence for gardens worthy of preservation and tax concession. Lists of outstanding gardens and landscapes are being drawn up, but as Mavis Batey of the Garden History Society has wisely warned, it will be no good asking for too many to be considered, and 200 is thought to be the optimum number. On this basis it can mean two or three partnership gardens at the most.

It has also been proved only too often that when it comes to preserving gardens the law is an unwieldy instrument, blundering to embalm a cobweb, for gardens are by their concept ephemeral and fragile. Gardens made by individuals are as insubstantial as the human span, and the partnership only tenuously extends the thread of permanence as far as an understanding guardian can be found. But the gardens of the partnership have strength in their number, and if they are seen as a collection, something on a par with Wren's City churches, perhaps there is a way to keep them for the 300 years that Lutyens dreamed of, if we have that long.[21] From the Survey on pages 159–76, twenty-four gardens are, at present, saveable. This hallowed two dozen are:

WOODSIDE because it was the beginning,
ORCHARDS as the symbol of what Surrey means to both partners,
GREY WALLS* for its geometry, DEANERY GARDEN for its unity,
ABBOTSWOOD for its marvellous planting opportunities,
MARSH COURT for its adventurous traditionalism,
FOLLY FARM for its sequence, the house out of doors,
THE HOO for its garden houses and tribute to seventeenth-century traditions,
AMMERDOWN* for its tribute to the eighteenth century,
HEATHCOTE for its Yorkshire ebullience,
LINDISFARNE's walled flower and vegetable garden, a Miss Jekyll legerdemain,
ASHBY ST LEDGERS as a symbol of all that is English, manorial and of the shires,
and NASHDOM for its superb use of a wonderful site.
Also HEYWOOD, with the most beautiful walled oval of several oval and circular designs,
LAMBAY CASTLE as the truest civilizing of a defensive home,
MILLMEAD because small is beautiful too,

---

*Indicates a garden where Miss Jekyll may not have done the planting but they were her gardens none the less.

HESTERCOMBE for its textures in stone and planting,
LITTLE THAKEHAM* for its experience of the third dimension,
TEMPLE DINSLEY for its rose garden and elegant brickwork,
GREAT MAYTHAM for its grandeur,
THE SALUTATION* for its symmetry, and EDNASTON MANOR, because it was the ending.
And of course, AMPORT HOUSE for Miss Jekyll's sake, and TYRINGHAM PARK as the great classical garden suited to Lutyens's reputation.

If the owners of these gardens – and over half of them are not private houses any more but in semi-public use as schools, offices, hotels, etc. – could be united to share information, plants, materials, ideas, to raise money and to open the gardens in sequences which would ensure a rest for both the gardens and their owners, it would seem possible to generate the restoration, and the continued enjoyment by many more people, of the gardens of this very special partnership.[22]

At the very last, I feel we must return to the garden-makers. 'A Lutyens house with a Jekyll garden' was once the outward symbol of good taste and financial success, a peculiarly apt and beautiful expression of the spirit of an age on the brink of extinction. I am sure that there are many like minds who will agree with my descriptions of the value of these gardens, and if I have not convinced others by now, then I fear it will not be. But what of the opinions of the two most concerned? Miss Jekyll went contentedly to her rest after a long life full of satisfactory labours, faithfully believing that her reward would be in heaven; however, I do think she should be vindicated in her service to life and art with a true demonstration of her planting in its rightful settings. Sir Edwin Lutyens, on the other hand, his great work of homage to his neglected God unfinished, did not leave so willingly, and these gardens were so important to him. Whatever new assessments of his work are made, no one can surely come nearer to knowing him than Christopher Hussey, his first biographer, who wrote at the end of his *Life of Lutyens*:

Sifting the layers of memory . . . it would seem that the gardens were the connecting pattern in his life. The lovely sequence from Miss Jekyll's at Munstead Wood to the enamelled carpets of Delhi, gardens of which the geometry left nothing to chance yet the forms and colours of nature were given their freedom, and the shapes of trees seen to greater advantage for their harmonized surroundings. These elements, and the light suffusing them . . . had been his first love . . . and remained a prime inspiration of his creative invention.[23]

Lutyens would have cared about the fate of his gardens, very much. In the last days of research for this book, I picked up by chance a copy of Lawrence Whistler's *The Image on the Glass*;[24] among the sublime illustrations of his most fragile craft was a picture of a Georgian crystal goblet, the gift of Lutyens to Lady Linlithgow, Vicereine of India, for her part in restoring Viceroy's House from the ravages of 'mistaken zeal' – the goblet was engraved, in deepest gratitude, from 'him who has most reason to be grateful'.

❧ APPENDIX A ❧

A LIST OF MISS JEKYLL'S COMMISSIONS 1880-1932

The following is a list of other gardens where Gertrude Jekyll contributed planting schemes from 1880 until her death in 1932. By far the greatest number of these gardens have been altered beyond recognition or disappeared altogether, therefore the list is in most part of antiquarian interest; however, the reference (R.P.G.) after a garden indicates that design and/or planting information survive in the Reef Point Gardens Collection, in the hope that some readers, finding themselves in possession of a 'Jekyll' garden, may gain some pleasure from the knowledge. A microfilm of the collection is in the care of the Garden History Society; inquiries to the British Architectural Library, R.I.B.A., 66 Portland Place, London WIN 3DH. (The list is adapted from Francis Jekyll's in his *Memoir* and from the Reef Point Gardens Collection, but makes no claim to be exhaustive – I know many people in Surrey alone who are convinced that they have Jekyll gardens, though their houses may not be on this list!)

1880
MUNSTEAD HOUSE, Godalming, Surrey (her mother)
SCALANDS, Robertsbridge, Sussex (Madame Bodichon)

1881
GISHURST COTTAGE, Weybridge, Surrey (G. F. Wilson). G. F. Wilson also consulted Gertrude Jekyll about the garden which is now the R. H. S. Wisley Garden, Ripley, Surrey.

1882
LONGWOOD PARK, (Huddersfield, Yorkshire). Dr M. J. Tooley (*Garden History, the Journal of the Garden History Society*, Vol. 8, No. 3, 1980) thinks that this is more likely to have been Longwood Park, 4 miles S.E. of Winchester, Hampshire.
OAKLANDS, Cranleigh, Surrey.

1884
A garden at Lower Eashing, near Godalming, Surrey (Mr Turnbull)
THE NORTH CANONRY, Salisbury, Wiltshire

1885
HANGERFIELD, Witley, Surrey
75 TILEHURST ROAD, Reading, Berkshire

1888
KNOLE, Cranleigh, Surrey

1890
LLANFAWR, Holyhead, Anglesey
GLOTTENHAM, Robertsbridge, Sussex (Mr B. Leigh-Smith)
HARBLEDOWN LODGE, Canterbury, Kent

1892
ASTON ROWANT, Oxfordshire
ENBRIDGE LODGE, Kingsclere, Hampshire

1893
EAST HADDON HALL, Northamptonshire

1895
TILECOTES, Marlow, Buckinghamshire
THE VICARAGE, Witley, Surrey
BANACLE COPSE, Culmer, Witley, Surrey (R.P.G.)
BANACLE EDGE, Culmer, Witley, Surrey
MAYHURST, Maybury Hill, Woking, Surrey
STRATTON AUDLEY, Bicester, Oxfordshire
GAZELEY, Marlow, Buckinghamshire
SEYMOUR COURT, Marlow, Buckinghamshire
STRATTON PARK, Micheldever, Hampshire
THE LODGE, Thames Ditton, Surrey

1896
MILFORD HOUSE, Milford, Surrey
THORNCOMBE PARK, Bramley, Surrey (R.P.G.)
BEAR PLACE, Wargrave, Berkshire

1897
HILLSIDE, Godalming, Surrey
WHINFOLD, Hascombe, Surrey (Arch: Sir Robert Lorimer) (R.P.G.)

1898
WEST DEAN PARK, Chichester, Sussex (R.P.G.)
WESTAWAY, Godalming, Surrey
NORMANSWOOD, Farnham, Surrey

MINNICKFOLD, Coldharbour, near Dorking, Surrey
MUNSTEAD ROUGH, near Godalming, Surrey (R.P.G.)

1900

HATCHLANDS, Clandon, Surrey (R.P.G.)
(now National Trust)

1901

HIGH BARN, Hascombe, Surrey (Arch: Sir Robert Lorimer)
(R.P.G.)
PRIOR'S FIELD, Puttenham, Surrey (Arch: C. F. A. Voysey
then T. Muntzer) (R.P.G.)
CAMILLA LACEY, Westhumble, Dorking, Surrey (R.P.G.)
ENTON LODGE, Witley, Surrey (R.P.G.)
HANLEY COURT, Bewdley, Worcestershire (R.P.G.)

1902

CHESWICK, Hedgerley Green, Buckinghamshire (R.P.G.)
ARUNDEL CASTLE, Sussex (R.P.G.)
HALE HOUSE, Ockley, Surrey (R.P.G.)
NEW PLACE, Haslemere, Surrey (R.P.G.) (Arch: C. F. A.
Voysey)
FRIAR'S HILL, Elstead, Surrey (R.P.G.)
LEYBOURNE, Witley, Surrey
SUTTON PLACE, near Guildford, Surrey (R.P.G.)
MUNSTEAD GRANGE, Godalming, Surrey (R.P.G.)
COTMATON, Lindfield, Sussex

1903

HALL PLACE, Shackleford, Surrey (now Aldro School)
(R.P.G.)

1904

OSBROOKS, Capel, Surrey (R.P.G.)
FIELD PLACE, Dunsfold, Surrey (R.P.G.)
BUSBRIDGE PARK, Godalming, Surrey (R.P.G.) (Arch: Sir
Ernest George)
BRACKENBURGH, Calthwaite, Cumberland (R.P.G.) (Arch:
Sir Robert Lorimer)

1905

BRAMLEY PARK HOUSE, Surrey
THE GRANGE, Hindhead, Surrey (R.P.G.)
LOSELEY HOUSE, Guildford, Surrey (R.P.G.)
TARN MOOR, Witley, Surrey

1906

TYLNEY HALL, Winchfield, Hampshire (R.P.G.)
HIGHCROFT, Burley, Hampshire (R.P.G.)
THORPE HALL, Louth, Lincolnshire
CÆSAR'S CAMP, Wimbledon Common, London SW
(R.P.G.)
THE MOORINGS, Hindhead, Surrey

1907

GREENWAYS, off Devenish Road, Sunningdale, Berkshire
(Arch: M. H. Baillie-Scott) (R.P.G.)
FIRGROVE, Godalming, Surrey (R.P.G.)
LITTLEHAY, Burley, Hampshire (R.P.G.)
BISHOPTHORPE PADDOCK, York (R.P.G.)
DYKE NOOK LODGE, Whatley Road, Accrington,
Lancashire (R.P.G.)

UPLANDS, Brook, Witley, Surrey (R.P.G.)
DURMAST, Burley, Hampshire (R.P.G.)
CLOSE WALKS, Midhurst, Surrey (R.P.G.)
LITTLECOTE, Lindfield, Sussex (R.P.G.)
OAK LEE, Lindfield, Sussex (R.P.G.)

1908

POLLARD'S WOOD, Fernhurst, Haslemere, Surrey
HOLLINGTON HOUSE, Newbury, Berkshire (R.P.G.)
PINECROFT, Graffham, Petworth, Sussex (R.P.G.)
PEPERHAROW PARK, near Godalming, Surrey (R.P.G.)
KING EDWARD VII SANATORIUM, Midhurst, Sussex (R.P.G.)
THE OLD MANOR HOUSE, Upton Grey, Winchfield,
Hampshire (R.P.G.)
RUNTON OLD HALL, Cromer, Norfolk (R.P.G.)

1909

HENLEY PARK, Henley on Thames, Oxfordshire (R.P.G.)
LEES COURT, Faversham, Kent (R.P.G.)
MOULSFORD MANOR, Moulsford, Berkshire (R.P.G.)
PRESADDFED, Valley, Anglesey (R.P.G.)
RIGNALLS, Great Missenden, Buckinghamshire (R.P.G.)
FRENSHAM PLACE, Frensham, Surrey (R.P.G.)
COWORTH PARK, Sunningdale, Berkshire (R.P.G.)
HEATHERSIDE HOUSE, Camberley, Surrey
HIGHMOUNT, Fort Road, Guildford, Surrey (R.P.G. and
Gardens for Small Country Houses)
STILEMANS, Munstead, Godalming, Surrey (R.P.G.)
WOODRUFFE, Worplesdon Hill, Brookwood, Surrey
(R.P.G.)

1910

DURBINS, Chantry View Road, Guildford, Surrey
(for Roger Fry)
SHEPHERD'S WELL, Forest Row, Sussex
GREAT ROKE, Witley, Surrey
CORNER HOUSE, Beckenham, Kent
ST EDMUND'S CATHOLIC CHURCH, Godalming, Surrey
OLD CROFT, Godalming, Surrey
CULMER, Witley, Surrey (R.P.G.)
LILLINGSTONE DAYRELL, Buckinghamshire
WEST SURREY GOLF CLUB, Milford, Surrey (garden for
Secretary's house) (R.P.G.)

1911

FAIRHILL, Berkhamsted, Hertfordshire (R.P.G.)
AMERSFOOT, Berkhamsted, Hertfordshire
STRUY LODGE, Beauly, Inverness (R.P.G.)
CHART COTTAGE, Seal, Sevenoaks, Kent (R.P.G.)
DRUMBANAGHER, Newry, Co. Down, N. Ireland
HYDON RIDGE, Hambledon, Surrey (R.P.G.)
NEWNHAM COLLEGE, Cambridge (the Sidgwick Memorial)
(R.P.G.)
LENTON HURST, Nottingham
VANN, Hambledon, Surrey
WOODCOTE, Whitchurch, Hampshire (R.P.G.)
MUNSTEAD GRANGE, Godalming, Surrey (R.P.G.)
BURGH HOUSE, Well Walk, Hampstead, London (R.P.G.)
SANDBOURNE, Bewdley, Worcestershire (R.P.G.)

1912

MONKSWOOD, Godalming, Surrey (R.P.G.)

TOWNHILL PARK, Bitterne, Southampton, Hampshire (R.P.G.)
MERROW CROFT, Merrow, Guildford, Surrey (R.P.G.)
J. G. PHILLIPS MEMORIAL, Borough Road, Godalming, Surrey (R.P.G.)

1913

MUNSTEAD OAKS, Godalming, Surrey (R.P.G.)
WARREN HURST, Ashtead, Surrey (R.P.G.)
FULMER COURT, near Beaconsfield, Buckinghamshire (R.P.G.)
HASCOMBE GRANGE, Hascombe, Godalming, Surrey (R.P.G.)
THE COPSE, Brook, Godalming, Surrey (R.P.G.)
HEATH COTTAGE, Puttenham, near Guildford, Surrey (R.P.G.)
WATERSIDE COPSE, Liphook, Hampshire (R.P.G.)
THE NURSE'S HOUSE, Culmer, Witley, Surrey (R.P.G.)
ORCHARDS, Great Missenden, Buckinghamshire (R.P.G.)

1914

FRANT COURT, Tunbridge Wells, Kent (R.P.G.)
GORSE BANK, Enton Green, Witley, Surrey
FIELD HOUSE, Clent, Stourbridge, Worcestershire (R.P.G.)
LUKYNS, Ewhurst, Surrey (R.P.G.)
HAWKLEY HURST, Petersfield, Hampshire (R.P.G.)
Garden for GODALMING POLICE STATION (R.P.G.)
THE RECTORY, Busbridge, Godalming, Surrey (R.P.G.)

1915

Garden for THE KING'S ARMS HOTEL, Godalming, Surrey
HIGHLANDS, Haslemere, Surrey
GARDEN COURT, Warwicks Bench Road, Guildford, Surrey (Arch: M. H. Baillie-Scott) (R.P.G.)
THE PHILIPSON MAUSOLEUM, Golders Green Cemetery, London NW11

1916

KESTON, High View Road, Sidcup, Kent
LITTLE CUMBRAE, Bute (R.P.G.)
LOWER HOUSE, Bowlhead Green, Witley, Surrey (R.P.G.)
KEYHAM HALL, Leicester
NEWCHAPEL HOUSE, near Lingfield, Surrey (R.P.G.)
80 CHESTERTON ROAD, Cambridge

1917

BARRINGTON COURT, Ilminster, Somerset (now National Trust) (R.P.G.)
23 VALE AVENUE, Chelsea, London SW3

1918

HOLYWELL COURT, Cliff Road, Eastbourne, Sussex (R.P.G.)
KILMEENA, West Byfleet, Surrey (R.P.G.)
KYLEMORE, Bradley, Great Grimsby, Lincolnshire (R.P.G.). See M. J. Tooley, *Garden History*, Vol. 8, No. 3, 1980.
BORLASES, Twyford, Berkshire (R.P.G.)
LEIGH MANOR, Cuckfield, Sussex
BURGATE, Dunsfold, Surrey (R.P.G.)

1919

WOOD END, Ascot, Berkshire (R.P.G.)
THE WHITE HOUSE, Wrotham, Kent (R.P.G.)

FAWKEWOOD, Sevenoaks, Kent (R.P.G.)
CHESTERTON OLD HALL, Bridgnorth, Shropshire
TUNWORTH DOWN, Basingstoke, Hampshire (R.P.G.)
NORMANSWOOD, Farnham, Surrey
THE OLD PARSONAGE, Gresford, Denbigh (now Clwyd) (R.P.G.)
MARKS DANES, Bruton, Somerset (R.P.G.)
PUTTENHAM PRIORY, near Guildford, Surrey (R.P.G.)
PEDNOR HOUSE, Chesham, Buckinghamshire (Arch: Forbes & Tait) (R.P.G.)
BRAMBLETYE, East Grinstead, Sussex (Arch: Forbes & Tait) (R.P.G.)

1920

LEYS CASTLE, Inverness (R.P.G.)
WALSHAM HOUSE, Elstead, Surrey (R.P.G.)
MOUNT STEWART, Newtownards, Co. Down, N. Ireland (R.P.G.)
DIDSWELL PLACE, Welwyn, Hertfordshire
KINGSWOOD, Shere, Surrey (R.P.G.)
DUNGARTH, Honley, Huddersfield, Yorkshire (Arch: G. H. Crowther) (R.P.G.)
GIRTON COLLEGE, Cambridge (garden borders) (R.P.G.)
BOVERIDGE PARK, Cranborne, Dorset (R.P.G.)
BROAD OAK, Seale, Farnham, Surrey
CAENWOOD TOWERS, Highgate, London N6 (Arch: L. R. Guthrie) (R.P.G.)
GRAYSWOOD HILL, Haslemere, Surrey (R.P.G.)
COPFORD HALL, Colchester, Essex
FOYLE RIDING FARM, Oxted, Surrey
38 HAMILTON TERRACE, London NW8 (for Sir Lawrence Weaver)
CHOWNES MEAD, Cuckfield, Sussex (R.P.G.)
BUTTS GATE, Wisborough Green, W. Sussex
GOLANDS HOUSE, Newchapel, Lingfield, Surrey (R.P.G.)
61 THE AVENUE, Kew, Surrey (for Mr Edward Jekyll) (R.P.G.)

1921

OAKLANDS, Wilmslow Park, Wilmslow, Cheshire (R.P.G.)
PALACE COTTAGE, Beaulieu, Hampshire
DRAYTON WOOD, Drayton, Norfolk (R.P.G.)
BRADSTONE BROOK, Shalford, Guildford, Surrey (R.P.G.)
CAMLEY HOUSE, Maidenhead Thicket, Berkshire
HILL TOP, Fort Road, Guildford, Surrey (R.P.G.)
YEW TREE HALL, Forest Row, Sussex
UPPER IFOLD HOUSE, near Dunsfold, Surrey (R.P.G.)
LITTLE WISSETT, Hook Heath Road, Woking, Surrey (R.P.G.)
28 ALBANY PARK ROAD, Kingston upon Thames, Surrey

1922

THE RIDGEWAY, Tittle Row, Maidenhead, Berkshire
ENTON HALL, Witley, Surrey (R.P.G.)
COURT LODGE, Knockholt, Kent
HASCOMBE COURT, Hascombe, Surrey (Arch: Miss C. Nauheim) (R.P.G.)
WATLINGTON PARK, Oxfordshire (R.P.G.)
BURNINGFOLD FARM, Dunsfold, Surrey (R.P.G.)
FISHERS, Wisborough Green, W. Sussex (R.P.G.)
THE GREAT HOUSE, Hambledon, Surrey (R.P.G.)
THE OLD PARSONAGE, Otford, Kent

A List of Miss Jekyll's Commissions

1923

172 Preston Road, Birkenhead, Cheshire
Fox Hill, Elstead, Surrey (R.P.G.)
Lainston House, Winchester, Hampshire (Arch: Forbes & Tait) (R.P.G.)
Memorial Cloister for Winchester School, Hampshire (Arch: Sir Herbert Baker) (R.P.G.)
Durford Edge, Petersfield, Hampshire (Arch: Unsworth & Triggs) (R.P.G.)
Wilbraham House, Wilbraham Place, Sloane Street, London SW3 (Arch: Oliver Hill) (R.P.G.)
35 Hamilton Terrace, London NW8
Southernway, St Martha's, Guildford, Surrey (R.P.G.)
Fox Steep, Crazies Hill, Wargrave, Berkshire (Arch: Oliver Hill) (R.P.G.)
Holmwood, Hambledon, Surrey (R.P.G.)
Kedleston Hall, Derbyshire (R.P.G.)

1924

Kildonan, Barrhill, Ayrshire, Scotland (for Mrs Euan Wallace, Lutyens's daughter Barbara)
Fisher's Gate, Withyham, Sussex
Hillside, Penarth, Glamorgan (now Gwent)
North Munstead, Godalming, Surrey (R.P.G.)
150 Balshagray Avenue, Jordanhill, Glasgow
Little Munton, Sunningdale, Berkshire (Arch: W. Sarel)
Garden for Messrs Hewitt & Co.'s Nurseries, Solihull, Warwickshire
Hall's Cottage, Frensham, Surrey (for Harold Falkner)

1925

Burnt Axon, Burley, Hampshire (R.P.G.)
Widford, Wydown Road, Haslemere, Surrey (R.P.G.)
The Wildernesse, Sevenoaks, Kent
Stowell Hall, Templecombe, Somerset (R.P.G.)
Combend Manor, Sapperton, Gloucestershire (Arch: S. H. Barnsley) (R.P.G.)
Hursley Park, Winchester, Hampshire (R.P.G.)
Merdon Manor, Hursley, Winchester, Hampshire (R.P.G.)
Little Beverley, Canterbury, Kent
Stonepitts, Seal, Sevenoaks, Kent (Arch: G. L. Kennedy) (R.P.G.)
The Glebe House, Cornwood, Dartmoor, Devon
The Old Lighthouse, St Margaret's at Cliffe, Kent (R.P.G.)

The Court, St Fagan's, Cardiff (R.P.G.)
Redcliff, Whittinghame, Prestonkirk, Scotland

1926

Woodlands, Saltburn-by-Sea, Yorkshire
Bestbeech St Mary, Wadhurst, Sussex (R.P.G.)
Three Fords, Send, Woking, Surrey (R.P.G.)
Woodhouse Copse, Holmbury St Mary, Surrey (Arch: Oliver Hill) (R.P.G.)
Roysted, Highdown Heath, Godalming, Surrey
South Luffenham Hall, Staffordshire (R.P.G.)
Ickwell House, Biggleswade, Bedfordshire (R.P.G.)
Old Glebe House, Woodbury, Connecticut, U.S.A. (R.P.G.)
Garden at West Barsham, Norfolk (Arch: John Page) (R.P.G.)
Beacon House, Droxford, Hampshire

1927

Little Haling, Denham, Buckinghamshire (Arch: W. Sarel) (R.P.G.)

1928

Lew Trenchard, Lew Down, N. Devon (R.P.G.)
Ponds, Seer Green, Beaconsfield, Buckinghamshire (R.P.G.)
Valewood Farm, Haslemere, Surrey (for Oliver Hill)
5 Hall Park Avenue, Westcliffe-on-Sea, Essex
The Priory, Hitchin, Hertfordshire (Arch: W. Sarel) (R.P.G.)
Hill Hall, Epping, Essex (R.P.G.)
Strood Park, Horsham, Sussex (R.P.G.)

1929

Garden for Moore Barracks, Shorncliffe Camp, Folkestone, Kent
Little Hoe, Rake Hangar, Petersfield, Hampshire (R.P.G.)
Reflections, Echo Pit Road, Guildford, Surrey
Marylands, Hurtwood, Surrey (Arch: Oliver Hill) (R.P.G.)
Wangford Hall, Brandon, Suffolk (R.P.G.)

1931

Springwood, Godalming, Surrey

1932

Cottage Wood, Walton on Thames, Surrey (R.P.G.)

191

APPENDIX B

ADDITIONAL NOTES ON LUTYENS'S COMMISSIONS

Lutyens also did a number of 'landscape' layouts:

1902

ROSSALL BEACH ESTATE, Lancashire. Layout plan for holiday home estate of 88 acres. Only a fragment carried out and surviving.

1910

HAMPSTEAD GARDEN SUBURB. Layout for Central Square published in Vol. 2 of *The Memorial*.

1919

BASILDON, Berkshire. Layout for almshouses and rectory around the church for Major J. A. Morrison. Layout and planting plans (R.P.G.) by Gertrude Jekyll but only a fragment carried out and surviving.

1930

RUNNYMEDE, Egham, Surrey. Lutyens planned the roads and the memorial pavilions at Runnymede to mark its bequest to the nation by the Fairhaven Trustees; 'pepper box' pavilions and lodges at the Windsor end, plus memorial piers, all survive, but approach road layout (designed in conjunction with his Bell Weir Bridge) has been changed.

1934

COCKINGTON, Devon. Layout for the Drum Inn and model village, of which only the Inn and related garden was built and survives.

Undated designs:

12 GROSVENOR SQUARE, London. Small town garden (R.I.B.A.D.) – the site has been re-developed.

ADDINGTON PARK, Kent. Survey and plans for garden layout (R.I.B.A.D). House demolished and garden overgrown – which is sad because this was Lutyens's first job for the Sofer-Whitburns, the eventual clients for Amport House (No. 96 in Survey, page 174).

WARLEY LEA, Great Warley, Essex. Layout plan (R.I.B.A.D.) for small formal garden for Miss Ellen Willmott. See note 37, p. 195.

TAVISTOCK SQUARE, London. Layout plan for Dame Louisa Blake Memorial and garden (R.I.B.A.D.).

ANGERTON HALL, Morpeth, Northumberland. Garden design mentioned in *The Memorial*, Vol. 1, list of Lutyens's Commissions.

STONEHOUSE COURT, Gloucestershire.

COPSE HILL HOUSE, Upper Slaughter, Gloucestershire. Lutyens was consulted over alterations to these houses, but whether he did anything to the gardens I do not know.

Overseas designs:

Besides Les Bois des Moutiers at Varengeville, Seine Inférieure (No. 22 in Survey, page 163), Lutyens designed two more gardens for the Mallet family – Les Communes near by, and one at Ranguin, Grasse, about which I know nothing. There were also several Spanish gardens, including one at El Guadalperal near Toledo (R.I.B.A.D.), of which I also know nothing (Lutyens's Spanish commissions are completely unexplored and might make a good thesis). There is a fantastic design in the R.I.B.A. collection for a house and garden, Harriman House in New York, which was apparently never built; also several gardens for Maharajahs done while he was in Delhi have apparently not survived.

NOTES

Introduction (pages 13–18)

1. J. B. Priestley, *The Edwardians*, Heinemann, 1970.
2. Francis Jekyll, *Gertrude Jekyll: A Memoir*, Jonathan Cape, 1934.
3. Lawrence Weaver's *Houses and Gardens by E. L. Lutyens* was first published by Country Life in 1913; it was later amended with new illustrations added, and re-issued as *Sir Edwin Lutyens' Houses and Gardens* after the war. The former has recently been published in a facsimile edition by Antique Collectors Club, 1981.
4. Francis Jekyll, op. cit., p. 19.

1. The Lady and the Architect (pages 19–32)

1. Sir Edwin Lutyens, foreword to Francis Jekyll, *Gertrude Jekyll: A Memoir*, Jonathan Cape, 1934.
2. Details of the Jekyll ancestors were collected by Sir Herbert Jekyll; these names and dates come from Francis Jekyll, op. cit., pp. 20ff. See also Betty Massingham's *Miss Jekyll: Portrait of a Great Gardener*, Country Life, 1966, p. 23.
3. The Poulett Thom[p]sons were, for a brief time in the early nineteenth century, the owners of Waverley Abbey House, built next to the Cistercian monastery ruins in a bend of the River Wey, south-east of Farnham. See my article on Waverley Abbey House, *Surrey*, Vol. 11, no. 6.
4. Bramley Park was built by J. T. Knowles between 1825 and 1837 for Capt. the Hon C. F. Wyndham (later the 4th Earl of Egremont). It was demolished in 1951.
5. The linking of the Rivers Wey (already a navigation to the Thames) and Arun was a scheme forwarded by the 3rd Earl of Egremont (of Petworth House) in the early nineteenth century. Building of the canal started in 1813; it branched off from the Wey at Stonebridge Wharf near Shalford, came through Bramley, then wound across via Cranleigh to Sidney Wood, Loxwood, to join the Arun near the old Manor House of Drungewick, about three miles north of Wisborough Green. Its course, partly dry, can still be followed on Ordnance Survey maps, and there is a Wey and Arun Canal society which hopes to restore it. Lord Egremont died in 1837 (to be succeeded by the owners of Bramley Park) but the impetus behind the canal's development was lost; despite the efforts of William Stanton, the renowned bargemaster at Bramley, the canal eventually closed in 1871.
6. The scene of Gertrude Jekyll's childhood, Bramley Park itself, is still very beautiful. The water has been left unmanaged, so that the streams and mill-ponds spread farther than they used to in some places and have become silted up in others. Herons and wild duck have made it their home, and the wild flowers that she loved – marsh marigolds, water iris, marsh orchid, twayblade and cranesbill – have come into their own. The descriptions of the park in her childhood will be found in *Children and Gardens*, Country Life, 1908.
7. The quotations from Gertrude Jekyll's diary are taken from Francis Jekyll, op. cit., p. 25.
8. ibid., p. 26.
9. The contorted tree roots of the Surrey lanes became almost an obsession – there are many prints of these photographs in the six albums which are part of the Reef Point Gardens Collection at Berkeley.
10. She presented much of her collection of 'Old West Surrey' objects, which are illustrated in the two books mentioned, to the Guildford Museum, in Quarry Street, Guildford.
11. Helen Allingham, the well-known painter of idyllic Surrey cottages, was born Helen Paterson in 1848. She was determined to be an artist though she had to struggle continually with the bias against women in the profession; with the support of her pioneering aunt, Laura Herford, she eventually entered the Royal Academy. She earned her living illustrating children's magazines and *The Graphic* and *Cornhill Magazine*. In 1874 she married the poet William Allingham, which allowed her to paint as she wished (watercolours) and to live in the country, at Sandhills, Witley. Many of the cottage paintings appeared in her first one-man show at the Fine Art Society in 1886. Miss Jekyll possibly visited this exhibition; she certainly knew Helen Allingham's paintings and admired them as records of a disappearing lifestyle, and as she was a comparatively near neighbour it is almost certain that she knew Mrs Allingham herself. Helen Allingham was elected a full member of the Royal Watercolour Society in 1890, but at about that time she moved from Surrey, though she did not stop painting. She died in 1926.
12. Barbara Leigh-Smith was born in 1827 into a 'family well known in English political circles for the sturdiness of its beliefs and the sterling worth of its banking accounts'. She longed to be an artist, and always had to satisfy this side of her personality by devoting some time to painting, at which she was good enough for her pictures to sell; however, her liberal upbringing had given her a conscience

about the inequalities of women in life and lack of opportunities for those less fortunate than herself. She ran a revolutionary co-educational, mixed society school in London with Octavia Hill (future founder of the National Trust) and Bessie Rayner Parkes (her lifelong companion in battle and mother of Hilaire Belloc); they also ran a non-militant campaign for reform in the status of women, pushing the Married Woman's Property Bill into Parliament in the 1850s to rectify the situation whereby a woman was the legal property, body, soul and belongings, of her husband or father. The Victorian establishment needed much persuading, and the Bill was only eventually passed, to their entire satisfaction, in 1893. Barbara's home, Scalands, on the family estate near Robertsbridge in Sussex, was her 'Castle of Defiance' in the style of an old Sussex manor house, surrounded by bluebells and nightingales. It was a favoured artistic retreat (Rossetti proposed to Lizzie Siddal there), where her friends gathered – Gertrude Jekyll was one of them, and she designed decorative schemes inside the house and garden arrangements outside. All Barbara's campaigning led to ill health, and on one of her recuperative trips to Algiers (then very fashionable) she met a French doctor, Eugene Bodichon, whom – to the surprise of all her friends – she married (see note 23 below). As Madame Bodichon she joined Emily Davies, Octavia Hill and Frances Buss in organizing (and she contributed a large sum towards it) the first college of women's higher education at Benslow House, Hitchin, in 1869; this eventually became Girton College, Cambridge. It would seem that Barbara's liberal mind, her ability to see the other side of the argument, her need for escapes to art, and the final breakdown of her health because of the all-round life she lived, have meant that her name is often forgotten when the roll of the more extremist militant feminists is read; however, she did much of their ground work for them. These notes come from a lovely (but forgotten) portrait – Hester Burton's *Barbara Bodichon*, John Murray, 1949.

13. From Francis Jekyll, op. cit., p. 77.

14. ibid., p. 76.

15. This was the impression of a Wargrave friend – George Leslie, from his book *Our River*, Bradbury Agnew, 1888 – quoted by Francis Jekyll, op. cit., p. 83.

16. The Blumenthals lived at 43 Hyde Park Gate, a house always open to their large circle of artistic and musical friends. 'Monsieur' Jacques Blumenthal was well known as a pianist and teacher at Queen Victoria's music-loving court, and composer of the light songs that the Victorian gentility loved. His wife, Leonie – 'Madame' – was what we would call a marvellous hostess. From Francis Jekyll, op. cit., p. 89.

17. See note 12 above.

18. Brabazon's cause has been vigorously championed in articles and exhibitions by Al Weil, an American art critic living in England. See 'Britain's Lost Impressionist', *The Antique Collector*, March 1974. Mr Weil has attributed Brabazon's downfall (or rather the decline of his reputation) to his jealously guarded amateur status, which meant that he rarely, if ever, parted with a painting – thousands of them were left at his home, Oaklands, at Sedlescombe in Sussex, at his death. When Brabazon's estate got into financial difficulties in the 1920s the paintings were flooded on to the market in too short a time – at first prices were higher than those paid for pastels and watercolours by Cézanne, but they soon dropped to give-away status, and Brabazon's reputation fell with the prices. There was an important exhibition at Hastings Art Gallery in 1976 which did something to restore confidence, and private collectors are now quite keen on his work. There have been several subsequent exhibitions and Brabazon's paintings are now selling, but it would be true to say that no major international gallery has yet given him recognition.

19. The quotes about embroideries are from Miss Jekyll's diary, and are taken from Francis Jekyll, op. cit., p. 87.

20. The letters from Lord Leighton are in a footnote in Francis Jekyll, op. cit., p. 87.

21. Patrick Trevor-Roper, *The World Through Blunted Sight*, Thames & Hudson, 1970.

22. Six volumes of albums in the Reef Point Gardens Collection show the results of Miss Jekyll's photographic efforts over thirty years – and she was very good. Her earliest efforts in the 1880s concentrate on details of the Surrey landscape and some of her friends, always interspersed with flower studies, either cut flowers from the garden or in the wild. As her life became more concentrated on Munstead Wood, so did her photography, and there are over 100 prints of her garden in its prime. The albums tell their own sad tale of how she could no longer cope with her fading eyesight – the last photograph in Vol. 6 (which tails off incompletely) is of the south border in all its glory. The date is August 1914.

23. As I have said above (note 12), all Barbara Leigh-Smith's friends were amazed and rather shocked when she married Dr Bodichon, who may have been tall, majestic and handsome but was also at his happiest riding in the desert or meditating wrapped up in a blanket. But they had much in common. He had been born into a noble Royalist and Catholic family, but had soon discovered republican sympathies and a desire to help the underdog – the opportunity came in Algeria, to which he was devoted, and where he was something of a legend for his healing powers. Their married life was to say the least unusual for the time – he rarely left Algeria and only briefly visited England (where he refused to adopt any drawing-room manners so only caused more shocks), so they spent part of each year apart, and part together in Algeria. They understood each other completely and were idyllically happy – a background of contentment against which both could carry on their idealistic battles. See also Hester Burton, op. cit.

24. Other myopic artists included: Matisse, Braque, Dufy, Derain, Pissarro, Degas, Renoir and Cézanne.

25. When Turner's 'Snow Storm – Avalanche and Inundation, a scene in the upper part of the Val D'Août' was exhibited at the Academy in 1837, *Blackwood's* magazine cried, 'Has any accident befallen Mr Turner's eyes?' Cf. *Turner 1775–1851*, the catalogue of the Turner exhibition, Tate Gallery, 1974, p. 158. Patrick Trevor-Roper (op. cit.) says that Turner's 'distortion and blurring of detail in later paintings was due probably to secondary astigmatism accompanying lens sclerosis', which amounted to a 'myopic' effect.

26. According to Patrick Trevor-Roper (op. cit.), Claude Monet too was myopic. His paintings of his garden at

Giverny certainly give that impression. See Claire Joyes, *Monet at Giverny*, Matthews, Miller, Dunbar, 1975.

27. This diary quote from Francis Jekyll, op. cit., p. 105.

28. William Robinson (1839–1935) came from Ireland as a young man to work in the Royal Botanical Society's Garden in Regent's Park, where one of his tasks was to make a collection of British wild flowers. While there, he met the editor of *The Times* and started to write on horticulture for that paper. From then on he never looked back, and his ability, energy and forthrightness soon won him the attention of the gardening world. He started his popular magazine *The Garden* in 1871 and continued as its editor until 1900, when he sold it to Edward Hudson, and E. T. Cook and Gertrude Jekyll were joint editors for a short time. William Robinson is the subject of a biography by Mea Allan, to be published by Faber & Faber in 1982.

29. William Robinson, *The English Flower Garden*, John Murray. Quotations are taken from the sixteenth edition, 1955.

30. ibid.

31. ibid.

32. Robinson's strictures were to be carefully heeded by the partnership. Lutyens learned to respect him in the early days; he gave a copy of *The English Flower Garden* to Princess Louise in 1897, he was working at Robinson's house, Gravetye Manor near East Grinstead, Sussex (now a hotel), the same year, and he asked Robinson to help out with a particularly difficult garden, Berrydowne, in 1899. See Lutyens Family Papers at the R.I.B.A. (Letters between E.L.L. and Lady Emily, LuE 3/10/1–29, February 1897, April 1897, 6 August 1899.)

33. Reference to Nathan Cole's *Royal Parks and Gardens of London* from Christopher Thacker, *A History of Gardens*, Croom Helm, 1979, p. 242.

34. From Francis Jekyll and G. C. Taylor (eds.), *A Gardener's Testament*, Country Life, 1937, p. 4. Paper by Gertrude Jekyll, 'Some Early Reminiscences', *Gardening Illustrated*, 27 August 1927.

35. In 1897, to celebrate the Diamond Jubilee of the Royal Horticultural Society, the Victoria Medal of Honour in Horticulture was instituted 'to be awarded from time to time to those deserving of special honour at the hand of the Society'. The first list made sixty awards, and among this list are the names of the 'wonderful company' of Miss Jekyll's gardening fraternity: Canon H. N. Ellacombe, Professor Foster, Dean Hole, Miss Willmott, G. F. Wilson, the Rev. Wolley-Dod. Miss Jekyll's award was 'as a designer of gardens' – she and Ellen Willmott were the only two women. See Harold R. Fletcher, *The Story of the R.H.S. 1804–1968*, Oxford University Press for the Royal Horticultural Society, 1969, p. 239.

36. George Ferguson Wilson retired as managing director of Price's Patent Candle Company in 1865 and came to live at Gishurst Cottage, The Heath, Weybridge, where Miss Jekyll designed a garden in 1881. He then built Heatherbank on Weybridge Heath, and bought sixty acres at Wisley to develop into a natural garden; Miss Jekyll also discussed ideas here with him. Wilson died in 1902, and in August 1903 the Wisley garden was taken over by the Royal Horticultural Society, with three trustees, Ellen Willmott, John Bennett-Poe (another friend of Miss Jekyll) and Cecil Hanbury.

37. Ellen Willmott was born in 1858; she inherited great spirit, energy and wealth and devoted all to her wide gardening interests. She also inherited her mother's garden at Great Warley in Essex, which she made even finer and more famous, especially because of her collection of roses. She wrote her great work *The Genus Rosa* (published between 1910 and 1914) from her rose collections, both in Essex and at her house and garden in France. Apart from roses she is remembered by many other plants named after her: *Potentilla nepalensis* 'Miss Willmott', Tulip Ellen Willmott, *Scabiosa caucasica* 'Miss Willmott' and several roses. Time, changing fortunes and her spinsterish ferocity forced the decline of her great gardens; Warley Place is a particular tragedy, in almost complete dereliction. See William T. Stearn, 'Ellen Willmott', *The Garden*, Vol. 104, No. 6, June 1979.

The R.I.B.A. have a drawing of a small formal garden (dated Feb. 1894) planned by Lutyens for a house at Great Warley for Miss Willmott. The house, now called Warley Lea, was built and the walled enclosure, which could have enclosed the garden, also survives.

38. Sir Michael Foster was Professor of Physiology at Cambridge and sometime Secretary of the Royal Society. He was a noted iris breeder, naming *Iris willmottiana* and *Iris warleyensis* after Miss Willmott and her estate in 1901 and 1912 respectively. See William T. Stearn, op. cit.

39. The story of Dean Hole of Rochester, who filled every space in the Cathedral Close with roses, is told in Betty Massingham, *Turn on the Fountains*, Gollancz, 1974.

40. The Ellacombes, father and son, H. T. and H. N., were vicars at Bitton (just across the River Avon from the Keynsham area of Bristol) for ninety-nine years between them. They planted 'rare and splendid' trees in the churchyard and kept a beautiful garden at the vicarage. Canon H. N. Ellacombe wrote *In My Vicarage Garden and Elsewhere* and *In a Gloucestershire Garden* in the 1890s.

41. The Mangles family were noted rhododendron breeders in the ideal woodland setting of their garden on Surrey sand at Littleworth Cross. *Hillier's Manual of Trees and Shrubs* (David & Charles, 1972) mentions: Beauty of Littleworth, a griffithianum hybrid with immense conical trusses of white crimson-spotted flowers, raised by Miss Clara Mangles about 1900; also Glory of Littleworth, a small, evergreen azaleodendron with creamy-white flowers raised by H. J. Mangles of Valewood Farm, Haslemere, and accepted by the R.H.S. Annual Meeting in 1911.

42. A detailed description of the colourful Lutyens ancestors is given by Mary Lutyens in *Edwin Lutyens by his daughter Mary Lutyens*, John Murray, 1980, pp. 1–6.

43. Charles Lutyens became quite famous as a painter of landscapes and horses, rather in the style of Herring and Fernley: he exhibited at the Royal Academy every year from 1862 to 1903. Further details in Mary Lutyens's beautiful book, op. cit., pp. 7ff. Charles Lutyens died in 1915, and there were exhibitions of his work at Eastbourne and Winchester in 1971. Mary Lutyens also notes that Landseer wanted to adopt Ned, but (hardly surprisingly) Mary Lutyens (his mother) objected, partly because Landseer was an alcoholic (op. cit., p. 10). What is interesting is that Charles Lutyens helped Landseer with the designs of the Trafalgar Square lions in 1859; eighty years later Edwin Lutyens added the fountains.

44. See previous note; Mary Lutyens, op. cit., p. 8.
45. Mary Lutyens, op. cit., p. 12.
46. From Sir Herbert Baker, *Architecture and Personalities*, Country Life, 1944.
47. The traditions of Surrey building that Lutyens absorbed are still all-pervasive in the Thursley area, and are especially well illustrated by a group of buildings on the road west from Thursley village, at the bend where the road crosses the Highcombe Bottom stream; approached from the village, it will be seen exactly how the angles of these buildings complement the slopes of the surrounding hills, and hint at Lutyens's favourite pitches for roofs and gables. At Bowlhead Green, an unspoiled hamlet on the east side of the A3, the Milford to Hindhead road, the Surrey that Helen Allingham painted and the young Lutyens saw is still intact.
48. This cottage still exists at Littleworth Cross. The R.I.B.A. Drawings Collection also has Lutyens's drawings for a thatched 'fowl house' with dovecote on top, designed for Harry Mangles. Perhaps it was the fowl house as well as the cottage drawing, dated 17 May 1889, which fascinated Miss Jekyll when she saw them at the tea-table?
49. Francis Jekyll, op. cit., from the foreword by Sir Edwin Lutyens.
50. ibid.

2. *The Making of Munstead Wood and the Early Surrey Gardens (pages 33-63)*

1. 'About Myself', see 'Some Early Reminiscences', *Gardening Illustrated*, 27 August 1927; quoted from Francis Jekyll and G. C. Taylor (eds.), *A Gardener's Testament*, Country Life, 1937, pp. 5-6.
2. The information for the Munstead Wood plan comes partly from a plan published in Gertrude Jekyll and Lawrence Weaver, *Gardens for Small Country Houses*, Country Life, n.d., p. 38, and partly from my own explorations of the site, which is now considerably altered.
3. From the foreword by Sir Edwin Lutyens to Francis Jekyll, *Gertrude Jekyll: A Memoir*, Jonathan Cape, 1934.
4. The broom squires were a people of gypsy origins who settled in the isolated valleys around Hindhead and Haslemere about the middle of the nineteenth century, and made their living selling 'besoms' of heather stems tied with grass to chestnut handles. They were turned into something of a folk legend by the artists and writers who came to this area when it became a Victorian retreat – S. Baring Gould's novel *The Broom Squires* was published in 1896, and Charles Kingsley is quoted as having thought them the epitome of rural dignity: '. . . civil, contented, industrious and often very handsome . . . dark haired and ruddy . . . swaggering in youth . . . but in old age, reserved, stately, courteous as a prince'. They were very much *of* their landscape.
5. Sir Edwin Lutyens's foreword to Francis Jekyll, op. cit.
6. Bargate stone is a rough sandstone, which was gathered from fields and heaths to make walls and cottages in south-west Surrey. Occasionally it was found in quarryable amounts, though these were never more than small village or farm quarries. Both Munstead Wood and Orchards had small quarries opened for their building. Now only one or two small quarries remain and these are only worked for repairs or additions to original buildings.

7. See Gertrude Jekyll, *Home and Garden*, Longmans Green, 1900, pp. 2-3.
8. ibid.
9. See William Robinson, *The English Flower Garden*.
10. The basis for this section is Miss Jekyll's own published plans of her borders at Munstead, modified by reference to her other writings. It must be understood, however, that as she was gardening at Munstead for over forty years, the garden was ever changing. However, I have tried to present her basic philosophies in the plans and illustrations I have used.
11. The Spring garden plan comes from *Colour in the Flower Garden*, Newnes/Country Life, 1908, p. 23, with modifications from Miss Jekyll's other published writings.
12. The plan for the Hidden garden is modified from that in *Colour in the Flower Garden*, p. 35.
13. The June garden plan is modified from that in *Colour in the Flower Garden*, p. 44.
14. The quotation from Harold Falkner's diary comes from Betty Massingham, *Miss Jekyll: Portrait of a Great Gardener*, Country Life, 1966, p. 69. Harold Falkner (1875-1966) was an Arts and Crafts architect living at Farnham whose talents were perhaps mis-directed because he did not need to earn a living; he was a great Farnham character, and a frequent visitor to Miss Jekyll during the last twenty years of her life – she had rather a weakness for architects! See my article on Harold Falkner in *Surrey*, Vol. 9, No. 6.
15. On a visit I paid recently to The Hut (which is now a separate house from Munstead Wood itself), I found the present owner carefully tending a descendant of the giant hogweed.
16. See Faber Birren (ed.), *The Principles of Harmony and Contrast of Colours and their Application to the Arts by M. E. Chevreul*, New York, Reinhold, 1967.
17. ibid.
18. ibid.
19. A grey garden plan will be found in *Colour in the Flower Garden*, p. 96.
20. Green garden plan from *Colour in the Flower Garden*, p. 98 see also page 185 for John Brookes's modern version of this colour scheme.
21. Herbaceous border plan from *Colour in the Flower Garden*, p. 53.
22. See Gertrude Jekyll, *Wood and Garden*, Longmans Green, 1899, pp. 109ff.
23. The correspondence and planting plans for the Blagdon border are in the Reef Point Gardens Collection (File X, Folder 221); on 17 October 1929 Ursula Ridley wrote: 'Now about the borders – I think they will be *quite* lovely and are exactly what I wanted. There are just one or two things – we can supply all the Dahlias, campanula latifolia, Nepeta, phlox and hollyhocks – . . . Then – Echinops don't seem to do at all well here – they have none of them come in the quarry and the gardener says he has tried them before without success. Could we substitute eryngium which do does well and which we have plenty of . . . Also the gardener says Crinums don't do at all well – but we have a great many white and mauve pinks . . .' Continuing in this vein, offering yellow scabious and wondering how big *Chrysanthema maxima* are, she ends: 'I *am* so grateful to you, and for all the trouble you take for me. I only *wish* you were able to come and see it all. With your help and

Father's the place could hardly be recognized for the improvements in it.'

24. Plan information from Reef Point Gardens Collection.

25. See *Colour in the Flower Garden*, p. 10.

26. Miss Jekyll's gaultheria appears to have been *G. shallon* – a vigorous, broad and leathery leaved shrub with pinkish-white flowers and purple berries – commonly used for game coverts and introduced here from North America in 1826 (see *Hillier's Manual of Trees and Shrubs*, David & Charles, 1972).

27. See *Home and Garden*.

28. The Hon. Emily Lawless was the client for one of Lutyens's earliest houses in a woodland near Shere in Surrey. Miss Lawless was a great naturalist and a keeper of a nature diary; she wanted no formal garden except lawn around the house with some heather planting which would melt into rhododendrons, azaleas and woodland. There is evidence that she and Miss Jekyll saw exactly eye to eye over woodland gardening, and today this garden preserves miraculously the spirit of the Munstead woodland, with occasional 'flowery incidents' and a nut walk surviving.

29. Miss Jekyll tells how a Rochdale mill 'lad' advertised for advice on a window box garden and she sent him the advice and plants 'of mossy and silvery saxifrages and a few small bulbs' plus some stones (for it was to be a rock garden), and how she rejoiced in the letters that came in return. (*Wood and Garden*, p. 185.)

30. See this chapter, note 6.

31. The Chances' original architect, whose plan they so disliked, was Halsey Ricardo (1854–1928) – probably not entirely by coincidence a member of the family that had bought Miss Jekyll's old home, Bramley Park. In spite of losing this job, Ricardo was a successful and flamboyant Arts and Crafts architect; his best known building, the Debenham house, 8 Addison Road, Holland Park, London, with its coloured glazed bricks in different hues and exotic excursions to the wilder shores of classicism, perhaps illustrates why he was out of sympathy with the Chances. William Chance (later Sir William) was a barrister and High Sheriff of Surrey for several years; Julia Chance was the daughter of Lt. Col. Edward Strachey (and therefore a cousin of Lytton Strachey) – and the little girl who sits on the steps at Orchards in the endpapers to this book was her niece, Dorothea Strachey.

32. Feldemore, a many-gabled house built in the 1850s and 1880s which seems to have been inspired not only by Alfred Waterhouse but by Philip Webb and Norman Shaw as well (both of them built houses in Holmbury St Mary, just down the hill), stands in wooded – and gaultheria-infested – grounds opposite what was Pasturewood (see note 33). Feldemore is now Belmont School, a preparatory school for boys, but occasionally its heyday returns, much to the enjoyment of everyone for miles around, when the Belmont Twelfth Night Ball takes over the house and gives it back its style.

33. Pasturewood is now the country branch of the Fabian Society and used for conferences and courses; it has been renamed Beatrice Webb House. The eminent Fabian John Parker, M.P. for Dagenham, is 'in charge', and he regards the garden, especially Miss Jekyll's rockery, as his great pleasure and relaxation.

34. Lutyens wrote that the Mirrielees were wonderfully easy to get on with, but his cases weren't unpacked and his hot water and shoes were left outside the door because of the timidity of the housemaid – 'An awful bore' – but the sick horses were fed on beef tea, butter and port wine! (Lutyens Family Papers.)

35. Lutyens Family Papers (R.I.B.A. Letters between E.L.L. and Lady Emily, June/July 1899). On 6 August 1899 Lutyens reports that William Robinson is being asked to help out at Berrydowne (E.L.L. to Lady Emily, 6 August 1899); a year later Emily wrote of the '19th solution' to the garden being tried (Lady Emily to E.L.L., 1900); Archibald Grove had had enough though, and was selling the house.

36. Most of Miss Jekyll's garden designs for the years 1890 to 1900 wanted no done for Lutyens, but there were two spates of her own commissions; in 1895 she did some Marlow gardens (Tilecotes, Gazeley and Seymour Court) and some at Witley in Surrey (of which The Vicarage survives), and Stratton Park, Micheldever, Hampshire (where Lutyens was building some cottages). In 1898 she worked at West Dean Park for Mrs William James (see Monkton House, No. 43 in the Survey, p. 166) and at Minnickfold, Coldharbour, near Dorking, and in both places her planting survives. The schemes seem to have been mostly for borders and rock and dry-wall planting.

37. Miss Jekyll seems to have done quite a lot of work at Charterhouse School, as she was a friend of Sir Frank and Lady Fletcher (he was headmaster from 1911 to 1935). Lady Fletcher made two gardens for school 'houses' – Saunderites and Northbrook – with Miss Jekyll's help, and both survive to some extent. The Rev. H. J. Evans was an assistant master from 1866 to 1900 and Hon. Chaplain from 1900 to 1906 – he had The Red House built a short way from the main school gates for his retirement, thus the commission for Lutyens certainly came via Miss Jekyll. I am indebted to Mr Fernandez-Arnesto and others at Charterhouse School for this information.

38. Mrs Earle wrote *Pot Pourri from a Surrey Garden* in 1897; two years later *More Pot Pourri* followed, then a *Third Pot Pourri* in 1903 and *Memoirs and Memories* in 1911. I feel that the passage quoted about Miss Jekyll's gardening efforts may have reflected the tensions of the time, for normally Mrs Earle was an affectionate and generous soul whom Ned and later his children came to adore. As I write, Mrs Earle is very much in vogue, and some people believe that she was the originator of many of Miss Jekyll's gardening ideas; but as to my story Miss Jekyll's reputation is secure – for where are Mrs Earle's sheaves of garden plans or her inspiration of a bright young architect?

39. This is a paraphrase of Lady Emily's own description from *A Blessed Girl: Memoirs of a Victorian Childhood 1887–1896* (Hart-Davis, 1953), much of which concerns her infatuation with Wilfred Scawen Blunt which was finally banished for ever by Ned Lutyens. It is a bravely written book.

40. A full description of Lutyens's courtship and marriage will be found in Mary Lutyens's book about her father: *Edwin Lutyens by his daughter Mary Lutyens*, John Murray, 1980, p. 28ff.

41. At the time of Emily's visit Miss Jekyll was still living in The Hut. Dressing 'rather like a man' must have been

descriptive of Miss Jekyll's preference for long-sleeved, generously-cut shirts, with perhaps a tie at the neck, and of course her gardening boots, made famous in the painting by William Nicholson.

3. *The Gardens of the Golden Afternoon (pages 64–95)*

1. These words are on a wall in the Hall of the Two Sisters in the Alhambra. Quoted from Desmond Stewart, *The Alhambra*, Reader's Digest/Newsweek, London/New York, 1974.

2. Lutyens Family Papers. On 10 September 1907 Lutyens wrote to Emily: 'There is that in art which transcends all rules – it is the divine (I use poor words) and it is what makes all the arts so absorbing and thrilling to follow – creating a furore.'

3. Gerald Balfour, M.P. was the brother of Arthur James Balfour, prime minister from 1902–5. The connection was important, for it was the entrée to the powerful Liberal families – where the Balfours led, the Tennants, Lyttletons and Asquiths soon followed.

4. Fisher's Hill in the Reef Point Gardens Collection (File I, Folder 15). The planting lists (typed and doubtfully originals) specify Drawings A B and C for planting around a tank, for large flower beds, a grey garden, a pergola, a dry wall and woodland banks – no drawings are there. The grey garden was possibly a parterre – '*Cineraria maritima* for edging the 5 middle beds', plus rosemary, *Eryngium oliverianum*, lavender, *Achillea* 'The Pearl', *Geranium ibericum*, small blue iris, cerastium, southernwood, catmint, white pinks, santolina, hyssop, pink hollyhocks and *Eryngium giganteum*, with *Stachys lanata* for more edgings. Choisya, escallonia, lavender, rosemary, skimmias, vines and verbena were planted against the house. It is a pity it is all gone.

5. David Lytton-Cobbold, the present owner of Knebworth House, has written to me (25 March 1979): 'My impression is that Lutyens but not Miss J was involved in the re-design of the formal garden at Knebworth (c. 1908) including in particular the pollarded lime avenues and the trompe l'oeil yew hedge. Sadly Lutyens's sketched lines on an earlier garden plan were rubbed out (not thinking they were important) by a garden consultant we employed a few years ago!' The Countess of Lytton is described by Elisabeth Lutyens in *A Goldfish Bowl*, Cassell, 1972.

6. Edward Hudson was the owner of a printing firm (Hudson & Kearns Ltd) which printed *Navy and Army* and *Racing Illustrated*, both known for their fine use of half-tone photographs. His idea for *Country Life Illustrated* (as it was first known), which was first published on 8 January 1897, was for a magazine dealing with sport in its widest sense, as understood by the English country gentleman. 'The finest pictorial printing machinery available' was imported and the highest quality of paper used. Hudson's co-directors were George and Frank Newnes and his own brother, William. Sports, gardening, dogs, horses and book reviews were well-established subjects before architecture came on the scene; the latter aroused Hudson's interest during trips round the country with his consumptive brother Henry, during which they constantly visited country houses, and this interest was reinforced by the meeting with Lutyens. Apart from all of Hudson's houses, Lutyens built the *Country Life* offices in Tavistock Street,

Covent Garden, in a style heavily influenced by Christopher Wren. This building still exists, and *Country Life* only left it in 1976 when it was bought by I.P.C. Magazines Ltd. The *Country Life* library of photographs, of which some have been used for this book, is an incredibly valuable collection of photographs of almost every house and garden of note in the British Isles during the past eighty years. See Bernard Darwin, *Fifty Years of Country Life*, Country Life, 1947.

7. Nairn and Pevsner, *The Buildings of England: Surrey*, 2nd edn revised by Bridget Cherry, Penguin, p. 378. This is sprinkled with the results of Nicholas Taylor's exhaustive research for every smallest sign of Lutyens's early works – I regard Mr Taylor as the ultimate expert on Lutyens's work, but for his projected definitive book we are still waiting!

8. Lindisfarne Castle is owned by the National Trust and is open daily during the summer season; it is necessary to consult both the current opening times and the tide tables!

9. Other Lutyens clients besides Hudson seemed to become 'hooked' – when the Rt. Hon. Alfred Lyttelton (see next note) sold Grey Walls he bought Wittersham House in Kent, which Lutyens altered for him, and he also altered a London house. Grey Walls was bought by William James, for whom Monkton House at Singleton in Sussex had been built (James was a legendarily rich American who had married an illegitimate daughter of Edward VII – with whom Lutyens, as well as everyone else, was fascinated; their son Edward James still owns Monkton). The Fenwick family owned both Abbotswood at Stow-on-the-Wold and Temple Dinsley and Hill House near Hitchin; in August 1917 Lutyens wrote: 'Bertie Fenwick wanted to sell Temple Dinsley and build again.' The War presumably put an end to this idea, as it did to almost everything else.

10. The client for Grey Walls was Alfred Lyttelton, the youngest of the 'Old Dozen', the children of the 4th Lord Lyttelton of Hagley Hall by his first marriage to Mary Glynne – 'the child who had cost his mother her life' (Betty Askwith, *The Lytteltons: A Family Chronicle*, Chatto & Windus, 1975, p. 159). Perhaps more than any other person, it is Alfred Lyttelton who in retrospect symbolizes the society for whom a Lutyens house with a Jekyll garden was the natural corollary of their lives. He was adored by all who knew him, and by thousands who only knew him by reputation as an outstanding cricketer, successful barrister and gentlemanly politician. He died of appendicitis in 1913 at the age of fifty-six.

11. Christopher Hussey, *Life of Lutyens*, Country Life, 1950, p. 99.

12. The 'adventurers' were the archetypal Lutyens clients – men who could appreciate in him the shades of their own modest beginnings and whose energy and drive was inhibited by no aristocratic restraint. They are perhaps the most fascinating group of clients of all – Amos Nelson of Gledstone (see Chapter 5), Julius Drewe 'the grocer' of Castle Drogo, the Player cigarette family with their lovely Ednaston Manor in Derbyshire, the Franklyns of Franklyn's Tobacco for whom New Place at Shedfield was built, and the unnamed gentlemen of the Vickers board who commissioned Abbey House at Barrow for the company.

13. From Christopher Hussey, op. cit., p. 100; he continues about Johnson: 'Lutyens came to love his courage, vigour

and honesty which, with more than a touch of flamboyance, he worked into the building.' Johnson lost one fortune, made another and then married – he became a fixture as a sporting gentleman at Marsh Court until the Second World War brought a final decline in his circumstances and obliged him to sell it. He died in 1949.

14. Lutyens and Johnson were both great fishermen – it was Lutyens's only country relaxation and the River Test thus had a great appeal. The love of river valleys was rather more symbolic though, according to Christopher Hussey (who, as well as knowing Lutyens through all his letters, drawings and buildings, knew him personally in his later years): maybe, coming from the waterless heaths of south-west Surrey, rivers were a special refreshment to him, but it also had something to do with their unquenchable sparkle of life.

15. See 'Some Problems of Garden Planning – Formal Gardens', an undated paper by Gertrude Jekyll in Francis Jekyll and G. C. Taylor (eds.), *A Gardener's Testament*, Country Life, 1937, p. 55. From this description of her 'ideal' water-lily pool, Marsh Court's can be imagined, but in *Wall and Water Gardens* (Country Life, 2nd edn, n.d., p. 141ff.) a similar description is accompanied by an illustration which is unlike Marsh Court's – this is not a Lutyens plan, and in the infuriating way of most of Miss Jekyll's book illustrations it is not identified. If anything, Marsh Court's keeping of the formal lilies near the house and completely within the 'hard landscape' area is much more fitting than this 'ideal' plan, which plonks a walled lily court in the centre of a grass terrace.

16. Also in *Wall and Water Gardens* (p. 161ff.) is an interesting paragraph about the owner of the name so many of the best water-lilies carry: 'A heavy debt of gratitude is owing to M. Latour Marliac of Temple-sur-Lot, France; for to him is due the credit of having perceived the adaptability of the various hardy species of Water-lily for purposes of hybridization, and for the yielding of a large variety of beautiful forms. It is to the labours of this gentleman that we owe the greater number of the beautiful flowers that we can now have in our ponds and tanks.'

17. From conversation with the present Lady Hylton, and from *In My Tower* by Walburga Lady Paget (Hutchinson, 1924) and the private papers of Mrs Viola Duckworth of Orchardleigh Park, Frome, it appears that the influence for the Italian garden at Ammerdown may have been the young Lady Hylton of the time, formerly Lady Alice Hervey: charming and cultivated, with a 'pretty wit and quick repartee', she was a considerable artist – she had worked with Walter Sickert and later designed the Wells Cathedral embroideries. She had visited Italy immediately after her marriage, was very interested in Italian history and literature, and when busy beautifying her new home it would seem appropriate to adopt the 'Italian' touch.

18. There were two notable exceptions where Miss Jekyll did not do the planting, Little Thakeham and The Salutation, because the owners were able gardeners themselves. Of Little Thakeham, Lutyens wrote in July 1904, 'the garden is wonderfully good – he [Ernest Blackburn] has made the pergola delightful' (Lutyens Family Papers). The Salutation was for Gaspard and Henry Farrer. The garden was clearly designed by Lutyens, but there is no evidence of original planting by Miss Jekyll.

4. Working Partnership (pages 96–131)

1. Miss Jekyll's words are from *Home and Garden*, Longmans Green, 1900, Ch. 22, 'Things Worth Doing'.

2. From a letter to Lady Emily Lutyens dated 8 April 1908. Lutyens Family Papers, R.I.B.A.

3. I say 'small' revolution because the partners were working at the end of the Arts and Crafts period, and the order and integrity in garden design that they practised would not long outlast their peak years, 1893–1910; the facile pencil and the free curve would win the day and a new naturalism was to take over in the 1920s. See my final chapter, 'A Reckoning', page 153.

4. All Lutyens's quotes on his theory of garden design come from his notes for the meeting with Mawson at the Architectural Association – and are in the letter to Lady Emily referred to in note 2 above.

5. 'Some Problems of Garden Planning', in Francis Jekyll and G. C. Taylor (eds.), *A Gardener's Testament*, p. 52.

6. See Francis Bacon's essay 'Of Gardens' in Matheson (ed.), *Selections from Francis Bacon's Writings*, Oxford University Press, 1952.

7. Lutyens visited Chesters on 23/24 April 1901 – see letter to Lady Emily in Lutyens Family Papers, R.I.B.A.

8. Sir Herbert Baker, *Architecture and Personalities*, Country Life, 1944.

9. Henry Ernest Milner (1845–1906) was the eldest son of the Victorian gardener Edward Milner, a pupil and later assistant to Joseph Paxton in his famous schemes for Chatsworth, the Crystal Palace and Prince's Park, Liverpool. Henry Milner was trained as an engineer, then went into partnership with his father and carried on the practice after Milner senior's death in 1884. He seems to have immediately turned against all the formalism his father had stood for; with his book *The Art and Practice of Landscape Gardening*, published in 1890, which was in fact Blomfield's target, he advocated another return to natural style, illustrated with what Miles Hadfield has called 'deplorable etchings'. See Alison Hodges, 'A Victorian Gardener: Edward Milner', *Journal of the Garden History Society*, Vol. V, No 3.

10. Blomfield's argument, as set out in *The Formal Garden in England* (with drawings by F. Inigo Thomas, Macmillan, 1892), p. 15, is that no true nature lover will be satisfied with a natural garden, content 'to sit in his rockery and suppose himself to be among the mountains', and so try and invoke natural landscape in a garden is contrived; but he who loves order, as dictated by the natural laws of the universe, will be happier with an enclosed space 'set out as the designer pleases'. Lutyens, of course, agreed more or less with Blomfield, but the pity of the partnership was that he never used Miss Jekyll's great understanding of plants in their natural habitats to make the successful and ordered transition from the formal garden around the house to the outside world. See my last chapter, 'A Reckoning', p. 153.

11. Miss Jekyll's perception of the woodland is from *Home and Garden*, p. 24 ff.

12. Lutyens was always concerned as to how his own eyesight would stand up to constant strain and pipe smoke.

13. Robert Lutyens, *Sir Edwin Lutyens: An Appreciation in Perspective*, Country Life, 1942.

14. Elisabeth Lutyens, *A Goldfish Bowl*, Cassell, 1972.

15. Thomas Mawson (1861–1933) was a practising town planner and landscape architect; the year after his debate with Lutyens (1909) he was appointed the first university lecturer in his subjects at Liverpool Department of Civic Design. He was President of the Town Planning Institute 1923/4 and the first President of the Institute of Landscape Architects in 1929; he was also the first person in this country to call himself a 'landscape architect', which thus had a great bearing on the adoption of this title for the new profession, who felt that architects did not know enough about nature to tamper with the non-built environment. Though this has largely been proved to be true it has not endeared them to architects – in particular Lutyens, who had the 'secret weapon' of Miss Jekyll down in Munstead Wood which meant that the partnership was an unbeatable entity, of which many were jealous. See my last chapter, 'A Reckoning', p. 153, and note 6 to that chapter.

16. From *Home and Garden*, Ch. 23, 'Living in the Hut'.

17. Lutyens met Barrie at Berrydowne Court in 1899; he designed the scenery for *Quality Street* at the Vaudeville Theatre in 1902, and also the set for the first production of *Peter Pan*. Later he altered Barrie's house in Adelphi Terrace, London. According to Mary Lutyens in *Edwin Lutyens*, p. 66, it was her father who invented Nana in *Peter Pan*.

18. In that they both rose from obscurity to be symbols of the Edwardian age, great contributors to the myths of patriotism and Empire but quiet and lonely men beneath the jingoism they are remembered for, Edward Elgar and Edwin Lutyens shared certain characteristics. They were both 'out' in society in the post-war period and met several times; because of this almost the only music Lutyens was aware of was Elgar's. In 1927, when his daughter Elisabeth was living with him for a while, she managed to discuss the subject with him and found out that he also liked Purcell (patriotism again); she also made him fascinated with the structural principles of music, 'stemming, as did architecture, from the Greeks'. See Elisabeth Lutyens, op. cit.

19. The note on the design of New Place is in the Reef Point Gardens Collection, File II, Folder 49.

20. From *Mary Lutyens*, op. cit., p. 195 – 'At the beginning of 1923 she (Lady Sackville) had given him a little grey Rolls Royce on the understanding that it was to be used for work and not for family outings. (He repaid her for it by degrees.) Father called his young chauffeur James because he had always wanted to step into a vehicle of his own and say "Home James".'

21. The notes from the Drogo planting schemes and the Marsh Court letters are in the Reef Point Gardens Collection (File VI, Folder 128; File II, Folder 44).

22. The Millmead plans and planting plans have been adapted by me from those published in Gertrude Jekyll and Lawrence Weaver, *Gardens for Small Country Houses*, Country Life, n.d., Ch. 1.

23. ibid.

24. From Alec Clifton Taylor, *The Pattern of English Building*, Batsford, 1962. The Tudor bricks were 9 inches × 4½ inches × 2¼ inches or slightly narrower; by the end of the seventeenth century the thickness had increased to 2½ inches and remained so till 1784, when a Brick Tax was introduced making a duty payable per 1,000 bricks used. The size was therefore increased, with bad results from the aesthetic viewpoint. The tax was repealed in 1850, but it was too late to retract, for bricks were being manufactured in large moulds and 3 inches thick became common. The narrow bricks are only made in small quantities – they were specially ordered when Lutyens used them, and are even rarer and more expensive now. I have found four companies which make comparable sizes: Freshfield Lane Brickworks, Danehill, Haywards Heath, Sussex RH17 7HH; Bovingdon Brickworks Ltd, Pudds Cross, Bovingdon, near Hemel Hempstead, Herts HP3 0NW; W. H. Collier Ltd, Marks Tey, Colchester, Essex CO6 1LN, and Redland Bricks Ltd, Redland House, Reigate, Surrey RH2 0SJ.

25. Daneshill Brickworks closed in 1976. Daneshill House is owned by Hampshire County Council and the garden is in a ruined state; see No. 50 in the Survey, page 167.

26. Gertrude Jekyll, *Garden Ornament*, 2nd edn revised with Christopher Hussey, Country Life, 1927. I have tried to avoid quoting from this edition as it was undoubtedly written from hindsight, after the gardens were made (the 1st edition was published in 1918); however, I feel this was an artistic judgement and therefore entirely Miss Jekyll's own.

27. The shortage of water on Munstead Heath, and the struggles of the houseowners who have come to live there since Miss Jekyll's day, are symbolized by the chief feature of the landscape now – a large and ornate water tower which supplies the Munstead community.

28. Lutyens Family Papers, R.I.B.A. (letter from E.L.L. to Lady Emily, 31 March 1911).

29. In 1939 Lutyens designed the Trafalgar Square fountains; one imagines that his loyalty to his godfather Landseer's lions overcame his Jekyll-inspired aversion to fountains – though those in Trafalgar Square are of the plainest kind. File X, Folder 224 (Miscellaneous) of the Reef Point Gardens Collection has some fascinating watercolour sketches (untitled, undated) of fountains of a very similar design, related to a sketch of an elaborate formal layout which multiplies and refines the pattern of Folly Farm's sunken rose garden (see colour pl. 16) – maybe this was what Lutyens would have liked to have done to Trafalgar Square?

30. Letter to Lady Emily, from the Lutyens Family Papers, R.I.B.A.

31. The letter about the Marsh Court planting is in the Reef Point Gardens Collection (File II, Folder 44).

32. ibid.

5. *The War and Afterwards* (pages 132–52)

1. Lutyens Family Papers, R.I.B.A. (E.L.L. to Lady Emily, LuE 16/4/1–4, 12 July 1917).

2. *Edwin Lutyens by his daughter Mary Lutyens*, John Murray, 1980, pp. 56–7.

3. ibid. p. 61.

4. Home and office combined were at 29 Bloomsbury Square until 1910, when the office moved to 17 Queen Anne's Gate. In 1914 the family moved to 31 Bedford Square, but in 1919 moved again to 13 Mansfield Street, which was to be Lutyens's home for the rest of his life. There was a separate 'Delhi' office from 1913 at 7 Apple Tree Yard, moving to 17 Bolton Street in 1924. In 1931

both offices moved to 5 Eaton Gate, and in 1942 everything came together again in Mansfield Street.

5. Elisabeth Lutyens, *A Goldfish Bowl*, Cassell, 1972. Speaking of her mother she also says: 'I have no criticism of her for her desertion of father, disruption of the home and the great harm her beliefs had on my health. I know she felt she had discovered a heaven or faith which were more important than earthly ties or responsibilities and that she only wished to share with those she loved what was to her, the greatest experience a human being could have. I'm sure she was not consciously aware of the hurt and harm that she caused. Father, alas, would have preferred her companionship, or at least her presence; that she should be a wife to him and hostess to his many friends and clients and provide a home to which he could bring them.'

6. The plan for The Green at Eckington, still covered with Lutyens's pipe ash, is in the estate office at Renishaw. Miss Jekyll's plans in the Reef Point Gardens Collection are mainly incomplete outlines, and where details have been filled in there are many alterations – on a summer border plan for the lawn garden she notes that 'Michaelmas daisies and Pyrethrum were too tall' and pink snapdragons, white galega and echinops were included in their places. These plans *c.* 1911/12.

7. Osbert Sitwell, *Great Morning, being the third volume of Left Hand, Right Hand,* Macmillan, 1948, p. 19.

8. Lutyens's international career began in 1910 when he designed the British Pavilion at the Rome International Exhibition of 1911; this building eventually became the British School in Rome. Later in 1910 he went to South Africa to design the Johannesburg Art Gallery and the Rand Regiments' War Memorial – over these he crossed swords with his old friend Herbert Baker, who was working in South Africa at the time and rather regarded it as his own territory.

9. Miss Jekyll's first book, *Wood and Garden*, was published in 1899, immediately followed by *Home and Garden* in 1900 (both by her first publishers, Longmans Green) – both these books were made up of her articles in papers and magazines. *Lilies for English Gardens* and *Wall and Water Gardens* (both published by Newnes/Country Life) followed in 1901, *Roses for English Gardens* in 1902, *Old West Surrey* in 1904, *Flower Decorations for the House* in 1907, *Colour in the Flower Garden* and *Children and Gardens* in 1908. For these ten years her life was fairly equally divided between her garden, her books and the Lutyens garden designs.

10. Miss Jekyll's garden commissions, from the list published in Francis Jekyll, *Gertrude Jekyll: A Memoir* and the surviving plans in the Reef Point Gardens Collection, with slight modifications by me, are printed as Appendix A, page 188.

11. From a booklet on Ednaston Manor Gardens, based on an article in *Derbyshire Countryside*, 1972. At the time of writing the Player family ownership of Ednaston Manor has come to an end with the death of Stephen Player, but the house has found new owners to carry on the garden traditions.

12. Lutyens Family Papers, R.I.B.A. (E.L.L. to Lady Emily, LuE 16/4/1–4, 12 July 1917).

13. According to the records of the Commonwealth War Graves Commission, Lutyens was chief architect for 128 cemeteries, though sometimes his assistants may have done the actual design and the division of responsibility is often impossible to make. The Reef Point Gardens Collection has drawings of the following: Warlincourt Halte British Cemetery, Saulty – Lutyens's office outline plan, October 1917, with notes (1,170 graves, clay soil, no hedges – in his hand), to which Miss Jekyll added planting details and further notes; Gezaincourt Communal Cemetery extension – Lutyens's office plans, April 1918, with her planting details; Hersin Communal Cemetery extension – complete planting details for French and British cemetery; Fienvillers near Arras – Lutyens's outline plan dated December 1918, with his own section through entrance and Great Stone elevation and Miss Jekyll's planting details (here some confusion arises, as according to C.W.G.C. records Fienvillers was designed by Capt. A. J. S. Hutton); Daours Cemetery – complete planting details; Auchonvillers planting details – not marked as Lutyens's plan and the cemetery, again according to C.W.G.C., was designed by Reginald Blomfield, for whom Miss Jekyll could have done the plans; La Neuville British Cemetery at Corbie – complete planting schemes. The most heartrending plan of all is for 'Trouville Hospitals' – thousands of graves on the site of the 14th Convalescent Depôt at Trouville which became the Trouville Hospital Area in February 1918; the cemetery is properly called Tourgeville Military Cemetery.

14. The Cenotaph of Sigismunda is mentioned and illustrated in *Home and Garden*. It was an enormous block of stone used for a seat beneath a birch tree and surrounded by hedges 'just north of the house', and looked down the summer borders from a point just beyond the pergola. The word 'cenotaph', meaning a sepulchral monument to someone whose body is elsewhere, was little used in English before 1918, and the seat was christened (presumably in allusion to the unseen but all-powerful Spirit of Munstead Wood) by one of Miss Jekyll's (many) friends who shared her fancy for etymology.

15. This quotation and the information about Lutyens's appointment and salary are taken from Gavin Stamp, *Silent Cities* – the catalogue of an exhibition of the Memorial and Cemetery Architecture of the Great War, first shown at the Heinz Gallery, 1977.

16. Time and circumstance made Lutyens concentrate on memorials after the war – not only the memorials for towns and villages, but ever afterwards an increasing stream of tombs and memorial stones for people he had known, including the Earl of Birkenhead at Charlton, Wiltshire; Lady Cynthia Mosley at Denham, Buckinghamshire; Earl Beatty in St Paul's; the Earl and Countess of Strathmore at Glamis, Forfar; Miss Sleath, the Lutyens's family nanny, at Knebworth; and of course Miss Jekyll, who is buried with Herbert and Agnes Jekyll in Busbridge churchyard, south of Godalming.

17. Professor A. S. G. Butler, *The Architecture of Sir Edwin Lutyens* (The Memorial, Vol. 2, p. 16–17), clearly regards Tyringham as the most worthy of Lutyens's garden designs – his long praise of the Temple of Music ends with the phrase: 'We are told that Lutyens liked sitting alone in this building, because, he said, he felt he had made no mistake.'

18. The plans for Amport House garden are in the Reef Point Gardens Collection (File VIII, Folder 173).
19. Details concerning the Dolls' House come from Clifford Musgrave, *Queen Mary's Dolls' House*, Pitkin Pictorials, 1971, also the Reef Point Gardens Collection, File X, Folder 226.
20. Elisabeth Lutyens, op. cit.
21. E. V. Lucas's description is quoted from Christopher Hussey, *The Life of Sir Edwin Lutyens*, Country Life, 1950.
22. The correspondence and plans concerning the Castle Drogo garden are in the Reef Point Gardens Collection (File VI, Folder 128) and the R.I.B.A. Drawings Collection/National Trust, Drewe Papers.
23. Thankfully, now that Castle Drogo is owned by the National Trust, the tennis court has given way to a green lawn. Lutyens was to use the enclosed circle as the climax of the most formal garden of all, that of Viceroy's House, New Delhi – filled with tiers of planting and a central pool, as he had devised it at Heywood so early in his career, it might justly be described as his ultimate garden feature. It is thus all the more frustrating that this particular example has been transferred to the top of a hill, where a central pool would be wholly inappropriate.
24. Plumpton Place correspondence etc. in Reef Point Gardens Collection (File X, Folder 222).
25. The correspondence and plans about the Blagdon quarry garden are in the Reef Point Gardens Collection (File X, Folder 221).
26. Nikolaus Pevsner, 'Building with Wit: The Architecture of Sir Edwin Lutyens', *Architects' Journal*, 1951. The planting of the Delhi garden was actualy supervised during 1928/9 by William Robertson Mustoe, who was from Kew and worked for the Horticultural Department in the Punjab until seconded to New Delhi from 1919 until 1931. From Gavin Stamp's notes on the Delhi exhibits in the catalogue for *Lutyens: The Work of the English Architect Sir Edwin Lutyens (1869–1944)*, an Arts Council exhibition at the Hayward Gallery, London, 1981/2.
27. Elisabeth Lutyens, op. cit., p. 70.
28. Munstead Wood was let to the Lutyens family in the summer of 1933; after that it had other tenants, and Francis 'Timmy' Jekyll, Miss Jekyll's nephew, lived in The Hut while he wrote his aunt's *Memoir*, for which he must have had free access to her belongings and drawings. It was when Francis Jekyll died in 1951 that everything was scattered, apparently by someone who did not know what they were doing. Presumably at this time the drawings were thrown out for waste paper (from which fate Beatrix Farrand rescued them), and many things were given away or auctioned. Unfortunately the valuers and auctioneers of Francis Jekyll's estate have not kept their records from this time.

6. *A Reckoning (pages 153–87)*

1. Lawrence Weaver, *Sir Edwin Lutyens' Houses and Gardens*, Country Life, 1925, p. xviii.
2. Much of the credit for the fact that we have the gardens and many of the houses must therefore go to the memory of Harry Mangles of Littleworth Cross, who realized that the son of his friend Charles Lutyens might be a suitable architect for Miss Jekyll.

3. For a complete list of Miss Jekyll's commissions, including gardens planned for other architects, see Appendix A, page 188.
4. Lutyens Family Papers, R.I.B.A.
5. Sir Herbert Baker, *Architecture and Personalities*, Country Life, 1944.
6. Thomas Mawson (1861–1933), the son of a Lancashire cotton warper, educated himself in horticulture and garden design and set up in practice in Windermere when he was twenty-three. His appointment as the first President of the Institute of Landscape Architects in 1929 was in recognition of a life spent advancing the ideas of design for the landscape in parks and gardens both here and overseas as a separate profession from that of architecture. Unlike Lutyens, lecturing was part of his stock-in-trade, and he was largely responsible for the establishment of civic landscape design as an academic subject in this country, after the example set in the United States. His designs have a strong element of similarity with Lutyens's work in garden design but are without Lutyens's clarity; neither had he a Miss Jekyll to restrain his planting. However, their legendary antipathy seems sad, and was probably based on social and professional misunderstandings. See David Mawson, 'Thomas H. Mawson', *Landscape Design*, August 1979. See note 15 to chapter 4.
7. Christopher Tunnard, *Gardens in the Modern Landscape*, Architectural Press, 1938.
8. The story of Brabazon's downfall is related in Chapter 1, note 18. As to the rest of Miss Jekyll's legacy – the scattering of the contents of Munstead Wood and The Hut after first her death, and then the death of Francis Jekyll in 1951, has meant that most of the things she made have disappeared into oblivion; of recorded objects, such as the embroidered panels she designed for Eaton Hall, and embroideries done for Edward Burne-Jones and Lord Leighton, there seems to be no trace. The Victoria & Albert Museum has a collection of antique Italian, Algerian and Tyrolean embroideries which she brought back from her travels, but nothing of her own that is identified. A small collection of her art objects will be found listed in the catalogue of the Arts Council Exhibition on *The Life and Work of Sir Edwin Lutyens* at the Hayward Gallery, London, November–February 1981/2; see also the catalogue of a smaller exhibition, *Gertrude Jekyll 1843–1932* at the Architectural Association School of Architecture, 34–36 Bedford Square, London WC1, November/December 1981.
9. Christopher Hussey, *The Life of Sir Edwin Lutyens*, Country Life, 1950, p. 525.
10. ibid., quoted from an article published in 1926 and an address to the Tomorrow Club in 1932.
11. Nikolaus Pevsner, 'Building with Wit: The Architecture of Sir Edwin Lutyens', *Architects' Journal*, 1951.
12. The budget for 29 Bloomsbury Square is quoted from Mary Lutyens, *Edwin Lutyens by his daughter Mary Lutyens*, John Murray, 1980, p. 54.
13. The mention of costs comes from the Lutyens Family Papers, various letters (R.I.B.A.).
14. Letter to the author from David Nelson, 4 January 1979.
15. Information about contractors is very scarce, but where something is known it has been added to the Survey. Many of the early houses, including Munstead Wood, Daneshill

and Orchards, bear a plaque with the architect, owner and builder named; there is also an album relating to Orchards, containing a photograph of the Thomas Underwood of Dunsfold building team and the names of the craftsmen.

16. In 1979, when old-fashioned flowers and natural gardening returned to the Chelsea Flower Show, I stood by a display of London pride, foxgloves and columbines for some time – almost everyone who approached made some comment about how pleased they were to see old favourites back again!

17. The information about Lutyens's involvement at Long Barn and his 'pervasive' influence at Sissinghurst is in a letter to the author from Nigel Nicolson, 8 March 1981.

18. The following articles appeared in *Country Life*:

Abbotswood: 15, 22 February 1913
Ammerdown House: 23 March; 2, 9 March 1929
Ashby St Ledgers: 27 July, 3, 10, 17 August 1951
Crooksbury: 15 September 1900; 6, 13 October 1944
Deanery Garden: 9 May 1903
Ednaston Manor: 24 March 1923
Folly Farm: 28 January 1922, 4 February 1922; 6 July 1961; 15 May 1975
Gledstone Hall: 13 April 1935
Goddards: 30 January 1904
Great Dixter: 4 January 1913
Great Maytham: 30 November 1912
Grey Walls: 9 September 1911
Heathcote: 9 July 1910
Hestercombe: 10 October 1908; 23 September 1976
Lambay Castle: 4 May 1912; 20, 27 July 1929
Lindisfarne: 7 June 1913
Little Thakeham: 28 August 1909
Marsh Court: 1 September 1906; 19 April 1913; 19, 26 March, 2 April 1932
Millmead: 11 May 1907
Munstead Wood: 8 December 1900
Nashdom: 31 August 1912
New Place: 9 April 1910
Orchards: 31 August 1901; 11 April 1908
Plumpton Place: 20 May 1933
The Salutation: 13, 20 September 1962
Temple Dinsley: 22 April 1911

19. Betty Massingham, 'Taste Maker in American Gardening: Louisa King's work and ideas', *Country Life*, 12 October 1978.

20. I quote from Michael Laurie, *An Introduction to Landscape Architecture*, American Elsevier Publishing Co./Pitman, 1976, p. 44: '. . . the elder statesman of garden design in California . . . is Thomas Church, who studied at Berkeley. He set up his practice in 1930. His work was extremely influential on the profession . . . and also helped, through *House and Home* and *Sunset Magazine*, to shape public opinion about the form and use of the domestic garden, small or large, in California and elsewhere.' *Southern Living* is one of the *Sunset* group and the high standard of design content has remained constant since Thomas Church's time. The article mentioned was 'Create a Classic Garden Border', *Southern Living*, April 1978.

21. Lutyens undoubtedly believed that his legacy was his work. Of Delhi he said: 'The Viceroy thinks only of what the place will look like in 3 years' time, 300 is what I think of.' Quoted from Christopher Hussey, op. cit., p. 282. (Maybe the Viceroy knew something Lutyens could not have known?) His attitude to eulogies and academic praise was rather different; Mary Lutyens remembers that he told her 'he could not understand a word of' a chapter on 'The Armature of Planes' contained in Robert Lutyens's *Appreciation* of his father, published in 1942. His opinion of the *Memorial* therefore can be imagined, and there can be no doubt that he would have wanted the *real* gardens to survive.

22. I make this as only a brief suggestion, as it does seem a possible way out, and several owners have said to me that they would like some encouragement to open their gardens on a limited basis. Really any scheme like this should encompass the houses as well (though opening houses is a *much* more difficult task), and I sincerely hope that one of the outcomes of the Arts Council exhibition on *The Life and Work of Sir Edwin Lutyens* held at the Hayward Gallery, London, November–February 1981/2, will be some sort of trust to guard his legacy.

23. Christopher Hussey, op. cit., p. 571.

24. Lawrence Whistler, *The Image on the Glass*, John Murray, 1975.

❦ BIBLIOGRAPHY ❦

BAKER, Sir Herbert, *Architecture and Personalities*, Country Life, 1944.

BIRREN, Faber (ed.), *The Principles of Harmony and Contrast of Colours and their Application to the Arts by M. E. Chevreul*, New York, Reinhold, 1967.

BURTON, Hester, *Barbara Bodichon 1827–1891*, John Murray, 1949.

BUTLER, A. S. G. and STEWART, George, *The Architecture of Sir Edwin Lutyens*, 3 vols. (1. *Country Houses*; 2. *Gardens, Washington, New Delhi*; 3. *Large Buildings*), Country Life, 1950.

COWLES, Virginia, *1913, The Defiant Swan Song*, Weidenfeld & Nicolson, 1967.

CROWE, Sylvia, *Garden Design*, Country Life, 1958.

EDWARDS, Joan, *Gertrude Jekyll, Embroiderer, Gardener and Craftsman* (Small Books on the History of Embroidery, no. 4), Bayford Books, 1981.

FLETCHER, Harold R., *The Story of the R.H.S. 1804–1968*, Oxford University Press for the Royal Horticultural Society, 1969.

GRADIDGE, Roderick, *Dream Houses: The Edwardian Ideal*, Constable, 1980.

HUSSEY, Christopher, *The Life of Sir Edwin Lutyens*, Vol. 4 of *The Memorial*, Country Life, 1950.

JEKYLL, Francis, *Gertrude Jekyll: A Memoir*, Jonathan Cape, 1934, with foreword by Sir Edwin Lutyens.

JEKYLL, Francis, and TAYLOR, G. C. (eds.), *A Gardener's Testament*, Country Life, 1937.

JEKYLL, Gertrude, *Wood and Garden*, Longmans Green, 1899.

—— *Home and Garden*, Longmans Green, 1900.

—— *Lilies for English Gardens*, Newnes/Country Life, 1901.

—— *Wall and Water Gardens*, Newnes/Country Life, 1901.

—— *Roses for English Gardens*, Newnes/Country Life, 1902.

—— *Old West Surrey*, Newnes/Country Life, 1904.

—— *Some English Gardens with paintings by George S. Elgood*, Longmans Green, 1904.

—— *Flower Decoration for the House*, Newnes/Country Life, 1907.

—— *Colour in the Flower Garden*, Newnes/Country Life, 1908.

—— *Children and Gardens*, Newnes/Country Life, 1908.

—— *Annuals and Biennials*, Newnes/Country Life, 1916.

—— *Garden Ornament*, Country Life, 1918.

—— *Old English Household Life*, Newnes/Country Life, 1925 (revised and rewritten from *Old West Surrey*).

JEKYLL, Gertrude, and HUSSEY, Christopher, *Garden Ornament* (revised edn), Country Life, 1927.

JEKYLL, Gertrude, and WEAVER, Lawrence, *Gardens for Small Country Houses*, Newnes/Country Life, 1912.

LUTYENS, Lady Emily, *A Blessed Girl: Memoirs of a Victorian Childhood 1887–1896*, Hart-Davis, 1953.

—— *Candles in the Sun*, Hart-Davis, 1951.

LUTYENS, Elisabeth, *A Goldfish Bowl*, Cassell, 1972.

LUTYENS, Mary, *Edwin Lutyens by his daughter Mary Lutyens*, John Murray, 1980.

LUTYENS, Robert, *Sir Edwin Lutyens: An Appreciation in Perspective*, Country Life, 1942.

MASSINGHAM, Betty, *Miss Jekyll: Portrait of a Great Gardener*, Country Life, 1966.

MASSON, Georgina, *Italian Gardens*, Thames & Hudson, 1966.

NICHOLSON, B. E., et al., *The Oxford Book of Garden Flowers*, Oxford University Press, 1973. This is much the most helpful book for Jekyll planting.

NICOLSON, Nigel, *Portrait of a Marriage*, Weidenfeld & Nicolson, 1973.

O'NEILL, Daniel, *Sir Edwin Lutyens, Country Houses*, Lund Humphries, 1980.

PRIESTLEY, J. B., *The Edwardians*, Heinemann, 1970.

ROBINSON, William, *The English Flower Garden*, John Murray, 16th edn, 1956.

SACKVILLE-WEST, Vita, *The Edwardians*, Hogarth Press, 1930.

SCOTT-JAMES, Anne, *Sissinghurst, The Making of a Garden*, Michael Joseph, 1975.

SERVICE, Alistair, *Edwardian Architecture*, Thames & Hudson, 1977.

SITWELL, Osbert, *Great Morning, being the third volume of Left Hand, Right Hand*, Macmillan, 1948.

STAMP, Gavin, *Silent Cities: An Exhibition of the Memorial and Cemetery Architecture of the Great War*, R.I.B.A., 1977.

STUART THOMAS, Graham, *The Old Shrub Roses*, Phoenix House, 1963.

TREVOR-ROPER, Patrick, *The World through Blunted Sight*, Thames & Hudson, 1970.

TUNNARD, Christopher, *Gardens in the Modern Landscape*, Architectural Press, 1938.

WEAVER, Lawrence, *The Houses and Gardens of E. L. Lutyens*, Country Life, 1913.

—— *Sir Edwin Lutyens' Houses and Gardens*, Country Life, 1921.

INDEX

Figures in *italic* type indicate illustrations. Black-and-white illustrations are referred to by page number (*24*), colour by plate number (*col. pl. 24*).

Abbotswood, Stow-on-the-Wold, Gloucestershire, *102*, 178, 186
Alhambra, the, 22, 64
Allingham, Helen (née Paterson), 22, 193
Ammerdown, Radstock, Somerset, 79–81, *79, 80, 81*, 124, 178, 186, 199
Amport House, Andover, Hampshire, 109, *123*, 141–3, *142, 144, 145*, 180, 187, col. pls. *23, 24*
Architecture and Personalities (Baker), 154
Arts and Crafts Movement, 15, 23, 97, 98
Arundel Castle, 14
Ashby St Ledgers, Northamptonshire, *122*, 179, 186

Bacon, Francis, 97
Baillie-Scott, M. Hugh, 153
Baker, Sir Herbert, 30, 97, 136, 153, 154
Barrie, Sir James, 94, 103, 200
Barrington Court, 14
Barton St Mary, East Grinstead, Sussex, 89–93, *90, 91, 92*, 179
Berrydowne Court, Overton, Hampshire, 60–61, *113*, 197, col. pl. *3*
Blagdon, Seaton Burn, Northumberland, 46, 48–9, 50, 150, *151*, 196
Blomfield, Sir Reginald, 98, 199
Blumenthal, Jacques and Leonie, 23, 194
Bodichon, Barbara (née Leigh-Smith), 22, 23, 25, 193–4
Brabazon, Hercules Brabazon, 23, 42, 194, col. pl. *2*
British Architectural Library (R.I.B.A.), 17
British Association of Garden Architects, 155
British Embassy, Washington, 147
Brookes, John, 43, *185*
Brydon, John, 97
Burne-Jones, Sir Edward, 22, 23
Burrows Cross, Shere, Surrey, 30
Butler, Professor A. S. G., 17, 201

Caldecott, Randolph, 30
California, University of, *see* Reef Point Gardens Collection
Castle Drogo, *see* Drogo
Cenotaph of Sigismunda, the, 36, 136
Cenotaph, the, 136
Chance, Julia (née Strachey) and William, 55, 56, 197

Charterhouse School, 197
Chevreul, Michel, 42
Cheyne Walk (No. 100), *184*
Children and Gardens (quoted), 20
Chinthurst Hill, Wonersh, Surrey, *107*, 109, 177
Colour circle, *43*
Colour in the Flower Garden, 44
Colour theories, 41–3, *43*
Commonwealth War Graves Commission, *see* War Graves Commission
Coneyhurst, Cranleigh, Surrey, 30
Country Life magazine, 15, 203
Crooksbury House, Farnham, Surrey, 53–4, 178

Daneshill, Basingstoke, Hampshire, 120, 179, *181*
Daneshill Brickworks, 120, 200
Dartington Hall, Devon, 182, 183
Deanery Garden, Sonning, Berkshire, 15, 65–8, *66, 67*, 69, 121, 178, 186
Dickson's of Newtownards, rose breeders, 142
Dillistone, George, 147
Dormy House, Walton Heath, Surrey, *182*
Drewe, Julius, 89, 110–11, 146–7
Drogo, Castle, Drewsteignton, Devon, 104, 107, 110–11, *112*, 146–7, 159, 177
Dry-wall planting, *116–19*, 142–5, *144–5*

Earle, Mrs C. W., 63, 64, 197
Eaton Hall, Cheshire, 23
Ednaston Manor, Derbyshire, *112*, 135–6, 180, 187, col. pl. *22*
Elgar, Sir Edward, 103, 200
Ellacombe, Canon H. N., 27
Ellacombe, H. N. and H. T., 195
English Flower Garden, The (Robinson), 26, 98

Falkner, Harold, 41, 196
Farrand, Beatrix, 16, 183
Fisher's Hill, Hook Heath, Woking, Surrey, 64, 178, 198
Folly Farm, Sulhamstead, Berkshire, 15, 93–5, *94, 95*, 178, 184, 186, col. pls. *13, 14, 15, 16*
Formal Garden in England, The (Blomfield), 98, 199
Foster, Sir Michael, 27, 195
Fulbrook, Elstead, Surrey, 107

Garden, The, 26
Garden History Society, 16, 186
Garden houses, *126*
Garden Ornament, 146, 154
Garden plans, *see* Layout plans
Gardens for Small Country Houses, 16, 111, 117, 154, 177
Gardens in the Modern Landscape (Tunnard), 155–6
George, Ernest, 30
George and Peto (office), 30, 97
Girton College, Cambridge, 23
Giverny, Monet's garden at, 25, 50
Gledstone Hall, Skipton, Yorkshire, 121, 138–9, *139*, 159, 180
Goddards, Abinger Common, Surrey, 58, 60, 177
Gordon, Georgina Duff, 23–4
Gravetye Manor, Sussex, *125*
Great Maytham, Rolvenden, Kent, 110, 121, 179, *179*, 184, 187
Great Morning (Sitwell), 133
Grey Walls, Gullane, Lothian, 70, 72, *74*, 178, 186, *col. pl. 6*

Hammersley, Charles, 19
Hampton Court, 124
Hazelhatch, Shere, Surrey, 53
Heathcote, Ilkley, Yorkshire, 108, *109*, 159, 179, 186
Herford, Laura, 21–2
Hestercombe, Taunton, Somerset, 15, 78, 82, 83–5, *84*, *85*, *112*, 122, *128*, 179, 184, 186, *col. pls. 8, 9, 10*
Heywood, Ballinakill, Eire, 78, 86–9, *86*, *87*, *88*, *89*, 179, 186
Hidcote Manor, Gloucestershire, 50, 182, 183
Hill, Oliver, 153
Historic Buildings Council, 185–6
Hole, Dean Samuel Reynolds, 27, 195
Home and Garden, 99, 103
Hoo, The, Willingdon, Sussex, *122*, 178, 186, *col. pls. 17, 18*
Houses and Gardens of E. L. Lutyens (Weaver), *see* Lutyens's *Houses and Gardens*
Hudson, Edward, 65, 68, 70, 148, 150, 198
Hunt, William Holman, 22
Hussey, Christopher, 17, 72, 154, 187

I.C.O.M.O.S. (U.K. Committee), 186
Image on the Glass, The (Whistler), 187
Imperial War Graves Commission, *see* War Graves Commission
Iris rills, *see* Water, design with

Jekyll, Edward Joseph Hill, 19, 21, 25
Jekyll, Gertrude:
   birth and family, 19, 193
   childhood and education, 20–22
   painter and craftswoman, 22–24
   exhibits at Royal Academy, 22
   love for Mediterranean plants, 22
   description of, at thirty, 22–3
   'folklore' collection, 21, 99, 193
   myopia, 24–5
   return to Surrey, 25–6
   gardening friends, 27
   buys Munstead Wood, 28

photograph (about 1880), 29
meeting with Lutyens, 13, 32
Munstead Wood garden, 34–53, *35*, *47*
Munstead Wood plant catalogue, *62*
colour theories, 41–3
woodland gardening, 33, 50–53, *52*
taste in gardens, 97, 98
perception and vision, 98–9
pattern of partnership with Lutyens, 14–15
portrait by William Nicholson, *135*
last commissions, 148–52
death of, 152
A Memoir (Francis Jekyll), 16, 23–4
list of commissions (1880–1932), 188–91
range of commissions, 14
awarded Victoria Medal of Honour, 195
Survey of gardens of partnership, 159–76
Jekyll, Herbert, 19, 25
Jekyll, Joseph (1754–1838), 19
Jekyll, Sir Joseph (1662–1738), 19
Jekyll, Julia (née Hammersley), 19, 27
Johnson, Herbert, 72, 131, 198–9
Johnson, Mrs Herbert, 131

Knebworth House, Hertfordshire, 14, 65, 198

Lambay Castle, Dublin Bay, Eire, 70, *70*, *71*, 100–*101*, 179, 186
Landseer, Sir Edwin, 28, 195
Lawless, Hon. Emily, 53, 197
Layout plans illustrated:
   Munstead Wood, 36
   Woodside, 54
   Orchards, 57
   Deanery Garden, 66
   Lambay, 70
   Grey Walls, 74
   Marsh Court, 75
   Ammerdown, 79
   Hestercombe, 82
   Heywood, 89
   Barton St Mary, 90
   Folly Farm, 94
   New Place, 105
   Heathcote, 109
   Millmead, 114
   Tyringham Park, 140
   100 Cheyne Walk, 184
Leigh-Smith, Barbara, *see* Bodichon, Barbara
Leighton, Frederic, Lord, 22, 23
Life of Lutyens (Hussey), 17, 187
Lethaby, William, 97
Lindisfarne Castle, Northumberland, 68, 104, 179, 186
Little Thakeham, Storrington, Sussex, 106, 109, 187, *col. pls. 11, 12*
Littleworth Cross, Surrey, 28, *31*, 32
Loseley House, Surrey, 14
Lorimer, Sir Robert, 153
Louise, H.R.H. Princess, Duchess of Argyll, 23
Lutyens, Charles Henry Augustus, 28, 195
Lutyens, Sir Edwin:
   birth, 28

Index

Lutyens, Sir Edwin—*cont.*
  childhood and family, 28
  education and training, 29–32
  meeting with Miss Jekyll, 13, 32
  meeting and marriage with Emily, 63
  early Surrey houses and gardens, 55–63
  inspirations to garden design, 96–7
  perception of design, 99, 101
  pattern of partnership with Miss Jekyll, 14–15
  letters to Lady Emily, 17
  photographs, 29, 101
  philosophy of garden design, 103
  family life, 132
  portrait by Augustus John, 134
  last years and death, 152
  Lutyens Memorial, The, 17, 157
  place in history of design, 154–7
  notes on additional landscape commissions, 192
  homes and offices, 200–201
  Survey of gardens made in partnership, 159–76
  Life of Lutyens (Hussey), 17, 187
Lutyens, Emily (née Lytton), Lady, 23, 63, 64, 151
Lutyens, Mary (née Gallwey), 28, 30
Lutyens Memorial, The (Butler, Stewart, Hussey), 17, 157
Lutyens's Houses and Gardens (Weaver), 15, 193
Lutyens, Robert, 99
Lyttelton, Hon. Alfred, 72, 178, 198
Lytton, Countess of, 63, 64

Mangles, family, 195
Mangles, Harry, 28, 32, 195
Marsh Court, Stockbridge, Hampshire, 72–3, 75, 75–8, 76, 77, 78, 107, 109, 123, 130–1, 178, 186, *col. pls. 19, 20, 21*
Mawson, Thomas, 96, 155, 200, 202
Merrist Wood, near Guildford, Surrey, 30
Millmead, Bramley, Surrey, 111, 114–120, 114, 115, 116, 118–19, 126, 177, 186
Milner, Henry Ernest, 98, 199
Millstones, 121, 123
Modern Painters (Ruskin), 22
Monet, Claude, 25, 50, 155, 194–5
Moore, Albert, 22
Morgan, William de, 22
Morris, Marshall, Faulkner & Co., 22
Morris, William, 22
Munstead House, Surrey, 25, 26
Munstead Wood, 13, 15, 28, 33, 109, 177, 178, 196
  building the house, 34
  garden, 34–53
  garden plan, 36
  north court, 35
  Spring garden, 37
  Hidden garden, 39
  June garden, 40
  main flower borders, 44–5
  planting, 47
  woodland gardening at, 50–53, 52
  plants for sale from, 62
  description from *Home and Garden*, 99
  decline of, 152

Nashdom, Taplow, Buckinghamshire, 120, 159, 186
Nelson, Sir Amos, 138, 159
New Place, Shedfield, Hampshire, 104–5, 105, 121, 179
Newton, Charles, 22
Newton, Mary (née Severn), 22

Old English Household Life, 21
Old West Surrey, 21
Orchards, Godalming, Surrey, 15, 55–8, 57, 58, 59, 107, 109, 178, 186, *col. pl. 7*

Park Hatch lodges, Hascombe, Surrey, 32, 33
Pasturewood, Holmbury St Mary, Surrey, 58, 60, 123, 197
Pavings, 121, 123, 124
Pergolas, 81, 83, 84, 126
Phillips Memorial, Godalming, 134
Planting plans illustrated:
  Munstead Wood, Spring garden, 37
  Munstead Wood, Hidden garden, 39
  Munstead Wood, June garden, 40
  herbaceous borders, 44–5, 48–9
  herb garden (Knebworth), 65
  terrace borders (Deanery Garden), 67
  kitchen borders (Barton St Mary), 91
  mixed borders (Barton St Mary), 92
  shade and dry-wall planting (Millmead), 118
  dry-wall planting, 119
  rose garden (Putteridge Park), 130
  raised rock garden (Amport House), 144–5
  wild planting (Blagdon Quarry), 151
Planting schemes:
  spring gardening, 36–8
  cottage gardening, 40–41
  herbaceous borders, 44–50, 67, 92, 93
  woodland gardening, 50–53
  jardins potagers, 56–8, 57, 91
  herbs (plant list), 62
  water-loving plants, 67, 75, 78, 78
  dry walls, 116–19, 142–5
  rose gardens, 130, 142
  war cemeteries, 136–8
Plumpton Place, Sussex, 70, 148, 148–9
Pools, *see* Water, design of
Pot Pourri from a Surrey Garden (Earle), 63, 197
Poynter, Edward, 22
Principles of Harmony and Contrast of Colour, The (Chevreul), 42–3
Putteridge Park, Luton, Bedfordshire, 130, 180

Queen Mary's Dolls' House, 104, 143

Red House, The, Godalming, Surrey, 62, 177, 197
Reef Point Gardens Collection, 16, 156, 194
Ridley, Viscountess (née Ursula Lutyens), 46, 50
Robinson, William, 25, 26–7, 35, 58, 61, 98, 125, 195
Rose gardens, 130, 142
Rossetti, Dante Gabriel, 22
Royal Horticultural Society, 27, 28
Royal Horticultural Society, Wisley Garden, 27
Royal Institute of British Architects, B.A.L., 17
Royal Parks and Gardens of London (Cole), 27
Ruskin, John, 22

Salutation, The, Sandwich, Kent, 110, *110*, 180, 187
Scalands, Robertsbridge, Sussex, 23, 34
Seats, *125*
Shaw, Richard Norman, 30, 97
Sissinghurst Castle, 50, 182, 183
Sitwell, Sir George, 89, 133
Solomon, Simeon, 22
Somerset County Council, 83, 85
South Kensington School of Art, 21, 30
Southern Living and *Sunset* tradition, 183, 203
Steps, 121, *122*
Stewart, George, 17
Stones of Venice, The (Ruskin), 22
Suburban Gardener and Villa Companion (Loudon), 27
Sullingstead, Hascombe, Surrey, 107
Surrey Archaeological Society, 15
Survey of gardens, 159–76
Sutton Place, Guildford, Surrey, 14

Temple Dinsley, Hitchin, Hertfordshire, 121, *126*, 159, 187
Terraces, 67, 69, 120–21, *179*
Thursley, Surrey, 28
Tigbourne Court, Witley, Surrey, 15, 60
Traylen's Bookshop, Guildford, Surrey, 17
Tunnard, Christopher, 155–6
Tyringham Park, Buckinghamshire, *140*, 140–41, 180, 187

Underwood, Thomas (builder), *124*, 182, 202–3

Viceroy's House, New Delhi, 14, 150–51, 187, 203
Villa d'Este, 22, 129

Walker, Frederick, 22
Wall and Water Gardens, 117
War cemeteries, 136–8, *137*, 201
War Graves Commission, 14, 136–8
War memorials, 136, 138
Warlincourt Halte B.C., Saulty, *137*
Water, design with, 75, 77, 78, *78*, 83, 85, *85*, 87, 94–5, *95*, 127–9, *128*, 139, *139*–41, *142*, *col. pls. 14*, *18*, *23*, *24*
Watts, George Frederick, 22
Weaver, Lawrence, 15, 17, 153
Webb, Philip, 22, 30, 97
Webb, Mr and Mrs Robert, 30
Westminster, Duke of, 23
Wild Garden, The (Robinson), 26
Willinghurst, Cranleigh, Surrey, 30
Willmott, Ellen, 27, 195
Wilson, George F., 27, 195
Witley Park, Surrey, *61*
Whistler, Lawrence, 187
Wood and Garden, 44
Woodside, Chenies, Buckinghamshire, 54–5, *54*, *55*, 177, 186, *col. pls. 4*, *5*
World Through Blunted Sight, The (Trevor-Roper), 24, 194
Wren, Sir Christopher, 97, 124, 152
Wyatt, James, 79, 83